Y0-EGI-437

Reading Strategies
for Today's College Student

Reading Strategies for Today's College Student

Rhonda Holt Atkinson
Central Missouri State University

Debbie Guice Longman
Southeastern Louisiana University

WADSWORTH
CENGAGE Learning

Australia • Brazil • Japan • Korea • Mexico • Singapore • Spain • United Kingdom • United States

WADSWORTH
CENGAGE Learning

Reading Strategies for Today's College Student
Rhonda Holt Atkinson/Debbie Guice Longman

Publisher: Michael Rosenberg

Acquisitions Editor: Stephen Dalphin

Development Editor: Laurie Runion

Editorial/Marketing Assistant:
Dawn Giovanniello

Technology Project Manager:
Joe Gallagher

Marketing Manager: Carrie Brandon

Advertising Project Manager:
Brian Chaffee

Senior Project Manager, Editorial
Production: Samantha Ross

Manufacturing Manager: Marcia Locke

Permissions Editor: Audrey Pettengill

Project Manager: Christine Wilson, IBC

Text Designer: Carol Rose

Cover Designer: Gina Petti

Compositor: Publishers' Design &
Production Services, Inc.

Cover Photograph: © Ron Chapple/
Getty Images

© 2006 Wadsworth, Cengage Learning

ALL RIGHTS RESERVED. No part of this work covered by the copyright herein may be reproduced, transmitted, stored or used in any form or by any means graphic, electronic, or mechanical, including but not limited to photocopying, recording, scanning, digitizing, taping, Web distribution, information networks, or information storage and retrieval systems, except as permitted under Section 107 or 108 of the 1976 United States Copyright Act, without the prior written permission of the publisher.

For product information and technology assistance, contact us at
Cengage Learning Customer & Sales Support, 1-800-354-9706

For permission to use material from this text or product,
submit all requests online at **cengage.com/permissions**
Further permissions questions can be e-mailed to
permissionrequest@cengage.com

Credits appear on page 371, which constitutes a continuation of the copyright page.

Library of Congress Control Number: 2004116547

ISBN-13: 978-0-8384-5710-8

ISBN-10: 0-8384-5710-X

www.wadsworth.com

Wadsworth
25 Thomson Place
Boston, MA 02210
USA

Cengage Learning products are represented in Canada by Nelson Education, Ltd.

For your course and learning solutions, visit **academic.cengage.com**

Purchase any of our products at your local college store or at our preferred online store **www.ichapters.com**

Printed in the United States of America
2 3 4 5 6 7 8 12 11 10 09 08

Contents

Preface to the Instructor

Reading Strategies for Today's College Student is designed for a basic developmental reading course (students reading at or below the sixth-grade level) or an ESL course. As college students, basic readers are faced with a variety of reading materials—textbooks, college catalogs, financial aid documents, correspondence and other information from institutions, articles from college newspapers, Web-based information—that they must navigate in order to achieve academic success. This textbook uses such text materials for exposition of instruction and reading activities.

We think you'll find that having students read the Student Introduction is an important first assignment. In the introduction, we explain how to use the book and its key features.

The first chapters are "Understanding Your New Environment" (Chapter 1) and "Reading for College" (Chapter 2). We present these topics at the start because we believe two factors contribute to college success. First, students need to operate from a position of strength. We believe that students' knowledge of themselves, their coursework, and the postsecondary environment gives them that strength. Second, students need to understand what to do with that knowledge. Everything college students do in life is a choice. The better they become at decision making, the more control they will have over their successes and failures. Chapter 1 introduces the *SOLVE* decision-making strategy, which is a system for thinking through choices and decisions. We also provide students with the reading techniques they need to make sense of themselves, college coursework, and collegiate institutions.

Any new language requires intensive language skills, and college language is no different. For that reason, the next five chapters focus on the language of college coursework. The use of a dictionary key as a tool for phonetic analysis in Chapter 3 ("Decoding New Words") gives students a reasonable and workable approach to figuring out unknown words. Chapter 4 ("Dictionary and Thesaurus") shows students how basic language reference books can help them form connected networks of meaning. The content of Chapter 5 ("Using Context") and Chapter 6 ("The Structure of Words") features numerous examples of words that college students routinely see and hear (e.g., *accreditation, adjunct, residency,* and *rigorous*). Students are instructed in finding meanings of new words through context clues or structural analysis. Chapter 7 ("Developing a

College Vocabulary") shows students where to find new words on campus and gives students a variety of concrete strategies for learning them.

The last five chapters build on word knowledge by providing students with the reading strategies for understanding main ideas (Chapter 8, "Reading for Main Ideas"), details (Chapter 9, "Reading for Details"), and drawing conclusions (Chapter 10, "Drawing Conclusions"). Today's college students must learn regardless of how information is formatted. Chapter 11 ("Reading Graphics") gives students strategies and practice in reading and comprehending a variety of visual formats, including charts, maps, and graphs. Because information often occurs in electronic as well as paper formats, Chapter 12 ("Using Online Information") clearly identifies features of the Internet and World Wide Web, and electronic features that are likely found on their campuses.

Key Features

- **Focus on reading fundamentals.** *Reading Strategies for Today's College Student* provides first-year students with clear, easy-to-understand basics for developing college-level vocabulary and reading strategies. As professors, we each have over 25 years of experience teaching reading and study strategies. As authors, we have written a variety of textbooks that focus on reading development (*Reading Enhancement and Development,* 7th Edition; *Vocabulary for College and Beyond; Strategic Thinking and Reading*) and learning strategies (*College Learning and Study Skills,* 7th Edition; *Study Methods and Reading Techniques,* 2nd Edition). The underlying theme in these books and our careers is a commitment to helping new college students succeed.

- **Focus on academic reading.** While the difficulty of the reading exposition in *Reading Strategies for Today's College Student* ranges from fourth- to sixth-grade level, as assessed by a standard readability formula, college readers are faced with materials at all levels of difficulty. This textbook uses such materials for exposition of instruction and reading activities. Students learn to read in this book what they will be reading from their first days on campus. *Reading Strategies for Today's College Student* is not just a reading book, but a book to help students get the most from their college experience.

- **Low reading level and conversational writing style.** Although the text's instructional information is written at a developmental level, we believe that the students for whom it is designed don't want to be treated as "remedial readers." Our conversational style provides informational content in easily understood context, while addressing students as adults.

- **Use of environmental text found at postsecondary institutions.** *Reading Strategies for Today's College Student* includes the kinds of challenging readings that postsecondary students and lifelong readers at all levels need to understand, such as textbook excerpts, college newspaper articles, financial aid information, websites, and short stories.

- **Pre-chapter guides that address different learning styles.** *Reading Strategies for Today's College Student* provides students with textual, visual, and interactive tools to learn effectively and assess background knowledge. Each chapter begins with a list of objectives to help students set learning goals; a chapter map to aid visual learners in understanding chapter content; written chapter outlines for logical learners; and a vocabulary assessment that helps students check their understanding of key terms before reading the chapter.

- **Vocabulary, comprehension, and writing activities for readings.** Exercises at the end of each reading provide additional opportunities to practice fundamental reading strategies the chapters address, such as decoding unknown words and finding main ideas. Answers to the exercises can be found at the back of the book, which allows students to chart their own progress.

- **Immediate comprehension check and application of strategies throughout chapters.** Quick Reviews and other exercises follow text sections, so students know at once if they understood and can apply what they learned. Answers to Quick Review exercises are located at the bottom of the page on which the Quick Reviews appear. Answers to application exercises can be found at the back of the text.

- **Writing Connection exercises.** Brief writing activities throughout the chapters give students opportunities to reflect on chapter content and respond in their own words.

- **Internet activities in every chapter.** Today's college students need to read online as well as in print formats. We have included a Learning Online section at the end of each chapter, which directs students to the website for this text. Students will find links to fun, interesting, and sometimes challenging websites, along with exercises that are relevant to chapter topics.

- **Post-chapter guides that facilitate understanding and reflection in different ways.** The text includes familiar reader-friendly pedagogical features. Chapter Summaries highlight key concepts, and Chapter Review questions help students determine if they understood main ideas and details. Less traditional pedagogy includes Action Summaries, which give students opportunities to create their own plans for evaluating strategies and integrating them into personal usage, and Chapter Vocabulary Review, which lets students evaluate their acquisition of new words.

- **Learning Tips.** Toward the end of each chapter, students will find a Learning Tip box. Each Learning Tip topic, ranging from assessing learning styles to forming study groups, from computing GPA to avoiding plagiarism, is designed to enhance students' college and study experience.

- **An appendix of readings.** The Appendix contains additional readings and exercises that instructors can use for testing, or students can use for extra study and practice.

Ancillaries

An Instructor's Manual to accompany *Reading Strategies for Today's College Student* includes strategies for teaching this course, sample syllabi, chapter tests, and suggested reading sources for students. To receive a copy, contact your Thomson Higher Education sales representative.

There is also a companion website, *http://developmentalenglish.wadsworth .com/atkinson-longman,* that includes web exercises, a glossary of chapter terms, flashcards and crossword puzzles to reinforce vocabulary, and links to fun and interesting websites related to reading. The site also features reading quizzes that provide students with an opportunity to apply and measure the reading skills they have gained in class. Each reading quiz contains a selection from a college textbook, followed by a series of comprehension and vocabulary questions. After taking the quiz, students receive immediate feedback on their responses.

Acknowledgments

We wish to thank our families who supported us in innumerable ways as we worked on this text. Our spouses, Tom and Richard, are our lifelong partners and personal cheerleaders. Our children, Rachel, Jacob, and Christopher, as well as the newest additions to our families, Anthony Arton and Carolin Suedkamp, allowed us the time we needed to work together on this project. Moreover, they helped us locate information, proof manuscripts, create answer keys, and develop website content.

We also wish to thank our colleagues at Southeastern Louisiana University in Hammond, Louisiana, and Central Missouri State University in Warrensburg, Missouri. Your friendship, collegiality, and professionalism inspire us.

Finally, we thank our publishing family for their hard work. Stephen Dalphin, Senior Acquisitions Editor, has provided us with vision and support. Laurie Runion, Developmental Editor Extraordinaire, has made all the difference in the development of this text (THANK YOU!) with her infinite suggestions and support. Samantha Ross, Senior Production Editor; Christine Wilson, Project Manager; Janet McCartney Parkinson, Copyeditor; Elsa van Bergen, Proofreader; and Carol Rose, Designer, have transformed our work.

Thanks, too, to our reviewers. We appreciate your assistance and insights.

Diane Amelotte, *Long Beach City College*
Andrée C. Fee, *Chesapeake College*
JoAnn Foriest, *Prairie State College*
Nancy Phillips, *Glendale Community College*
B. Meredith Tumlin, *Gadsden State Community College*

Student Introduction

Starting Off on the Right Foot

Congratulations! You are about to begin an exciting new journey! Whether you're enrolled in a community college, university, technical institute, vocational school, junior college, or other program, we want you to start off on the right foot.

Do you know what it means to *start off on the right foot*? The ancient Romans thought it was unlucky to enter a house or room with the left foot first. Wealthy Romans placed servants at the door to make sure that visitors came in on the right foot. Your college wants you to start off on the right foot. There are no servants to help you, so your success at college is up to you. Here are a few steps to help you start off on the right foot during your first weeks of school.

1. **Get to know your school.** Find important places on campus. You probably already know where your classes meet. It's a good idea to get the phone numbers, office numbers and email addresses of your instructors. You also need to know where to find basic campus services. These include:

   - student center
   - health center
   - financial aid office
   - library
   - computer lab
   - disability support services
   - learning centers

   Your campus phone book is a good place to look for these. You can also call the campus operator for help.

2. **Mix and mingle.** Get to know the people in your classes. Introduce yourself to at least one person in each class. When you meet new people, tell them about yourself. If you need help or advice, let others know. Faculty, staff, and other students may know how to help you. This helps you create a support network.

Get to know the resources on your campus. If your campus has a newspaper, read it regularly. Most newspapers have a calendar that lists campus activities, meetings, or other events.

3. **Get organized.** Once you get a course outline or syllabus from each class, make a term planner. Here's what you do: First, buy or make a monthly calendar with large squares for writing. Also get a copy of your school catalog's academic calendar. Second, take your monthly calendar and write in all holidays, school vacations, and academic due dates. These might include the last day to add or drop a course, registration for next term, and so on. Third, using your course outlines, write test dates and due dates for papers or other projects on your calendar. Fourth, write in personal dates like family time, doctor appointments, and so on.

4. **Go to class.** Go to your classes each time they meet—even if your instructors don't take attendance. You're the one going to college. You want to get the most from your classes. Do all the readings and homework. Before class, take three to five minutes to look over your reading assignments. When possible, sit at the front of the classroom. Be sure to take notes. Take another three to five minutes to look over your notes as soon as possible after each class.

5. **Work for yourself.** Do all the readings and homework you are assigned. Learning is not a spectator sport. Just as physical workouts exercise your body, reading and doing homework gives your brain a workout. Nobody can exercise for you, and nobody can learn for you. If you want to succeed, you have to do the work.

6. **Stay healthy.** Get enough sleep. Eat good foods. Exercise. College can be a busy time. It's easy to forget about your health, so make sure to take care of yourself.

7. **Get help when you need it.** If you have trouble in a class, talk to your instructor. If you need to make an important decision, visit the counseling center. If you need help paying for classes, go to the financial aid office. Start your school year off on the right foot by getting the help that you need to succeed in college!

How to Use This Book

This book can help you become a better reader. It includes a **table of contents**, 12 **chapters**, an **appendix**, a **glossary**, an **answer key**, and an **index.** For this book to be helpful, you need to know where each of these is and how to use them.

You'll find the **Contents** at the front of the book. This tells you the title of each chapter, what's inside each chapter, and the pages on which the chapters start.

Each chapter starts with "Objectives" like the ones below:

OBJECTIVES

After you finish this chapter this chapter, you should be able to

- Use context to identify parts of speech
- Get meaning from different kinds of context clues

Objectives tell you what you should know or be able to do after you finish a chapter. If you look at them before reading the chapter, they will help you know what to learn.

Next comes the "Chapter Outline." This shows you the topics in each chapter and helps you see the order of ideas.

CHAPTER OUTLINE

I. Using Context to Identify Parts of Speech

II. Using Context Clues to Find Meaning

    A. Text Context Clues

        1. Punctuation Clues

        2. Definition Clues

    B. Bridging Context Clues

        1. Contrast Clues

        2. Comparison Clues

        3. Example Clues

    C. Experiential Context Clues

After the Objectives and Chapter Outline, you will see a "Chapter Map" like the one on the next page. A chapter map shows a chapter's main ideas in a picture. It helps you see how ideas work together.

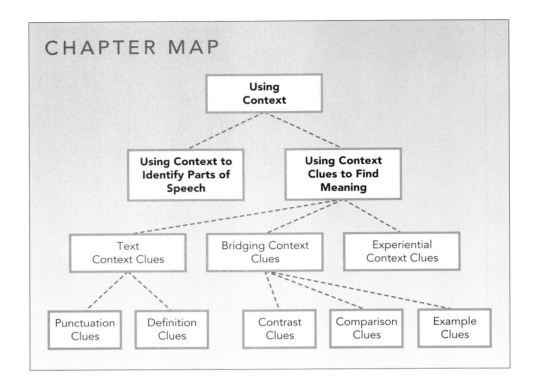

Next comes the "Vocabulary Check." The words in the Vocabulary Check are words that come from the chapter. They are shown in the order that they appear in the chapter. Some will be words you know, but some will be new words. You will be asked to rate them before you read. If you see a new word, you will rate it a 0. If you have seen the word before, but don't know what it means, you will rate it a 1. If you think you know what the word means, you will rate it a 2. If you know the word and can use it when you speak or write, you will rate it a 3. You will be asked to rate the terms again at the end of the chapter to help you see what you learned.

Included in the Vocabulary Check is a "Pronunciation Guide." The Pronunciation Guide will help you know how to say the words so you can add them to your everyday vocabulary. The way the words look in this column show you how they can be said aloud. If this is new to you, Chapter 3 tells how to use a pronunciation guide, and you may want to read it right away. You will also find a key to using the pronunciation guide on the inside covers of your book.

VOCABULARY CHECK

Before-Reading Ratings	Vocabulary Words	Pronunciation Guide (How do I say this word?)	After-Reading Ratings
	literal	ˈli-t(ə-)rəl	
	text context clues	ˌtekst ˈkän-ˌtekst ˈklüz	

Chapters also contain features within them to help you learn. **Major headings** and **subheadings** show how ideas work together. **Major headings** point out key topics. **Subheadings** divide a key topic into parts. For example, Chapter 5 contains 2 major headings. The first major heading is

Using Context to Identify Parts of Speech.

The second major heading is

Using Context to Find Meaning.

This part contains three subheadings. These are Text Context Clues, Bridging Context Clues, and Experiential Context Clues.

You will also see **boldfaced** words in dark print within the chapters. These are the same words you rated in the "Vocabulary Check" at the start of the chapter as well as other important words. Seeing these words in the chapters will help you to understand their meanings better. Most chapters contain **figures** and **tables** like the ones on page 256. These are special features that will help you organize ideas.

You will find several "Writing Connections" in each chapter. These are questions that ask you to think about what you've learned. They also help you think about new ideas. "Quick Reviews" appear at the end of sections. These true/false quizzes will help you know if you understand what you just read. The answers to the Quick Reviews can be found at the bottom of the page they're on. You'll also find lots of different **exercises** throughout each chapter. These let you practice what you've learned right away. The answers to these exercises can be found in the back of the book.

The end of each chapter also includes features to help you learn. College success involves more than reading skills. That's why every chapter includes a "Learning Tip" box. The information in these boxes give you tools to make the most of college. They include topics like:

- how to form a study group

- how to make the best use of your time

- how can you remember what you learned

- how to get along with your instructors

A "Chapter Summary" lists the chapter's main points and helps you review what you just read. The "Chapter Review" asks questions to help you find out what you've learned. You can use what you've learned in the "Action Summary" at the end of each chapter. These will help you make your new skills part of your daily life. The "Learning Online" section shows you where to go on the World Wide Web to learn more about a chapter topic or skill. The "Chapter Vocabulary Review" asks you to look again at the vocabulary words at the beginning of the chapter. This will help you check your understanding of chapter terms.

Finally, you should skim or quickly read the titles of the readings in the **Appendix.** This has the kinds of readings you'll find in college classes and on college campuses. These include readings from campus newspapers and websites. There are exercises that follow the readings. They will also help you practice your understanding of what you read and your vocabulary skills.

At the back of the book, you'll find a **Glossary.** This is like a dictionary. It defines the key vocabulary terms in each chapter. You'll also find an **Index.** This will help you find information by page number.

It's All about Your Success!

Each author of this book has worked with college students for more than 25 years. We know the college scene. We know students. We wrote this book to give you the skills and knowledge you need for college reading. What we don't know is your college. We don't know you.

A priority of every college is **retention.** This means that your school wants you to stay in school until you graduate. To do this, they offer services to help students succeed. That's why your school offers the course that uses this book.

Your college also hired teachers. Their job is to help you learn. But, teachers can't read your mind. They can't help you if they don't know you need help. If you don't understand something, you need to ask questions until you do.

We—your authors, your teachers, and you—have the same goal: for you to succeed in college. Let's go!

CHAPTER 1

Understanding Your New Environment

OBJECTIVES

After you finish this chapter, you should be able to

- Tell how to get the most from your college experience
- List the steps in **SOLVE** (a problem-solving method)

↳ON TEST

CHAPTER OUTLINE

I. Getting the Most from Your College Experience

II. Deciding What to Do: *SOLVE*

    A. **S** : Identify **S**ituations

    B. **O**: Think of **O**ptions

    C. **L** : Think of **L**ogical Outcomes

    D. **V** : Mo**V**e Forward

    E. **E** : **E**valuate Your Choice

CHAPTER MAP

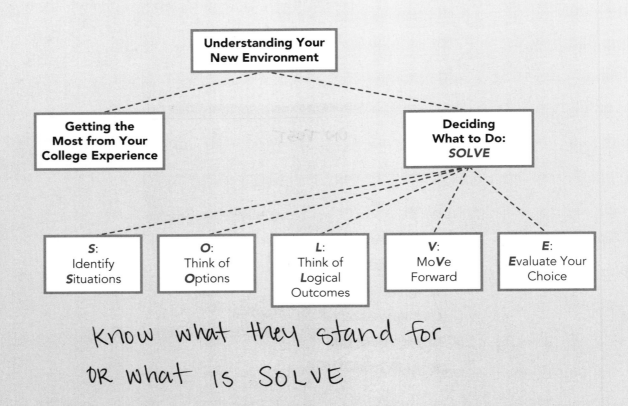

Understanding Your New Environment

Getting the Most from Your College Experience

Deciding What to Do: *SOLVE*

S: Identify **S**ituations

O: Think of **O**ptions

L: Think of **L**ogical Outcomes

V: Mo**V**e Forward

E: **E**valuate Your Choice

Know what they stand for
OR what IS SOLVE

VOCABULARY CHECK

Below are the vocabulary words you will need to know in this chapter.

If you see a word that's brand-new to you, write a 0 in the "Before-Reading Ratings" column. If you have seen the word before but don't know what it means, write a 1. If you think you know what the word means, write a 2. If you know the word and can use it in a sentence, write a 3.

If you wrote a 0 or 1, look up the word in the Glossary at the back of the book. Then, after reading the chapter, look at these words again and rate them in the "After-Reading Ratings" column. (The Chapter Vocabulary Review at the end of each chapter will tell you how to do this.)

If you come across new words in the chapter that are not on this list, underline them or write them in your notebook, and look them up in your dictionary. Write down their meaning. (If you need to review using a dictionary, go to Chapter 4.) This will help you increase your vocabulary.

Before-Reading Ratings	Vocabulary Words	Pronunciation Guide (How do I say this word?)	After-Reading Ratings
3	faculty	ˈfa-kəl-tē	
2	distance learning	ˈdis-tən(t)s ˈlərn-iŋ	
1	college catalog	ˈkä-lij ˈka-tə-ˌlȯg	
3	student handbook	ˈstü-dənt ˈhand-ˌbu̇k	
2	culture	ˈkəl-chər	
3	*SOLVE*	ˈsälv	
1	acronym	ˈa-krə-ˌnim	
1	learning styles	ˈlərn-iŋ ˈstī(-ə)lz	
2	logical thinker	ˈlä-ji-kəl ˈthiŋk-ər	

know these words
for test

Before-Reading Ratings	Vocabulary Words	Pronunciation Guide (How do I say this word?)	After-Reading Ratings
	global thinker	ˈglō-bəl ˈthiŋk-ər	
	visual learner	ˈvi-zhə-wəl ˈlərn-ər	
	auditory learner	ˈȯ-də-ˌtȯr-ē ˈlərn-ər	
	tactile learner	ˈtak-təl ˈlərn-ər	
	kinesthetic learner	ˌki-nəs-ˈthe-tik ˈlərn-ər	

> **There is no more vulnerable human combination than an undergraduate.**
>
> *John Sloan Dickey*
>
> President, Dartmouth University (1945–1970)

Welcome to college! So, how do you feel? Happy? Nervous? Maybe a little scared? Worried about all the work you have to do? There's a good chance you feel all of this and more. As John Sloan Dickey shares in the quote to the left, vulnerability (feeling helpless or at risk) is common in undergraduates. Many students just starting college feel this way. One way to feel good about your college life is to have success. In this book, we will share with you an important way to become successful—by becoming a better reader!

You will read a lot in college. The chapters in this book will help you build reading skills. One of the meanings of reading is *to figure out.* Your college success depends on your skills in reading—or figuring out—classes, people, situations, and even yourself. You need these skills right away. This chapter will help you "read," or figure out, your new campus. It gives tips and new ideas for making the most of your college days. It will also help you learn to make good choices.

As you read this chapter and the other chapters in this book, you will be learning a lot of new vocabulary words. If you come across a word that you don't know, underline it or write it in a notebook, then look it up in a dictionary. Write its meaning. If you need a dictionary review, take a quick look at Chapter 4. The more effort you put into learning new words, the faster you will become a better reader.

Getting the Most from Your College Experience

College is more than going to class. It is more than taking tests. Looking at your goals, dreams, and the world around you is also part of college life.

To get the most from college, you need to know who and what can help you here.

First, you need to know that college will not be like other schools. You must prove yourself in each class you take. Your new **faculty** (professors or teachers) don't know you. They don't know if you were a good student at other schools. They don't know if you were a high school dropout. Your age, experience, and background don't matter. They don't know if you like, dislike, or fear their subjects. You must finish more work in less time. You may have hundreds of pages to read for one class. Only two or three tests may decide your grade. There may be no homework due one week. A test, paper, or project could be due each day of the next week. No one will make sure you do your homework except you. You may have **distance learning** classes (online courses that do not take place in campus classrooms). In these classes, you often control the speed of the course. You may never meet your classmates or instructors face-to-face.

Second, you need to figure out your learning style. What is the best way for you to learn? One way to find out is by doing the Learning Tip box called "Reading Your Learning Styles" on page 13. Knowing how you learn best will help you use your time wisely. Stop now and go to the Learning Tip box. Take a few minutes to do the short tests to see what kind of learner you are.

Third, you need to learn about others around you. College students come from different backgrounds. They have different experiences. Each person you meet adds to your college experience. To learn from others, you must get to know them. You can start by meeting people in your classes. You might try introducing yourself to one person in each class. You may also want to exchange phone numbers or email addresses.

Fourth, you need to know how to find important places on campus. You already know the buildings and rooms where your classes meet. It's also a good idea to know where to find your instructors. You will need their phone numbers, office numbers, and email addresses. You also need to know where to find basic campus services. These include places like the student center, health center, and library. If you don't have a computer, you will have to find a computer lab. If you need help in a class, you might need to find a tutor. Tutors are fellow students who know a subject well. They can help you if you have problems in a class. Calling the campus operator can help you find a certain department. Your campus phone book is also a good place to find information. You can also search your campus website for what you need. Advisors, instructors, or other students are sources of help, too.

Fifth, you need to have a **college catalog** *and a* **student handbook.** These are filled with good information. They will tell you the rules of your college. The college catalog also contains information about courses and degrees.

Sixth, you need to learn about the **culture,** *or the customs, of your campus.* For instance, if your campus has a newspaper, read it regularly. Most newspapers have a calendar that lists campus events. You can learn when and where to go for concerts, art shows, plays, guest speakers, and sports events. Or, you can look on the bulletin boards in each building. These often give helpful information about your school's culture. Here you might find when the chess club meets or where you can try out for a part in a play.

Seventh, you need to meet people and form your own support group. A support group is made up of people who know you and want to help you. As you meet others, tell them about your interests, needs, and goals. The better people know you, the more they can help you. Your support group can include faculty, staff, and other students.

EXERCISE 1.1   **Who and what can help you at your campus? Where can you find help when you need it?** Use the worksheet below to help you learn about yourself and your campus. To find this information, try using your college catalog, your student handbook, your campus newspaper, and campus bulletin boards.

1. List each of your classes in the first column of the chart below. In the second column, write the name of one student in each class, along with their phone numbers and email addresses. In the third column, write your instructors' names, phone numbers, email addresses, and office numbers. (Hint: You might find this information on the syllabus your instructor gave you.)

Class	Students' names, phone numbers, and email addresses	Instructors' names, phone numbers, email addresses, and office numbers
	Nina (805) 264-3322 becerra_ni@hotmail.com	
	Nicole Guerrero 347-7693 nicoleguerrero67@yahoo.com	

2. List three services or activities you can find at the student center.

   1. _____

   2. _____

   3. _____

3. List three services or activities you can find at the bookstore.
   1. pencils
   2. note pads
   3. books

4. List three services or activities you can find at the health center.
   1. medicine
   2. first aid
   3. acute care

5. List three activities or organizations on your campus.
   1. New Paper
   2.
   3.

6. Where is the financial aid office located? Admission Office

7. List three services available at the library.
   1. Books
   2. Resource
   3. Tutors

8. Where can students use computers on campus? The LRC class

9. List the name, phone number, email address, and campus address of your advisor. Carol Brown 922-8256 303 East Plaza Dr,

10. What is the name of your campus newspaper?_____
    Where can you get a copy of the newspaper? _____

11. What is the Internet address of your campus website? _____
    www.sbbcollege.com

12. List three kinds of information you can find on your campus website.
    1. Classes
    2. registration
    3. financial aid

13. Go to the "Reading Your Learning Styles" box on page 13. Write what you found out about your learning style. What kind of thinker are you? Logical? Global? Or both? _I came up with both_ _for my learning style._

_____

Which way do you learn best? Are you a visual learner? An auditory learner? A tactile/kinesthetic learner? Or a mix of different types? _I am a tactile/kinesthetic learner_ _lear from doing._

QUICK REVIEW

Circle the correct answer. Check your answers at the bottom of the page before reading the next section.

1. A college catalog can help you learn more about your campus. (T) F

2. If you know your learning style, you will use your time better. (T) F

3. In college, you only learn in class or from faculty. T (F)

Deciding What to Do: **SOLVE**

Many college experiences involve choices. Should you go to class? Should you stay at home? Should you study, or should you party? Should you spend money or save it? Should you join this group or that one?

Many students are not used to a lot of choices. Parents, teachers, spouses, friends, bosses, and others may have helped them make choices before. But now students must decide for themselves. How can they—and you—know what to choose?

SOLVE is a way to help you think about your choices. *SOLVE* is an **acronym.** An acronym is a word that is made from key letters in a phrase. For the acronym *SOLVE*, the *S* comes from *Identify **S**ituations*. The *O* comes from *Think of **O**ptions*. The *L* comes from *Think of **L**ogical Outcomes*. The *V* comes from *Mo**V**e Forward*. The *E* comes from ***E**valuate Your Choice*. Using the steps in *SOLVE* can help you when you have to make a decision.

S: Identify Situations

Identifying a situation is the first step in *SOLVE*. To identify a situation, you write the decision you have to make. This will help you see the problem more clearly. It lets you see how a problem fits into the big picture of your

Quick Review Answers: 1. T   2. T   3. F

life. It helps you know if the problem is large or small. For example, in college you have to decide on a major. This is an important decision. Let's pretend you are interested in art and biology. You have to decide if you want to get a degree in art or in biology. Your first step is to state the problem, that is, to write it. Until you put it in words, it will be harder to make a decision.

O: Think of Options

Once you write the problem, your next step is to find ways to solve it. So, how do you decide what to major in—art or biology? At this stage, you think of every option or choice. Just remember, there are no right or wrong choices in this step. How do you do this? First, be curious and open to new ideas. Look at the college catalog. What classes will you have to take in biology? Do they interest you? Second, write lots of ideas. Some ideas will be easy to think of. Why do you like biology? What do you like about art? If you need help with ideas, talk to friends or faculty. If you want to know about a biology degree, for example, talk to a biology professor. If you're curious about an art degree, talk to an art professor. Third, make a list of your choices. This keeps you from forgetting about them. And last, don't be afraid to make a wrong turn. You are only thinking of your options, not making any final decisions yet.

L: Think of Logical Outcomes

Once you list your options, try to think of outcomes (what will happen) for each choice. Make a list of the positive (good) and negative (bad) sides to each choice. For instance, you might make the following list of "good" and "bad" sides to getting a degree in biology.

"Good" Sides to Getting a Degree in Biology	"Bad" Sides to Getting a Degree in Biology
1. Biology is something I do well.	1. I would have to move far away to get a good job.
2. I can find a good job with a degree in biology.	2. I would miss my family and friends.
3. I could make a lot of money.	3. I would miss not being able to work with art every day.
4. My family and friends would be proud of me.	

Once you have looked at possible outcomes, then set a deadline for making your choice. This gives you a time limit. Maybe your deadline will be after taking three science classes and three art classes. Once you make a choice, you need to try it on for size, so don't set a deadline that is too soon.

V: Mo**V**e Forward

Now that you've made a decision, it is time to move forward toward your goal. The steps you take will help you learn if the choice you made is the best one for you.

To move toward your goal, you must first *accept or support your choice.* You have carefully looked at your options. You feel good about your choice, and you need to think about it in a positive way. Second, *don't depend on others for success.* For instance, setting up a biology study group the week before final exams seems like a good choice. But what if group members get sick? What if they don't show up? If you depend only on the group for study, you may be unhappy with your grade. Third, *ask others for support.* This may seem like the opposite of the last suggestion, but there is a difference. Here, you do not depend on others. You use them only for help and support. They give you information, advice, and friendship. Fourth, *think about being a success.* Some people think about their mistakes over and over. If they get a bad test grade, they feel like their college life is over. They might think they will fail the next test, too. Then what happens? They fail just as they thought they would. Last, *avoid self-destruction.* In other words, don't make choices that can hurt you. For instance, when it's time to study, do you study in busy or noisy places where it's hard to concentrate? Do you try to study in the student center, or at home with kids playing, or with your friends? Think about how you could help yourself succeed. You could set up a quiet study area in your bedroom or dorm room. You could choose a quiet place like the library. You could turn off the phone. You could ask someone to babysit for a few hours.

E: **E**valuate Your Choice

You did it. You saw a situation that required a choice. You thought of options. You thought about results. You made a choice. But, did it work?

If it did, great! If not, don't worry. Most decisions can be changed. For instance, maybe you chose to major in biology. You knew you were interested in biology. You knew you would get a good job. But, now you are halfway through your classes and find that you hate science. This was not the right choice for you.

Do you have to stick to your choice? If a choice isn't working, what should you do? Be unhappy? Think that your life is over? No. You can think about your decision again and make a new choice. How do you know if the choice you made is a good one? Table 1.1 can help you decide.

Table 1.1   Did You Make the Right Choice?

1. Was there a choice to be made?
2. Are you happy with the outcome?
3. Have you given your choice enough time to work?
4. Were there any options that you did not think about?
5. Were you right about the good and bad results of the choice you made?
6. Was there anything about the situation or the options that you failed to think about?

EXERCISE 1.2   **From money to relationships, everyone has problems. You may be wondering how to pay your bills. You might not know what to major in. You might not get along with a family member or roommate. Which problem is most pressing for you now?** Use each of the steps in *SOLVE* to help you make a choice about that problem.

1. Identify a problem that you want to solve. _How to pay bills_

2. Describe the problem. _Not having income_

3. How important do you think the problem is in your life? Is it a big problem or a small one? _Big problem_

4. State the problem as clearly as possible. _Not having money to pay with_

5. Identify three options that can solve the problem and complete the following worksheet for each one.

Option 1:	
Positives (Good)	Negatives (Bad)

Option 2:	
Positives	Negatives

Option 3:	
Positives	Negatives

6. Which of the above options would you like to learn more about?

   _____

   Why? _____

7. Are you ready to make a decision yet? If so, what is your decision?

   _____

8. What steps can you take to move forward? _____

   _____

QUICK REVIEW

Circle the correct answer. Check your answers at the bottom of the page before reading the next section.

1. *SOLVE* is a way to help you think through choices. T F
2. Thinking of options is the first step in *SOLVE*. T F
3. You must come up with options on your own. T F
4. After making a choice, it is not a good idea to change your mind. T F

WRITING CONNECTION

Respond to the following on a separate sheet of paper or in your notebook.

What part of *SOLVE* do you think is hardest for you? Why?

Quick Review Answers: 1. T   2. F   3. F   4. F

LEARNING TIP
Reading Your Learning Styles

Are you right-handed or left-handed? Try writing your name with the hand that you don't usually write with. It probably feels strange. Writing like that takes more effort. Just as you find it is easier to use one hand rather than the other, you have ways of learning that are easier for you. These are your **learning styles**. When you know your learning styles, you can study better and you can learn more quickly.

Brain Styles

Scientists once thought that each side of the brain worked in different ways. New research says this is not so. It says your thinking is either called logical or global. (We'll talk about what these two words mean after you answer the questions below.) The next exercise helps you know what way of thinking is most comfortable or easiest for you.

EXERCISE

Answer the following questions. Circle your answer as you read each question.

1. How do you make decisions?
   A. I usually go with my first ideas.
   B. I think about my choices for a long time.
2. Which do you remember better?
   A. names
   B. faces
3. How do you make plans?
   A. I like to plan ahead.
   B. I like doing things at a moment's notice.
4. When talking with others, which do you like more: listening or speaking?
   A. I like being the listener.
   B. I like being the speaker.
5. What do you pay attention to when listening to a speaker?
   A. I pay attention to what the speaker says.
   B. I pay attention to the speaker's body language (the movements and mannerisms of a person).
6. Do you like to set goals for yourself?
   A. yes
   B. no

7. How would you describe your study area?
   A. messy
   B. neat and well-organized
8. Do you often know how much time has passed without looking at a clock?
   A. yes
   B. no
9. How do you write papers?
   A. I write down my thoughts as they come to me.
   B. I plan what I'm going to write.
10. What do you remember more about a song?
    A. the words
    B. the tune (music)
11. Are you good at remembering things?
    A. yes
    B. no
12. When you doodle (write or draw or scribble for fun), what do you doodle?
    A. shapes
    B. words
13. Put the palms of your hands together and lock your fingers. Which thumb is on top?
    A. left
    B. right
14. How do you plan your day?
    A. I make a list of what I want to do.
    B. I just let things happen.
15. Are you good at telling or showing your feelings?
    A. yes
    B. no
16. What do you usually do during an argument?
    A. I listen and consider the point of view of the other person.
    B. I insist that I am right.

Now circle your answers in the boxes on the next page. The row that has more answers circled shows the brain style that is more comfortable for you. If most of your answers are in the "Logical" row, then you are stronger as a **logical thinker.** If most of your answers are in the "Global" row, then you are a stronger **global thinker.** If the numbers are the same in both rows (or if they are different by 1 number), you are both a logical and a global thinker.

Logical:	1B	2A	3A	4B	5A	6A	7B	8A	9B	10A	11A	12B	13A	14A	15B	16B
Global:	1A	2B	3B	4A	5B	6B	7A	8B	9A	10B	11B	12A	13B	14B	15A	16A

What does this mean? If you are a **logical thinker,** you like details and order. You prefer lectures, readings, and outlines. You like to think about one idea for a long time. You enjoy concepts or ideas. You like things that involve numbers or words (e.g., math or word puzzles and games). You prefer information and facts that are true. When you can use information, you learn best. You like to plan when you will do things. You like to be in charge of what you do. You like objective tests where you can choose answers. These include multiple choice, true-false, or matching questions.

If you are a **global thinker,** you like see how information works together. You like main ideas more than details. You like to take pieces of information and put it together. You enjoy subjects like geometry or writing. You like to see information visually, like maps and charts. You prefer reading and listening. You think about more than one project at a time. You like subjective tests with essay or short-answer questions. They let you show how you can think creatively.

You may find that you are neither a logical nor a global thinker. Rather, you are a bit of both. In this case, you learn by combining features of each type.

Sense Styles   *of learners on test*   _know these styles!!_

There are different ways to get information, and you may prefer one more than others. These learning styles involve your senses. Some people are **visual learners.** They learn best from what they see. Some people are **auditory learners.** They learn best from what they hear. Some people are **tactile** or **kinesthetic learners.** Tactile learners learn best when they can touch things. Kinesthetic learners like to do things. Both tactile and kinesthetic learners like to be actively involved. Which are you? The next exercise helps you find out.

EXERCISE   Check the statements that describe you best.

Visual Learner

   ✓   I remember information better if I see it.

       I understand better when I watch people as they speak.

   ✓   I need a quiet place to get my work done.

_____ When I take a test, I can see my textbook pages in my head.

___✓___ I need to read directions, not just hear them.

_____ Music or other sounds bother me when I study.

_____ I don't always get the meaning of a joke.

___✓___ I draw pictures while I take notes.

_____ I have trouble following lectures.

_____ Some colors bother me.

___✓___ I remember faces better than names.

___✓___ I like to watch someone else do something before trying it myself.

_____ I often use flash cards and study guides.

_____ The one thing I need in life is TV.

___6___ **Total number of points**

Visual Learner

_____ My papers and notebooks always seem messy.

___✓___ When I read, I keep my place on the line with my finger.

_____ I do not follow written directions well.

___✓___ If I hear something, I will remember it.

_____ Writing has always been difficult for me.

_____ I often don't read words correctly (i.e., _them_ for _then_).

___✓___ I would rather listen and learn than read and learn.

_____ I'm not very good at figuring out someone's body language.

___✓___ Pages with small print or fuzzy print are hard for me to read.

_____ My eyes get tired quickly, even though my vision checkup is always fine.

_____ I remember names more easily than faces.

_____ I learn best when someone tells me what to do.

_____ I often use audio tapes to study.

_____ I like to learn in study groups.

_____ The one thing I need in life is music.

___4___ **Total number of points**

Tactile/Kinesthetic Learner

_____ ✓ I start a project before I read the directions.

_____ ✓ I hate to sit still for long periods of time.

_____ ✓ I like to learn by doing.

_____ I can handle multiple tasks.

_____ ✓ When solving problems, I try one answer and if it doesn't work, I try something else.

_____ I like to read while riding an exercise bike.

_____ I often take study breaks.

_____ I have a hard time giving step-by-step instructions to others.

_____ ✓ I am good at sports.

_____ ✓ I use my hands when describing things.

_____ ✓ I like to rewrite or type my notes after class.

_____ I remember what was done, not what was seen or talked about.

_____ ✓ When studying for a test, I often reorganize my notes or create maps.

_____ The one thing I need in life is sports.

_____ 8 **Total number of points**

Count the check marks you made in each section. Each check mark counts for 1 point. In what section did you have 10 or more checks or points? A score of 10 points or more in one section means that may be a style that works for you. Where did you get the highest number of points? In the "Visual Learner" section? Then you are a visual learner. You learn best by seeing information. In the "Auditory Learner" section? Then you learn best by hearing. Or in the "Tactile/Kinesthetic Learner" section? Then you learn best by being actively involved.

In which section did you get the second highest number of points? This is the section that supports or helps your best learning style. For example, let's say you scored highest in the Visual Learner section and second highest in Auditory Learner section. This means you learn best by seeing, but listening also helps you to learn.

CHAPTER SUMMARY

1. To do well in college, you need to read books, people, and situations. This book provides instructions and directions to improve your reading skills.

2. You can increase your success in college in several ways. First, you need to know the differences between college and other kinds of school. Second, you need to learn about yourself, others, and your college culture. Third, you need to know where to find useful places. Fourth, you need to know how to use a college catalog and student handbook. Fifth, you need to form your own support groups.

3. This book, together with your course instructor, provides you with skills and knowledge for college reading success.

4. *SOLVE* helps you make informed choices when making decisions.

CHAPTER REVIEW

On a separate sheet of paper, answer the questions below.

1. What does *reading* mean?
2. Describe *SOLVE* and list the steps in the process.
3. What did you learn about your learning styles? How can you use this to become a better learner?

ACTION SUMMARY

• Which ideas from this chapter do I already use?

_____

_____

• Which ideas from this chapter are new to me?

_SOLVE_____

_____

• The best idea I learned from this chapter is . . . . Why?

_the SOLVE because it helps me_____

_see out of the box._____

• Ideas from this chapter I would like to try are . . . .

_SOLVE._____

_____

• How will I put the new ideas I've learned into action?

Use it when I have a choice that is difficult to make.

LEARNING ONLINE

The World Wide Web provides many tools for learning about college success. Go to http://developmentalenglish.wadsworth.com/atkinson-longman to find the website for *Reading Strategies for Today's College Student*. This website is designed for students using this book. Here you will find:

• fun and interesting websites related to reading
• web exercises and reading quizzes that will help you become a better reader
• a list of chapter objectives
• a glossary of terms used in the chapter
• flashcards
• crossword puzzles

CHAPTER VOCABULARY REVIEW

Go back to the "Vocabulary Check" at the beginning of the chapter. Now that you've read this chapter, rate how well you understand the vocabulary words in the "After-Reading Ratings" column. If you rate any word less than a 3, read the information about that term again.

CHAPTER 2

Reading for College

OBJECTIVES

After you finish this chapter, you should be able to

- Describe reading and study plans
- Know how to set goals for reading
- Identify ways to make sense of what you read
- Describe ways to review actively

CHAPTER OUTLINE

I. Reading and Study Plans

    A. Three Types of Reading and Study Plans

        1. SQ3R

        2. SQ4R

        3. PQRST

II. Step 1: The Overview

    A. Three Types of Chapter Guides

        1. Pre-Chapter Guides

        2. Intra-Chapter Guides

        3. Post-Chapter Guides

    B. Three Types of Chapter Overviews

        1. Previewing

        2. Outlining

        3. Mapping

III. Step 2: Setting Learning Goals

IV. Step 3: Reading and Checking Understanding

V. Step 4: Active Review Strategies

CHAPTER MAP

5 min {
① Preview
② Question
③ Intra-chapter guides a)maps

Take notes {
④ Read chapter → Aloud
⑤ Re-Read
⑥ Questions

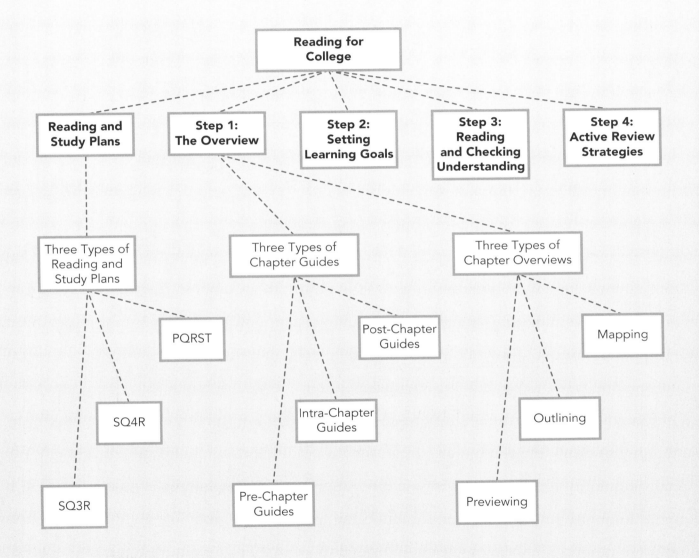

VOCABULARY CHECK

Below are the vocabulary words you will need to know in this chapter.

If you see a word that's brand-new to you, write a 0 in the "Before-Reading Ratings" column. If you have seen the word before but don't know what it means, write a 1. If you think you know what the word means, write a 2. If you know the word and can use it in a sentence, write a 3.

If you wrote a 0 or 1, look up the word in the Glossary at the back of the book. Then, after reading the chapter, look at these words again and rate them in the "After-Reading Ratings" column.

If you come across new words in the chapter that are not on this list, underline them or write them in your notebook, and look them up in your dictionary. This will help you increase your vocabulary.

Before-Reading Ratings	Vocabulary Words	Pronunciation Guide (How do I say this word?)	After-Reading Ratings
	reading and study plan	'rē-diŋ ən(d) 'stə-dē 'plan	
	overview	'ō-vər-ˌvyü	
	pre-chapter guides	prē-'chap-tər 'gīdz	
	intra-chapter guides	'in-trə-'chap-tər 'gīdz	
	post-chapter guides	'pōst-'chap-tər 'gīdz	
	previewing	'prē-ˌvyü-iŋ	
	outlining	'aùt-ˌlīn-iŋ	
	mapping	'map-iŋ	
	mnemonics	ni-mä-nikz	

KNOW THE VOCAB

> **You've really got to start hitting the books because it's no joke out here.**
>
> *Spike Lee*
>
> Twentieth-century American Filmmaker

At first, college looks easy. You have lots of time. There are few demands. You're in class a few hours a week. There's no homework due yet. Some instructors don't take attendance. Some don't collect homework. You have new places to go, new people to meet. Your life as a college student *is* easy . . . until you have to take tests. Quickly, you learn college is no joke. You've got to "hit the books"—that is, you have to open them, read them, *and* understand what you've read. But how do you really hit the books? It takes more than just looking through the pages and chapters. Hitting the books requires a plan.

Reading and Study Plans

[handwritten note: Have an idea on what these are →]

Have you ever read a page or a chapter, and still didn't know what it was about? Maybe you were just looking at the words but not understanding them. If so, you know that looking and learning are not the same. Looking is just seeing the words. Learning is knowing what the words, pages, and chapters mean. Reading is a skill—one that you must practice. Learning to read better is a process that takes time and effort. Think about a skill you have. Are you good at a sport, like basketball? Can you bake a cake that your family loves? Do you play the guitar? Now think about when you first developed your skill. Maybe you couldn't sink a basket the first few times on the court. Your first cake might not have tasted very good. And the first song you tried to play might have made your dog howl. But following a plan helped you improve your skill. In sports, you have a game plan. In baking, you have a recipe. In music, you have notes to follow. You had to spend time trying to get better and following the plan until you were good at your skill. Reading and learning are no different. You have to practice and spend time doing them until you get better. You also have to have a plan—a **reading and study plan.** That is what you will learn in this chapter.

Three Types of Reading and Study Plans

[handwritten note: 1. SQ3R 2. SQ4R 3. PQRST]

Most reading and study plans use a word or an *acronym* (a word made from a letter—usually the first letter—of each word in the plan) to help you remember their steps. Three of the most common study plans are SQ3R, SQ4R, and PQRST.

SQ3R

[handwritten note: SURVEY QUESTION READ RECITE REVIEW]

One of the most well-known plans is called *SQ3R*. Each letter in SQ3R stands for a learning step. The *S* stands for *Survey.* In the Survey step, you look over what you need to read. The *Q* stands for *Question.* In this step you ask questions about what you are going to read. This helps you set learning goals. Next come three *R*s. The first *R* stands for *Read.* At this step, you begin to read. The second *R* stands for *Recite.* This means that you say out loud what you read and what you remember. The third *R* stands for *Review*. Here, you look back over what you read to help you remember it.

SQ4R

Another reading and study plan is called *SQ4R*. It includes all the steps in SQ3R of *Survey, Question, Read, Recite,* and *Review*. But it also adds a fourth *R: wRite*. In this last step, you write about what you read.

PQRST

A third common reading and study plan is *PQRST*. The steps in this plan are: *Preview* (looking ahead at what you will read), *Question, Read, Summarize* (looking back at what you read), and *Test* (seeing if you remember what you read).

Each of these plans is a little different from the others, but the steps are similar. The goal of each plan is the same—to help you read and study better. The next section will discuss each step in more detail.

QUICK REVIEW

Circle the correct answer. Check your answers at the bottom of the page before reading the next section.

1. Reading and study plans help you become an active learner. **(T)**   F

2. Setting goals is the first step in most reading/study plans.   T   **(F)**

3. The last step in most reading and study plans is a review of information.   **(T)**   F

Step 1: The Overview (KNOW all this!!)

Your first step in a reading and study plan is an **overview**. This is the *survey* or *preview* stage in SQ3R, SQ4R, and PQRST. An overview is a quick look at a chapter or book. This gives you an idea of what the chapter or book is about. You look for information that you already know. You look at how the chapter is organized. You look at the text features, such as the chapter guides. You try to decide which text features are most important.

Three Types of Chapter Guides

How do you know which features in a chapter are most important? The chapter itself can provide clues in the pre-chapter guides, the intra-

Quick Review Answers: 1. T   2. F   3. T

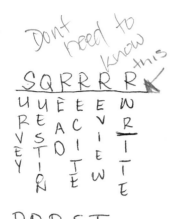

Don't need to know this

S Q R R R R
U U E E E W
R E A C V R
V S D I I I
E T O T E T
Y I T E W E
  O N T   E
  N   E

P Q R S T
R U E U E
E E A M S
V S D M T
I T M A
E I   R
W O   I
  N   Z
      E

chapter guides, and the post-chapter guides. (All textbooks are different, but you will usually find features like these.)

Pre-Chapter Guides

Some clues are at the beginning of a chapter. They tell you about chapter content—what's in the chapter. These are called **pre-chapter guides.** Pre-chapter guides include the following:

- Chapter title—The chapter title tells you what the chapter is about. You can ask yourself: Based on this title, what do I think will be covered in this chapter? What do I already know about this topic?

- Chapter introduction—The chapter introduction tells you the important ideas in the chapter. You can ask yourself: What do I need to learn from this chapter? (How did the introduction to this chapter on page 23 let you know what this chapter is about?)

- Pre-reading questions—Pre-reading questions show you what is important in a chapter. You use these to answer questions while you read. You can ask yourself: What questions does the author think are important?

- Key terms—Key terms show what words are important in the chapter. You can ask yourself: What words are new to me? Which words do I already know? (In this book the key terms are found in the "Vocabulary Check.")

- Chapter outline or map—The chapter outline or map shows you how the chapter is organized. You can ask yourself: How does this chapter organize ideas? (This book has both chapter outlines and chapter maps.)

- Chapter objectives—Chapter objectives tell you what you should know after reading the chapter. You can ask yourself: What does the author want me to know or do? (This is also a feature used at the beginning of each chapter in this book.)

Intra-Chapter Guides

Some clues are in the chapter. They help you find your way through a chapter. These are called **intra-chapter guides.** Intra-chapter guides include the following:

- Headings/subheadings—Headings and subheadings point out important information. You can ask yourself: What do the headings look like? What do the subheadings look like? How do headings and subheadings work together? (In this book, the Level 1 headings, which are the most important headings, look like this: Level 1 Headings. The Level 2 headings, which tell more about the information under the Level 1 headings, look like this: Level 2 Headings. The Level 3 headings, which tell more about the information in the Level 2 headings, look like this: Level 3 Headings. The Level 4 headings—which tell more information about the Level 3 headings—look like this: **Level 4 Headings**.

- Key terms in context—The key terms in context show how vocabulary words are used in the chapter. You can ask yourself: Do I know this word? What does it mean? How is it used? (In this book, key terms are in **boldfaced** text the first time they are used.)

- Text boxes—Text boxes give you more information about a chapter topic. You can ask yourself: Why is this box important? How does it fit into the rest of the chapter? (Look on page 42 for an example of the text boxes used in this book.)

- Different typefaces—Typefaces are the different style of letters used in a book. Some typefaces are in a different color. Some are bolded **like this** or in italics *like this*. Some are underlined <u>like this</u>. Different typefaces show important information. You can ask yourself: What do the different typefaces mean? (Take a quick look through this book and see where you find bolded or italicized text.)

- Graphics—Graphics are visual aids that show ideas in picture form. Graphics can include figures, charts, photographs, and maps. You can ask yourself: Why are these visual aids included? What do they show? What do they mean? (Chapter 11 shows a number of different types of graphics.)

- Marginal notes—Marginal notes can be found in the white space of a page, usually on the left or right side of the page. These notes give you extra information about a topic in the chapter. You can ask yourself: Why are these marginal notes important? How do they relate to the text?

Post-Chapter Guides

Some clues are at the end of a chapter. They help you make sure you understand chapter content. These are called **post-chapter guides.** Post-chapter guides include the following:

- Chapter summary—The chapter summary reviews main ideas. You can ask yourself: What does the author think are the main point(s) of the chapter? (Take a quick look at the chapter summary for this chapter on page 44.)

- Review questions—Review questions help you test your understanding of what you read. You can ask yourself: What information did I understand? What information did I not understand? What should I review? (Look at the chapter review questions at the end of this chapter on page 44)

- Terms—If key terms are not shown at the start of chapters, they might be shown at the end. You can ask yourself: Did I understand the important words in the chapter? What words do I need to study further?

- Suggested readings—Suggested readings tell you where you can read more on the chapter topic. You can ask yourself: Do I need more information? What more can I learn about the chapter topic?

Three Types of Chapter Overviews

Now that you know the clues to look for, let's talk about three different ways to get an overview: previewing, outlining, and mapping. Read the description of each one, try each one, and then choose the one that works best for you.

Previewing

Previewing a chapter means you look through it before reading it. But it is much more than just looking at pages. It is a careful study of what is in each chapter. If you use the chapter guides, a preview will help you know what you need to learn in each chapter. Be sure that you write down what you preview. This keeps you on target and makes previewing active. Below are the preview steps you need to know.

1. **Read the chapter title.** Write the chapter title at the top of a sheet of paper. This is your preview page.
2. **Read the introduction or first paragraph of the chapter.** Ask yourself: What is this chapter about? In just a few sentences, write the answer to this question below the title of your preview page.
3. **Read the headings and subheadings in the chapter.** Answer the question: How do the headings and subheading work together?
4. **Read the first sentence or paragraph under each heading and subheading.** This tells you what is important in each section. Answer the question: What is the main idea under each heading? Write these on your preview page.
5. **Pay attention to graphics.** How are tables, maps, figures, or photos used in the chapter? Answer the question: How will these help me when reading this chapter? Note key graphics on your preview page.
6. **Note any different typefaces (boldface, underlining, *italics*).** Where do you see boldfaced words? Which words are underlined? Are any words in italics? Answer the question: How will the different typefaces help me when reading this chapter?

7. **Read the last paragraph or summary.** This will help you see what is important in the chapter. Compare it with the main idea of the first paragraph. Answer the question: What is the main idea in the last paragraph or summary? Write this on your preview page.

8. **Read the objectives at the beginning of the chapter.** Write them on your preview page. Answer the question: What should I learn from this chapter?

9. **Read the list of key terms at the beginning or end of the chapter.** Write the words on your preview page. Answer the question: Which words do I know? Which words are new to me?

Outlining

The second type of overview is making an outline. **Outlining** shows which ideas are the most important, and which are less important. Outlining also show how ideas relate to each other.

In an outline, the chapter title is the topic. Headings are major points. Subheadings show minor points. Information within headings and subheadings tell important or additional facts.

Outlines can be formal or informal. Below is a formal outline of this chapter. Formal outlines use Roman numerals (I, II, III, and so on). You place these on the left side of the page or margin. They show main concepts. Ideas that support the main concepts are indented (moved in). These are shown by capital letters (A, B, C, etc.). Lesser details are indented further. Arabic numerals (1, 2, 3) mark them.

FORMAL OUTLINE

I. Reading and Study Plans
   A. Three Types of Reading and Study Plans
      1. SQ3R
      2. SQ4R
      3. PQRST
II. Step 1: The Overview
   A. Three Types of Chapter Guides
      1. Pre-Chapter Guides
      2. Intra-Chapter Guides
      3. Post-Chapter Guides
   B. Three Types of Chapter Overviews
      1. Previewing
      2. Outlining
      3. Mapping
III. Step 2: Setting Learning Goals
IV. Step 3: Reading and Checking Understanding
V. Step 4: Active Review Strategies

Outlines don't need to be formal. The idea is to mark information visually so you can see connections within it. Informal outlines use the indented format of formal outlines. To make informal outlines clear, you divide major headings and sections by drawing a line between them. Use symbols, dashes, or checks to show rank. Here is an informal outline of this chapter:

INFORMAL OUTLINE

Reading and Study Plans
- — Three Types of Reading and Study Plans
  - • SQ3R
  - • SQ4R
  - • PQRST

Step 1: The Overview
- — Three Types of Chapter Guides
  - • Pre-Chapter Guides
  - • Intra-Chapter Guides
  - • Post-Chapter Guides
- — Three Types of Chapter Overviews
  - • Previewing
  - • Outlining
  - • Mapping

Step 2: Setting Learning Goals

Step 3: Reading and Checking Understanding

Step 4: Active Review Strategies

Mapping

The third way to get an overview is creating a map. In **mapping**, you make a drawing like a map to show how written ideas work together. Mapping gives you a visual overview, or a picture, of the chapter. Look at the chapter map at the beginning of this (or any) chapter, and then read the steps below about mapping a chapter.

1. Take a sheet of paper and write the first major chapter heading in the top left corner. (This is a Level 1 heading.) Decide if you want to draw boxes or circles (or any other shape) around the major headings. In this chapter the first major heading is "Reading and Study Plans."

2. If there are subheadings (Level 2 headings) in the section, write them below the Level 1 major heading. Use lines to join them to the major heading. In this chapter, the first subheading is "Three Types of Reading and Study Plans."

3. If there is another level of subheadings (Level 3 headings), write them below the Level 2 subheadings. Use lines to connect them to the Level 2 subheadings. In this chapter, the Level 3 subheadings are "SQ3R," "SQ4R," and "PQRST."

4. In some books, there may even be a Level 4 heading. If that is the case, continue the process above.

5. Start this process again when you come to the next Level 1 heading. In this chapter, the next major heading is "Step 1: The Overview."

6. Repeat the steps until the end of the chapter.

EXERCISE 2.1

What kinds of chapter guides are in your textbooks? For this exercise, you will need paper, this book, and two textbooks from other classes.

1. Divide a piece of paper into three columns. Label the first column *Pre-Chapter Guides*. Label the second column *Intra-Chapter Guides*. Label the third column *Post-Chapter Guides*.

2. Pick a chapter in this book. Find the chapter guides and write them in the correct columns.

3. Do Step 2 again, using a textbook from one of your other classes.

4. Choose a third textbook. Do Step 2 again.

5. In a paragraph, tell which book had the chapter guides you liked most. Explain why you liked them.

EXERCISE 2.2

You need to try all of the overview strategies to know which one works best for you. Choose a textbook from one of your other classes. You can use one of the textbooks you used in Exercise 2.1. Complete the following exercise on a piece of paper.

1. Write down a preview of one chapter.

2. Make a formal or informal outline of one chapter. (The chapter does not need to be the same as the one used for Step 1.)

3. Create a chapter map of one chapter. (The chapter does not need to be the same as the one used for Steps 1 or 2.)

4. In a paragraph, tell about the overview you liked best. Explain why you liked it best.

QUICK REVIEW

Circle the correct answer. Check your answers at the bottom of the page before reading the next section.

1. Authors give clues about what is important in texts.   **T**   **F**

2. An overview helps you review information after reading.   **T**   **F**

3. There is only one correct way to get an overview of information.   **T**   **F**

Quick Review Answers: 1. T   2. F   3. F

WRITING CONNECTION

Respond to the following on a separate sheet of paper or in your notebook.

Which previewing strategy fits your learning style best? Why? (If you need to, go back to the "Learning Tip" on page 13 in Chapter 1.)

Step 2: Setting Learning Goals

Your second step in a reading and study plan is to set learning goals. For many students, the goal of reading is just to finish. But finishing is not the point of college reading. *Learning* is the point. If you read without thinking, you miss the point. Setting learning goals before you begin reading gives you a purpose, or reason, for reading. Setting learning goals makes reading active. This means you take actions to make your learning happen.

Asking questions while reading is a good way to set learning goals. Some books have questions in the headings or subheadings. As you read, you try to answer these questions. This makes reading active. But not all texts have questions. So where do you get your questions? You can use *questioning words* to turn headings and subheadings into questions. Tables 2.1 and 2.2 show questioning words for main ideas and details.

When you ask questions, you want to find the important ideas in a section. Three questioning words that help you find these are *why, how,* and *what* (see Table 2.1). A question that begins with *why* asks for reasons. A question that begins with *how* helps you find a way. A question that

Table 2.1   Questioning Words for Main Ideas

If You Want to Know . . .	Then Ask . . .
a reason	Why?
a way	How?
a purpose or definition	What?
a fact	What?

Table 2.2   Questioning Words for Details

If You Want to Know . . .	Then Ask . . .
a person	Who?
a number or amount	How many?/How much?
a choice	Which?
a time	When?
a place	Where?

begins with *what* helps you find a purpose, fact, or definition. For example, look at the first major heading in this chapter. It is "Reading and Study Plans." Using questioning words, you could ask yourself:

• What are reading and study plans?

• How do I use reading and study plans?

• Why should I use reading and study plans?

You can also use questioning words to help you find details. Look at Table 2.2. Knowing details helps you understand what you've read more fully. After reading a section in a textbook, you can ask yourself *who, how many* or *how much, which, when,* and *where.* The questioning word *who* asks for a person's name. *How many* or *how much* asks for a number or amount. *Which* asks you to make a choice. *When* and *where* ask for a time and place. For example, if you were reading a chapter on the Vietnam War in your history book, you could ask yourself:

• Who was the president of the United States during the Vietnam War?

• How many soldiers fought in the Vietnam War?

• How much money did the United States spend on the Vietnam War?

• Which countries fought in the Vietnam War?

• When did the Vietnam War begin? When did it end?

• Where is Vietnam?

   Other chapter guides help you set learning goals, too. For example, chapter objectives tell what you should know or be able to do after reading a chapter. Post-chapter guides also can help you set learning goals. Some authors put review questions at the end of a chapter. Reading them before reading the chapter helps set reading goals. You can look for the answers as you read.

EXERCISE 2.3 **Asking questions about information you get from overviewing helps you set learning goals.** Choose one of the outlines or maps you made in Exercise 2.2. On a separate sheet of paper, rewrite the outline or map in question form. Use the questioning words in Tables 2.1 and 2.2.

QUICK REVIEW

Circle the correct answer. Check your answers at the bottom of the page before reading the next section.

1. Finishing a chapter is the point of college reading. T F

2. Turning chapter headings and subheadings into questions is one way to set learning goals. T F

3. Chapter objectives and review questions can also be used to set learning goals. T F

Step 3: Reading and Checking Understanding

Your third step in a reading and study plan is reading and checking understanding. You have practiced getting overviews, and you know how to set learning goals. The next step is reading and understanding. You try to make sense of what you read. You organize it so you can remember it.

When you read a page or a chapter, you usually know right away if you have understood the information. If you didn't understand, what do you do? Like many students, you might read the passage or page again. If you understand after the second reading, you can summarize it. You can write about what you know. But, what do you do if you don't understand after the second reading?

There could be several reasons you are having problems. Maybe you can't focus on the reading. Maybe it seems like the reading is taking a very long time. Below are some common reading problems and ways to solve them.

1. **I can't concentrate or stay focused.**
   - Find a quiet place to read. Turn off the TV or music. Go to the library or a quiet room away from people.

Quick Review Answers: 1. F 2. T 3. T

- Study in short blocks of time over a longer period. Maybe you could read three or four pages, then take a short break. Stand up and walk around. When you come back, review what you read before, then read a few more pages.

- Find a place and time when you won't be bothered. Keep paper, pens, sticky notes, and highlighters in this area. Make this your "office" and go there to work.

- Before you begin reading and studying, decide what you want to get done. Then study until you meet this goal.

2. **I just don't understand what I'm reading.**

   - Read the page or section again.

   - Use the questioning words in Table 2.2 to look for details.

   - Read out loud what is confusing you. Sometimes reading it out loud will help you understand. That's because you know some words when you hear them but not when you read them silently.

   - Write the important ideas of sections in your own words.

   - Look in another book. You can find books on the same subject in your campus library. (Chapter 12 gives you information on using the Internet to find books you need at your campus library.) The authors of these books may explain topics in ways that are easier to understand. You can return to your text for more information, if needed.

   - See your instructor or a tutor. Both are there to help you when you need it. Don't be afraid to ask for help.

   - Form a study group. Get together after reading a chapter so you can talk about it. (The "Learning Tip" box on page 74 in Chapter 3 tells how to form a study group.)

3. **It's taking me a long time to read one chapter!**

   - It's okay to take your time reading. Read difficult chapters as slowly as you need to. Read easier chapters more quickly.

   - Practice reading different materials. Try reading magazines, newspapers, and novels. Your practice with these will increase your reading speed.

   - Take a speed-reading course. Some campuses offer workshops that give suggestions to help you read faster. Your instructor or advisor can help you find one.

   - Read for fun! Find books on topics that you like and enjoy them. The more you learn to enjoy reading, the easier it will become for you.

QUICK REVIEW

Circle the correct answer. Check your answers at the bottom of the page before reading the next section.

1. Reading out loud can help you understand what you've read. **T** **F**

2. Lack of concentration is not a common reading problem. **T** **F**

3. Studying for big blocks of time will make learning easier. **T** **F**

Step 4: Active Review Strategies

The fourth and final step in your reading and study plan is using active review strategies. Reviewing is more than just rereading. Reviewing, like learning, must be an active process. Reviewing helps you remember what you read. Active review strategies make learning last. In most classes, you will have to recall what you have read. You will have to show your professors what you learned. Reviewing will help you do this. It will help you to study better. Here are some review strategies to try.

- Make concept maps like the one you learned to do in the section "Three Types of Chapter Overviews." Look at them or redraw them again and again.

- Make flash cards. Write review questions and answers, main ideas, or other information from chapters on index cards or note cards. Read through them until you can remember the information written on the cards.

- Change chapter objectives, key words, and major headings into questions. Use them to make a study guide for yourself.

- Answer the review questions at the beginning or end of chapters. Study the answers until you know them.

- Meet with a study group. Go over the review questions and your study guides. You can even use your flash cards with your study group.

- If there are chapter objectives in your book, do you understand them? Can you do them? If not, go back and find what you need to learn.

- If there is a chapter summary, check to see that you understand the points in it. If not, find them in the chapter and reread those sections.

- Look at the first major heading in your chapter, and then write everything you can recall about that topic. Look back to make sure you didn't leave anything out. Do the same for the other major headings.

Quick Review Answers: 1. T   2. F   3. F

- If there are review tests at the end of chapters, be sure to take them.

- Take the study guides that you have made and read them out loud.

Here is something important for you to think about: *When* you review is as important as what you do to review. Many students cram. This means they wait until the night before a test to start studying. Some students even wait until right before a test to start reviewing. Last-minute study is more stressful. It is hard to remember what you've learned when you are worried about the time. And it is difficult to get a good grade when you don't give yourself enough time to study. Like practicing other skills, it's better to plan many short reviews. Review sessions don't need to be long. They can be only 5 or 10 minutes. Table 2.3 shows how you might plan an hour-long study session. It includes a brief review. It also has a planned break. You need breaks in your study sessions. The break gives information time to soak into your brain.

Table 2.3 Sample 60-Minute Study Session

10 minutes	Survey information by creating a map or outline of what you will read. For instance, perhaps your instructor assigned Chapter 5 in your history text.
2 minutes	Set a learning goal. For example: My learning goal is to read and make notes for the first ten pages of Chapter 5.
30 minutes	Read and make notes for Chapter 5.
8 minutes	Review your notes for Chapter 5. This quick review provides immediate practice of what you've learned.
10 minutes	Take a break. The break gives your brain time to rest. It also helps the brain store what you've learned.

WRITING CONNECTION

Respond to the following on a separate sheet of paper or in your notebook.

Which of the active review strategies have you used? Which one will you try? Why?

QUICK REVIEW

Circle the correct answer. Check your answers at the bottom of the page before reading the next section.

1. Reviewing should be an active process. **T** **F**

2. A single long review is better than several short reviews. **T** **F**

3. Learning does not need the same kinds of regular practice that other skills require. **T** **F**

4. Taking breaks while studying makes it difficult for you to remember what you are studying. **T** **F**

EXERCISE 2.4 **Active review increases recall.** Now that you've read this chapter, you can use one of the active review strategies in "Step 4: Active Review Strategies" to help you learn the content. Write a paragraph on why you chose the strategy you used.

EXERCISE 2.5 **Some study plan steps can be used with other types of readings.** On page 38 is a section from a college catalog. Read the general education requirements that appear there. On a separate sheet of paper, do the following:

1. Set goals for reading by changing each heading to a question, like "What are general education requirements?"

2. Write these questions on paper on a separate sheet of paper. Answer them after you read the information.

3. Get a copy of the general education requirements for your school. These should be in the college catalog or on your college website.

4. Write a paragraph that compares the two sets of requirements. How are they alike? How are they different?

Quick Review Answers: 1. T   2. F   3. F   4. F

GENERAL EDUCATION REQUIREMENTS

Tools of Learning 18

1 Students must take coursework that helps them learn and use information. This should include writing (6 hours), math (3 hours), oral communication (3 hours), computer skills (3 hours), and critical thinking (3 hours). These courses become learning tools.

Humanities and Social Sciences 18

2 Students must learn to think about themselves and the world around them. This includes literature (3 hours), culture (3 hours), history and government (6 hours), and social sciences (6 hours).

Sciences 3-4

3 Students must learn about the scientific process. They should develop skills for exploring ideas. One course should include a lab. Sciences requirements include biological (3–4 hours) and natural sciences (3–4 hours).

Personal Development 7

4 Students must have the competencies they need for lifelong success. Students may choose any 2 of the following: Student Success Seminar (1 hour), physical education (1 hour), service learning (1 hour), ROTC (1 hour), personal health (2 hours), or career planning (1 hour).

VOCABULARY   These vocabulary words are in the catalog page above. Answer each question. For words you do not know, check your dictionary.

1. A *competency* is a _____.
   A. skill
   B. strategy
   C. process
   D. technique

2. A *requirement* _____.
   A. can be done
   B. is suggested
   C. must be done
   D. has already been done

3. *Oral communication* involves _____ language.
   A. written
   B. spoken
   C. translated
   D. foreign

VOCABULARY BUILDER

List five words from the catalog section and/or from your college's information that are new to you. Look up each word in a dictionary. Write down what it means. (If there is more than one meaning, choose the one you think fits best.) Use the word in a sentence of your own.

1. mnemonics - memory tricks

2. previewing - an advance showing or introductory.

3. diagraph - a pair of letters joined to form a glyph (ae)

4. syllable - unit of organization to form a unit of speech.

5. Schwa - an unstressed and toneless neutral vowel sound in any language.

COMPREHENSION

How much did you understand in the reading? Read the questions below and circle the correct answer.

1. What is the total number of learning tool credits required?
   A. 12 hours
   B. 15 hours
   C. 18 hours
   D. 21 hours

2. Which of the following is true?
   A. The number of learning tool hours is more than the number of humanities and social studies hours.
   B. The number of learning tool hours is less than the number of humanities and social studies hours.
   C. The number of learning tool hours is equal to the number of humanities and social studies hours.

3. Which of the following is described as a competency for lifelong success?
   A. computer literacy
   B. critical thinking
   C. service learning
   D. written communication

EXERCISE 2.6   **Some study plan steps can be used with other readings—even information found on the Internet.** Preview the article below from a government website first, then do the following:

1. Set goals for reading by changing each heading to a question. For example, the second heading could become "How can you decide where and how to serve?"

2. Write your questions on a separate piece of paper. Leave several blank lines between each question.

3. Read, and make a note when you find the answers to your questions.

4. Write the answers below each question.

5. What is the main idea of the website? Write your answer at the bottom of your page.

AMERICORPS: ARE YOU UP TO THE TASK?

1   Put your values to work through AmeriCorps. Make a community safer. Help a kid learn. Protect the environment. Whatever your interest, there's an AmeriCorps program that needs you. It needs your courage, your skills, and your dedication.

2   Do something special, something **unique,** or something exciting. Are you up to the challenge?

You decide where and how to serve.

3   Each year, more than 40,000 members serve with programs in every state in the nation. You can tutor kids in your own community, or build new homes for families far away from your home. **Restore** coastlines or help families traumatized by domestic violence. You might do the work yourself, or help others serve by planning projects and getting volunteers. Whatever you do, there's an AmeriCorps challenge just waiting for you.

Get an education, experience, and skills.

4   You'll learn teamwork, communication, responsibility, and other essential skills that will help you for the rest of your life. And you'll gain the personal satisfaction of taking on a challenge and seeing results.

You will be able to pay your bills.

5   You'll receive a small living allowance, health insurance, student loan deferment, and training. Plus, after you finish your **service,** you'll receive a $4,725 education award to help pay for college, grad school, vocational training, or to pay off student loans. Serve part-time and you'll get a **portion** of that amount.

Choose from nearly 1,000 national and local groups.

6   You can be an AmeriCorps member with any of the programs that make up AmeriCorps. There are national groups like the American Red Cross, Habitat for Humanity, and Boys and Girls Clubs. There are also local community centers and places of worship. Find the program you want in the area where you want to serve. Or you may choose to serve in AmeriCorps*VISTA or AmeriCorps*NCCC.

Source: The Corporation for National and Community Service.

VOCABULARY   These vocabulary words are in the section you just read. Answer each
question. For words you do not know, check your dictionary.

1. *Unique* means _____.
   A. ordinary
   B. usual
   C. unusual
   D. complete

2. *Restore* means _____.
   A. buy again
   B. purchase
   C. return to original form
   D. to store again

3. A *portion* is _____.
   A. a part of something
   B. a magical drink
   C. a room divider
   D. a harbor for ships

VOCABULARY   List three words from the reading whose meanings you do not know. Look
BUILDER   up each word in a dictionary. Write down what it means. (If there is more
than one meaning, choose the one you think fits the best.) Use the word in a
sentence of your own.

1. _____

   _____

2. _____

   _____

3. _____

   _____

COMPREHENSION   How much did you understand in the reading? Read the questions below
and circle the correct answer.

1. Which of the following was NOT identified as a way to serve in
   AmeriCorps?
   A. make communities safer
   B. build homes
   C. tutor high school students
   D. serve in the military

2. Which of the following was NOT identified as a national group in which AmeriCorps participants can serve?
   A. Democratic and Republican political organizations
   B. Boys and Girls Clubs
   C. a local church
   D. Habitat for Humanity

3. After completing service in AmeriCorps, each person receives $4,725, which can be used for all of the following EXCEPT:
   A. learning how to be a car mechanic
   B. paying off school loans
   C. going to a private college
   D. paying off personal expenses

LEARNING TIP

Memory Tricks

all of this on test!!

Remembering what you have read is often easier said than done . . . or is it? **Mnemonics** are memory tricks. They help you remember and recall information. Different mnemonics work with different learning styles, like the ones you read about in Chapter 1. Using the style best for you helps you recall more with less work.

Which mnemonic works best? The answer depends on the information and your learning style (see Chapter 1). The best way is to try different mnemonics and see which ones you like best.

Mnemonic	Description	Example	Global	Logical	Visual	Auditory	Tactile/Kinesthetic
Acronym	Words made from a letter—usually the first letter—of concepts you need to recall	ROY G. BIV The letters in these words stand for the colors of the rainbow: **Red, Orange, Yellow, Green, Blue, Indigo, and Violet.**		Y	Y		Y

Mnemonic	Description	Example	Global	Logical	Visual	Auditory	Tactile/Kinesthetic
Acrostic	Sentence or phrase made from the first letter of concepts you need to recall	**Please Excuse My Dear Aunt Sally.** The first letter in each word stands for the order of operations in math—**P**arentheses, **E**xponents, **M**ultiply, **D**ivide, **A**dd, **S**ubtract.		Y	Y		Y
Association	Humorous or extreme ideas; these can include pictures you visualize to make ideas more seem more real	To recall that the Second Amendment of the Bill of Rights is the right to bear arms (that is, the right to own guns), you could think of the two "arms" of a bear.	Y		Y		Y
Location	Helps you remember how information looks (highlighted in the text, boldfaced term) or where it is found (top of the page, under a picture)	Add meaningful doodles like ✓, ☺, !, → or color	Y		Y		Y
Word Games	Make rhymes (words that sound alike) or songs; look for patterns in words	"*i* before *e* except after *c*" to remember the order of the letters *i* and *e* in words		Y	Y	Y	Y

CHAPTER SUMMARY

1. Reading and study plans help you learn more actively.
2. Chapter guides help you find important information in a book.
3. An overview is the first step of a reading and study plan. Chapter guides give clues. You use these guides to preview, outline, or map a chapter.
4. Learning goals help you set purposes for reading. Your own questions, the chapter's review questions, or the chapter's objectives can help you create learning goals.
5. As you read, you must check your understanding.
6. Short and active reviews over several study sessions will increase your recall.

CHAPTER REVIEW

On a separate sheet of paper, answer briefly but completely.

1. What goes into a reading and study plan for learning?
2. What is the purpose of an overview?
3. Give an example of a pre-chapter, intra-chapter, and post-chapter guide. Tell the purpose of each.
4. List three ways to get an overview of a chapter.
5. Other than grades, how can you check your understanding?
6. Why is it important to set goals for learning?
7. Describe the characteristics of a good review session.

ACTION SUMMARY

- Which ideas from this chapter do I already use?

  _____

  _____

- Which ideas from this chapter are new to me?

  _____

  _____

- The best idea I learned from this chapter is . . . . Why?

  _____

  _____

- The ideas from this chapter I would like to try are . . . .

  _____

  _____

- How will I put the new ideas I've learned into action?

  _____

  _____

LEARNING ONLINE

Go to http://developmentalenglish.wadsworth.com/atkinson-longman to find the website for _Reading Strategies for Today's College Student._ This website is designed for students using this book. Here you will find:

- fun and interesting websites related to reading
- web exercises and reading quizzes that will help you become a better reader
- a list of chapter objectives
- a glossary of terms used in the chapter
- flashcards
- crossword puzzles

CHAPTER VOCABULARY REVIEW

Go back to the "Vocabulary Check" at the beginning of the chapter. Now that you've read this chapter, rate how well you understand the vocabulary words in the "After-Reading Ratings" column. If you rate any word less than a 3, read the information about that term again.

Decoding New Words

OBJECTIVES

After you finish this chapter, you should be able to

• Tell how to use a dictionary pronunciation key

• Identify consonant sounds by themselves and in blends and digraphs

• Compare vowel sounds and their uses

• Tell why decoding doesn't always work

CHAPTER OUTLINE

I. **A–Z Review**

II. **Consonants**

    A. Blends and Digraphs

    B. Silent Letters

III. **Vowels**

    A. Syllables

    B. Short Vowel Sounds

    C. Long Vowel Sounds

    D. Y Sounds

    E. Vowel Pair Sounds

    F. Schwa Sounds

IV. **Decoding Warning**

STUDY THIS WHOLE CHAPTER

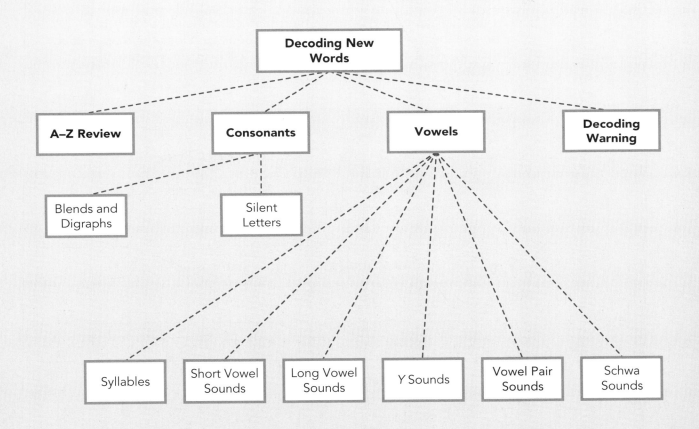

Decoding New Words

A–Z Review

Consonants

Vowels

Decoding Warning

Blends and Digraphs

Silent Letters

Syllables

Short Vowel Sounds

Long Vowel Sounds

Y Sounds

Vowel Pair Sounds

Schwa Sounds

Prefix Root Suffix

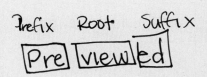

Pre view ed

VOCABULARY CHECK

Below are the vocabulary words you will need to know in this chapter.

If you see a word that's brand-new to you, write a 0 in the "Before-Reading Ratings" column. If you have seen the word before but don't know what it means, write a 1. If you think you know what the word means, write a 2. If you know the word and can use it in a sentence, write a 3.

If you wrote a 0 or 1, look up the word in the Glossary at the back of the book. Then, after reading the chapter, look at these words again and rate them in the "After-Reading Ratings" column.

If you come across new words in the chapter that are not on this list, underline them or write them in your notebook, and look them up in your dictionary. Write down their meaning. This will help you increase your vocabulary.

Before-Reading Ratings	Vocabulary Words	Pronunciation Guide (How do I say this word)	After-Reading Ratings
	consonants	ˈkän(t)-s(ə-)nənts	
	vowels	ˈvau̇(-ə)lz	
	pronunciation key	prə-ˌnən(t)-sē-ˈā-shən ˈkē	
	blend	ˈblend	
	digraph	ˈdī-ˌgraf	
	silent letter	ˈsī-lənt ˈle-tər	
	syllable	ˈsi-lə-bəl	
	short vowel sound	ˈshȯrt ˈvau̇(-ə)l ˈsau̇nd	
	long vowel sound	ˈlȯŋ ˈvau̇(ə)l ˈsau̇nd	
	schwa	ˈschwä	

KNOW THESE

"You say *potato*
and I say *potahto*
You say *tomato*
and I say *tomahto*

From the RKO Picture
Shall We Dance

Music by George
Gershwin. Lyrics by
Ira Gershwin.
Performed by
Fred Astaire and
Ginger Rogers

If you took the learning style quiz in Chapter 1, you already know your learning style. (If you did not, go back to Chapter 1 and take this quiz.) People learn in different ways. You learn better when you use the methods that fit you best. Don't compare how you learn with the way other students learn. Some people can look at information one time and know it. Other people need to see, hear, write, and use information to know it.

What does your learning style have to do with decoding, or understanding, a word? It has *everything* to do with decoding a word! If you are a visual learner, you need to see how words look. When you see a new word, you will need to look at the letters in it. You need to look for patterns of letters that you know. (We'll talk about some of these patterns in this chapter.)

If you are an auditory learner, you learn best by hearing. You need to hear how words sound. When you see a new word, you will need to change, the letters of the word into their sounds. (In this chapter, we'll talk about what sounds different letters make.)

Decoding words is different for tactile or kinesthetic learners—people who learn by touch or movement. You may not be able to figure out a word by how it looks or sounds. Instead, you may need to write it down, or mark it on the page where it is written. (Throughout this chapter, you'll do many exercises to help you learn to do this.)

A–Z Review

The twenty-six letters of the alphabet build words. Some letters are **consonants.** Twenty letters are always consonants: *B, C, D, F, G, H, J, K, L, M, N, P, Q, R, S, T, V, W, X,* and *Z.* Some are **vowels.** Five letters are always vowels: A, E, I, O, U. The letter *Y* is unique. Sometimes it is a vowel, and sometimes it is a consonant. Look at Table 3.1, which shows vowel and consonant letters.

You sometimes need a key to help you decode words. A dictionary holds that key. In your dictionary, you will find a **pronunciation key.** This key shows the sound of each letter or combination of letters. You will find the pronunciation key inside the cover of your dictionary, or within the first few pages. Table 3.2 shows an example of a dictionary's pronunciation key.

Table 3.1   Vowel and Consonant Letters

Vowels	a		e		i		o		u		y	
Consonants	b	c	d	f	g	h	j	k	l	m	n	p	q	r	s	t	v	w	x	y	z

Table 3.2 Sample Dictionary Pronunciation Key

Letter(s)	Example(s)	Your Example
a	sat, fact, battle	
ā	day, pail, shape	play
ər	bird, further, alert	
ä	father, stop	
b	bib, bubble	
ch	church	
d, dd	did, filled, waddle	
e	wet, steady	
ē	see, eve, clear	
ə	sofa, item, circus, easily, cannon	
f	fine, life, skiff, phase, laugh	
g	get, giggle, big	
h	hop, ahead	
hw	when, wheel	
i	pill	
ī	tie, by	
ir	near, deer, pier	
j	jump, budge, ginger	
k	kick, cat, technique	
l	lit, little, pillow	
m	mom, climb, hammer	
n	no, open, known, gnome, thinner	

Letter(s)	Example(s)	Your Example
ŋ	finger, ring, singing	
ō	joke, over, hope, grow	
ȯ	caught, law, coarse, horrid	
ȯi	oil	
u̇	hook	
ü	loot	
ou	out, south	
ȯr	boar, door, horse	
p	pop, happy	
r	rip, soar	
s	soap, rice	
sh	shot, wish, sure, nation	
t	tin, light, topped	
th	thank, bath	
_th_	that, then, bathe, mother	
y	yard, young	
u̇r	poor, tour	
v	vote, five	
y	yard, young	
w	will, twelve	
z	zoo, xerox	
zh	treasure, rouge	

Take a look at how the key works. Let's say you want to look up the word *act* in your dictionary. Next to the word you might see "ăkt." To find out what that *a* means, you look for that symbol in the pronunciation guide. Next to the symbol you might see words like *sat, fact,* and *battle.* That means that when you look up a word and see *a,* it has the sound of *ă* in *sat, fact,* and *battle.* If you look up the word *flea* in the dictionary, you would see "flē." When you look ē up in the pronunciation guide, you might see the words *see, eve,* and *clear.* This means *flea* has the same "e" sound as these words. You can change some of the examples in Table 3.2 to words that you like better.

QUICK REVIEW

Circle the correct answer. Check your answers at the bottom of the page before reading the next section.

1. Letters are either consonants or vowels. **T** **F**

2. The letter *X* can be a consonant or a vowel. **T** **F**

3. The pronunciation key in a dictionary helps you spell words. **T** **F**

✗ ~~WRITING CONNECTION~~

Respond to the following on a separate sheet of paper or in your notebook.

Based on the learning style quiz you took in Chapter 1, how do you learn best? Explain how you can use your style to decode words more effectively.

EXERCISE 3.1   **Your own examples may be more helpful than those given in a pronunciation key.** Write your own examples of letter sounds in the last column of Table 3.2. Try to think of your own words, or go to the pronunciation guide in your dictionary and write in the words that are used as examples there. (The pronunciation guide can be found in the first few pages of a dictionary. See Chapter 4 if you need more information.)

Consonants ← KNOW DEFFENITION FOR

Most letters are consonants. You hear a consonant when your lips, tongue, or teeth stop the air coming out of your mouth. Consonants often give a word its beginning or ending sounds. For instance, think about where your lips, tongue, and teeth are as you say these words: *bat, ship, loss, gust, chum.*

Quick Review Answers: 1. T   2. F   3. F

In each word, your lips, teeth, or tongue affects how the word starts and stops. The pronunciation guide in Table 3.2 shows how consonant sounds (as well as vowel sounds) are said.

You may have noticed that some sounds in Table 3.2 are made by more than one letter. Some consonants (like *c, d, g, q, s,* and *x*) have more than one sound. A list of these with tips for decoding them appears in Table 3.3.

Table 3.3   Consonants with Two or More Sounds

Letter	Sound	Example	Decoding Tip
c	c (soft *c*)	city cell cyst	If *c* is followed by the letters *e, i,* or *y,* it usually has the sound of *s* (like *city*). This is called the *soft c* sound. If it followed by any other letter, it has the sound of a *k* (like *cat*). This is called the *hard c* sound.
	k (hard *c*)	cat arc class	
g	j (soft *g*)	gin gem gym	Like *c,* the letter *g* has both hard and soft sounds. The soft sound (the sound *j*) is usually used when the letters *i, e,* or *y* follow *g* (like *gym*). But, some words have the hard *g* sound when *i* or *e* follows *g.* These include *gift, girl,* and *get.*
	g (hard *g*)	gift gate go egg glass	
d	d	done dad middle admit	When *d* appears at the start or end of a word, it always has the sound of *d* (like *dad*). It also has the sound of *d* when it appears as a double letter (like *middle*). Unfortunately, there's no clear rule for the sound of *d* in the middle of a word. In most cases, it will be the *d* sound, but sometimes it will be the sound of the letter *j* (like *educate*).
	j	schedule educate soldier	

(continued)

Table 3.3   Consonants with Two or More Sounds (*continued*)

Letter	Sound	Example	Decoding Tip
q(u)	kw	**qu**een **qu**it s**qu**irrel quilt	The letter *q* differs from all other consonants. In English, the vowel *u* always follows the consonant *q*. In these words, *u* does not act like a vowel. Instead, it combines with *q* to form either the blended sound *kw* or the sound of *k*. If *qu* appears at the beginning or close to the beginning of a word, it usually has a *kw* sound (like *quit*). If it appears in the middle of a word or is followed by the letter *e,* it has a *k* sound (like *technique*).
	k	tech**niqu**e mos**qu**ito u**niqu**e	
s	s	self sand less	When a word begins with the letter *s* (like *self*) or ends with double *s* (like *less*), it has the usual sound of *s*. If the letter *s* appears between two vowels or ends a word but is not doubled, it has a *z* sound (like *rose*). If the letter *s* is followed by the letters *ure,* it usually has a *zh* sound (like *treasure*). In a few cases—such as *sure* or when doubled before the letters *ure*—it has an *sh* sound (like *pressure*).
	z	rose lies prison	
	zh	treasure pleasure	
	sh	sure assure pressure	

Letter	Sound	Example	Decoding Tip
x	z	xylophone Xerox	The letter *x* rarely begins a word. When it does, it has a *z* sound (like *Xerox*). In most words, *x* appears at the end or in the middle of word. In these cases, *x* has the sound *ks* (like *fox*). When the letter *e* precedes *x*, it has the sound of *gz* (like *exam*).
	ks	fox toxic next	
	gz	exam extra	

Blends and Digraphs ◄Know DEFF

When two or more consonants appear together, they sometimes form a **blend** or **digraph**. In a blend, each consonant's sound is heard. For example, in the word *flea*, you can hear the sounds of *f* and *l*. In a digraph, two or three consonants combine to form a new sound. For example, in the word *she*, the letters *s* and *h* make a single sound. Some letters, such as *b, c, d, f, g, p, q, s*, and *t*, often begin a blend. The letters *l, m, n, r*, and sometimes *t* often complete the blend. Blends are found in words such as *blast, grape, stray, plan*, and *staff*. Other consonants, such as *h, j, v, x, y*, and *z*, are never in blends. Table 3.4 lists blends and examples. The blends in the table that are in boldfaced letters appear only at the ends of a word or syllable (such as *ft* in *lift* or *ld* in *wild*). Table 3.5 lists digraphs, the sounds they form, and examples.

Table 3.4 Common Blends and Examples

Blend (hear each letter)	Example	Blend	Example
bl	**blue**	fr	**free**
br	**brass**	fl	**fly**
cl	**class**	**ft** (occurs at the end of a word)	**lift**
cr	**cram**	gr	**grade**
dr	**drop**	gl	**glass**

(continued)

Table 3.4   Common Blends and Examples (*continued*)

Blend (sound out the letter)	Example	Blend	Example
ld (occurs at the end of a word)	wild	sk	skate
lt (occurs at the end of a word)	tilt	sm	small
mp (occurs at the end of a word)	camp	sn	snow
nd (occurs at the end of a word)	kind	sp	spoon
nk (occurs at the end of a word)	sink	squ	squash
nt (occurs at the end of a word)	sent	spl	split
pl	play	spr	spring
pr	prop	st	stop
sc	scam	str	strike
scr	scrap	sw	swipe
sl	slim	tr	try

Table 3.5   Digraphs, Sounds, and Examples

Digraph	Sound	Examples	Digraph	Sound	Examples
ch (one sound)	ch	chill church chum	ph	f	phone graph
	sh	chef chute	sh	sh	show rush
	k	chorus schedule technical	th	*unvoiced* th	bath think
gh	f	laugh rough		*voiced* th	them bathe

Silent Letters ← *KNOW DEFF.*

When two consonants appear together in some words, one consonant is a **silent letter.** For example, in the word *know,* the letter *k* is silent. In the word *comb,* the letter *b* is silent. Table 3.6 lists consonant pairs with silent letters, the sound that is heard, and examples.

Table 3.6 Consonant Pairs with Silent Letters

Silent Letter Combinations	Silent Letter(s)	Sound	Examples
mb	b	m	**bomb** **tomb** **climb**
ck	c	k	**clock** **sick**
gh	gh	no sound	**through** **right**
gn	g	n	**sign** **gnat**
kn	k	n	**know** **knife**
ld	l	d	**could** **should** **would**
wh	h	w	**whisper** **whip**
wr	w	r	**wrong** **write**

(continued)

Table 3.6   Consonant Pairs with Silent Letters (*continued*)

Silent Letter Combinations	Silent Letter(s)	Sound	Examples
double consonants	bb, dd, ff, gg, ll, mm, nn, pp, rr, ss, tt, zz	one consonant sound	ribbon addition staff giggle bell common running happy stirred less fitting buzz

QUICK REVIEW

Circle the correct answer. Check your answers at the bottom of the page before reading the next section.

1. You hear a consonant when your lips, tongue, or teeth stop the air coming out of your mouth. **(T) F**

2. Two or fewer consonants form blends and digraphs. **T (F)**

3. In a digraph, the first consonant is heard and the second consonant is silent. **T (F)**

EXERCISE 3.2   **Sometimes the only way to know which sound a letter has is to say it.** Say each of the words at the top of the next page out loud. If you are not sure how to pronounce them, look them up in your dictionary. As you'll see, some of the consonants in these words are boldfaced, such as the *x* and *s* in *Texas* and the *ch* and *c* in *technical*. Now look at the table below the words. It includes six of the twenty consonants. Figure out which consonant sound is being made in each word, then write it in the table next to the correct sound. For example, the word *cage* goes with the letter *c*, in the *k* row. Hint: Some words (like *congress*) will go in more than one category. Some categories may not have any words in them.

Quick Review Answers: 1. T   2. F   3. F

Texas	cage	express	xylem
congress	exact	rag	exam
rice	technical	educator	requirement
space	quilt	reduce	specific

Letter	Sound	Words
c	s (soft c)	
	k (hard c)	*cage*
g	j (soft g)	
	g (hard g)	
d	d	
	j	
q(u)	kw	
	k	
s	s	
	z	
	zh	
	sh	
x	z	
	ks	
	gz	

EXERCISE 3.3   **Practice pays off in vocabulary development.** Say the words below out loud. If you are not sure how to pronounce them, look them up in your dictionary. If a word has a blend (each consonant's sound is heard), underline the blend. If a word has a digraph (consonants combine to form a new sound), circle the digraph. If the word has a silent consonant (consonant's sound is not heard), cross out the silent letter. Then write the words in the correct category. For example, in the word *stamp* you would underline the *st*, then write it in the "Blend" column because you can hear both the *s* and the *t*. Hint: Some words will go in more than one category.

shift   grade   first   past   inspire
craft   comb   knew   shadow   praise
class   stamp   attack   written   shall
prince   plastic   gnarl   spell   cheese

Blend	Digraph	Silent Consonant
stamp shift craft class prince grade plastic first past spell inspire praise	Shift Shadow Shall Cheese	Comb Knew Shall Written gnarl attack

Vowels

A group of letters must have one or more vowels (*a, e, i, o, u,* or *y*) to form a word. In vowels, your teeth, lips, or tongue do not stop sounds. Instead, the sounds are formed by the way you open your mouth. For instance, think about the shape of your mouth at the end of these words: *bee, boy, buy, bay.* Your mouth shapes the word's sound.

Syllables

A **syllable** forms each time your mouth opens and makes a vowel sound in a word. This is why you can count syllables by placing a hand under your chin. When you open your mouth, your chin moves down. This movement indicates a syllable has been formed. For instance, place your hand under your chin and say these words: *cold* (1 syllable), *jacket* (2 syllables), *telephone* (3 syllables), *impossible* (4 syllables).

Short Vowel Sounds

When a word or syllable has one vowel, it is often said to have a **short vowel sound.** For instance, say the words *cabin, bed, lipstick, hot,* and *sun.* The vowel sound(s) you hear in each one is the short sound for that vowel. Table 3.7 shows one-syllable and two-syllable words with short vowel sounds. As you look at the words in Table 3.7, you will see that they form rhyming families. Rhyming families are groups of words that look and sound similar.

When the letter *r* follows a single vowel, it changes the short sound. Say the word *bat.* Now say the word *bar.* Can you hear how the *r* changes the sound? Table 3.7 also lists words in which the letter *r* affects the sound.

Table 3.7 Words with Short Vowel and *R*-Controlled Sounds

Vowel	One-Syllable Examples	Two-Syllable Examples	*R*-Controlled Sounds
a	bat, cat, fat, hat, splat cast, fast, last, mast, vast band, hand, land, stand	candle, handle after, rafter landing, standing	bar dart carton market marvel startle sparkle

(continued)

Table 3.7   Words with Short Vowel and *R*-Controlled Sounds (*continued*)

Vowel	One-Syllable Examples	Two-Syllable Examples	*R*-Controlled Sounds
e	bet, jet, met, net, pet, set beg, keg, leg, peg bell, dell, fell, sell, swell	better, wetter bending, sending beckon, reckon	her herd inert jerk perk
i	big, dig, pig, swig, twig hilt, jilt, lilt, silt, tilt bin, fin, gin, pin, tin, twin	blister, sister riddle, fiddle little, whittle	dirt first shirt stir
o	cop, hop, mop, pop, stop boss, loss, moss, toss block, dock, jock, stock	jogging, logging hobby, lobby bond, pond	born fortune lord horn porous
u	cub, hub, nub, pub, stub bunt, grunt, hunt, stunt bunch, hunch, lunch	hulking, sulking bumpy, frumpy under, thunder	burst blurt curse hurt lurch nurture

Long Vowel Sounds

Vowels also have long sounds. In these sounds, the sound of the vowel is the same as the vowel's name. For instance, the **long vowel sound** of the letter *a* sounds like *a*. Say the word *rain*. The vowel sound you hear is the long vowel sound of *a*. Long vowel sounds happen most often when there are two vowels in a word or syllable and only one vowel sound, such as in *race* (long *a* sound) or *neat* (long *e* sound). The three rules below work for most long vowel sounds. Table 3.8 shows examples for each rule.

1. If a word or syllable ends in vowel-consonant-*e,* the vowel is long and the *e* is silent. Examples include *cape, line,* and *hope.*
2. If two vowels come together in a word, the first vowel is long and the second vowel is silent. Examples include *pain, team,* and *soap.*
3. If a single vowel ends a word or syllable, the vowel has a long sound. Examples include *he, go,* and *flu.*

Table 3.8   Examples of Long Vowel Rules

Consonant-Vowel-Silent *E*	Two Vowels Together	Single Vowel at End of a Syllable
date, gate, hate, late, mate, rate ace, face, lace, mace, pace, place, race gale, male, pale, sale, stale, whale fade, jade, made brake, cake, flake, lake, make, rake	bay, day, hay, stay, sway brain, drain, plain, rain	ba-con ba-sic ra-ting fa-king na-ture la-bel
gene	beet, feet, meet, street deal, heal, peal, seal beam, cream, dream, ream, steam, stream bean, dean, lean, mean beep, deep, keep, steep	she be de-cide de-sign be-lieve de-value se-cret de-tail de-liver be-gin
dine, fine, line, mine, nine, pine, vine bride, hide, ride, slide, stride, wide bite, kite, mite, quite, site dime, chime, lime, mime bike, hike, like, spike, strike	cried, died, dried, fried	hi si-lent twi-light
bone, clone, hone, lone, stone, tone broke, coke, joke, poke doe, foe, hoe, toe, woe dole, hole, mole, stole, whole cope, dope, hope, lope, mope, rope	boat, coat, float, moat soap cloak, oak, soak	go zero o-zone ro-bot sto-len go-ing no-tice pro-test
brute, cute, flute, jute, mute dune, June, tune crude, dude, nude, rude	blue, clue, cue, due, hue, rue, sue	flu Cu-ban u-nite tu-ba tu-na mu-sic

Y Sounds

The letter *y* has different uses and sounds, depending on where it comes in a word. When *y* is a word's first letter, it acts like a consonant, such as in *you* or *yell*. At other times, it acts like a vowel, such as in *gym, fly,* or *pretty*. The vowel sound of *y* depends on where it is found. When *y* is in the middle of a word or syllable, it has the sound of a short *i*, as in *gym*. When *y* is at the end of a one-syllable word, it has the sound of long *i*, as in *fly*. When *y* is at the end of a word with more than one syllable, it has the sound of long *e*, as in *pretty*. Table 3.9 shows sounds of *y* by where it appears in a word.

Vowel Pair Sounds

Just as two consonants sometimes join to form a new sound in a blend, two vowels sometimes join to form a new sound, such as in *food* or *through*. Some pairs form a single new sound, such as in *coin* or *toy*. Other pairs can have several different sounds, such as in *rough* or *through*. Table 3.10 lists common vowel pairs and examples.

Schwa Sounds

If you say the word *America,* you will hear another vowel sound at the beginning and end. This is called the **schwa** sound. It is the most common vowel sound in the English language. It is pronounced "uh," like in the word *allow*. The schwa sound is often heard in words of more than one syllable. In a pronunciation key, the schwa sound is shown as an upside-down *e* (ə). Any vowel can make the schwa sound. Below is a list that shows the sound of schwa in different words.

- The *a* is schwa in *allow.*
- The *e* is schwa in *synthesis.*
- The *i* is schwa in *confident.*
- The *o* is schwa in *police.*
- The *u* is schwa in *medium.*
- The *y* is schwa in *syringe.*
- The *ou* is schwa in *nervous.*
- The *io* is schwa in *potion.*
- The *iou* is schwa in *cautious.*

Table 3.9 Y Sounds by Position in the Word

Y at the Beginning of a Word or Syllable	Y in the Middle of a Word or Syllable	Y at the End of a One-Syllable Word	Y at the End of a Multi-Syllable Word
yell yellow yes you young yours youth	anonymous antonym gym hymn myth syllable	by cry fly my shy try sty	any baby funny hardly many penny sunny tardy tiny

Table 3.10 Vowel Pairs That Form New Sounds

Vowel Pair	Examples
au/aw	awful, law, pawn, saw, slaw, tawdry caught, haul, naughty, taught
oi/oy	boil, coil, coin, hoist, point, poise, rejoice, soil, toil boys, toy, joy, royal
oo	book, brook, hood, hook, look, stood tooth, booth, room, broom, loose, caboose, noose, food, mood, spoon
ou	ought, cough, fought through, wound could, would, should rough, tough, enough hound, pound, found, sound, around, ground, sprout, out, shout, mouth, south
ow	crowd, towel, trowel, sow, cow, shower, tower, power, down, town, plow, brown, frown, crown, drown tow, crow, low, mow
ew	threw, blew, drew, crew, jewel

QUICK REVIEW

Circle the correct answer. Check your answers at the bottom of the page before reading the next section.

1. You hear a vowel when your lips, tongue, or teeth stop the air coming out of your mouth. T **F**

2. Only five letters can ever be vowels. T **F**

3. Vowels have long sounds when the sound of the vowel is the same as the name of the vowel. **T** F

4. The short *a* sound is the most common vowel sound in the English language. T **F**

EXERCISE 3.4

Learning vowel sounds takes practice. Say each of the words below out loud. If you are not sure how to pronounce them, look them up in your dictionary. If a word has a short vowel sound, like in *lift* or *stand*, circle the letter that makes the short vowel sound, then write it in the left column. If a word has a long vowel sound, like in *scream* or *mice*, underline the letters that form the long vowel sound and write them in the middle column. If a word has an *r*-controlled vowel sound, like *far* or *torn*, put a box around the *r*-controlled vowel, then write it in the right column.

brisk *1*   plume *2*
shelf *1*   shunt *1*
please *2*   harm *3*
star *3*   shame *2*
scream *2*   deed *2*
dice *2*   pit *1*
text *1*   port *3*
prime *2*   sport *3*

Short Vowel Sound	Long Vowel Sound	R-Controlled Vowel Sound
~~text~~ Brisk Shelf text shunt Pit	Shelf please scream dice Prime Plume shame deed	brisk Star harm Port sport

EXERCISE 3.5   **Identifying the sound of Y in a word depends on where it occurs.** Say each of the words below aloud. If you are not sure how to pronounce them, look them up in your dictionary. First, underline the letter *y* in every word. If the *y* in a word has a consonant sound like in *year* or *young*, write the word in the first column. If *y* has a short *i* vowel sound like in *gym*, write it in the second column. If *y* has a long *i* vowel sound like in *fry*, write it in the third column. If *y* has a long *e* vowel sound like in *baby*, write it in the last column. Hint: One word fits into two columns.

yolk	pry	electricity	paralysis	year
sky	you	chemistry	history	ply
mythological	industry	synthesis	polygamy	biology

Y as a Consonant	Y as a Vowel (Short *I* Sound)	Y as a Vowel (Long *I* Sound)	Y as a Vowel (Long *E* Sound)
York Year You	Paralysis mythological synthesis Polygamy	Pry sky ply	electricity Chemistry history industry polygamy biology

EXERCISE 3.6   **Vowel pairs form many different sounds.** Say each of the words below out loud. If you are not sure how to pronounce them, look them up in your dictionary. Underline the two-letter vowel combination that forms the vowel sound. Next, write the words by vowel sound in the correct row. For example, in the word *soon*, you would underline *oo*, then write *soon* next to the "*oo* as in *room*" row. Some rows may not have any words that match their sounds.

bought	shoot	scoundrel	prawn	stewed
flow	scour	awesome	foil	mistook
power	august	haughty	choice	ahoy
stoop	nook	alloy	screw	groom

Vowel Pair	Words
au as in *taught*	haughty august
aw as in *draw*	awsome, prawn
oi as in *join*	foil, choice
oy as in *joy*	alloy, ahoy
oo as in *room*	stoop, nook, shoot, groom, mistook
oo as in *book*	micstook, nook
ou as in *cough*	brought
ou as in *through*	
ou as in *could*	
ou as in *tough*	
ou as in *pound*	Scoundrel, scour
ow as in *cow*	power
ow as in *crow*	flow
ew as in *blew*	stewed, screw

Decoding Warning

English is a great language. But it can be a hard language to learn. Read this section below that takes a funny look at the English language:

If GH can stand for P as in hiccough
If OUGH can stand for O as in dough
If PHTH can stand for T as in phthisis
If EIGH can stand for A as in neighbor
If TTE can stand for T as in gazette
If EAU can stand for O as in plateau
Then the right way to spell POTATO should be:

GHOUGHPHTHEIGHTTEEAU

Some basic rules apply to most English words. But words don't always follow the rules. English is a language that contains words from many other languages. For example, *jury* comes from French. *Ranch* comes from Spanish. *Algebra* comes from Arabic. *Chimpanzee* comes from the African Kongo dialect. Each language has its own rules. And sometimes people in different parts of the country pronounce words differently. For example, the word *pecan* is often pronounced as 'pe-kän in southern states. It is pronounced as, pē-'kan elsewhere in the United States. Early spellings of a word were not always the same. For example, the words *strop* and *strap* have the same meaning. Rules, then, sometimes work. Sometimes they don't. What can you do?

Keep in mind that if a word is hard for you to decode, it's most likely hard for other students to decode, too. Ask your instructor, classmates, friends, or family questions about words. Listen carefully to the people around you as they speak. Notice how words look. Write them down for yourself. Make a set of note cards for each of your courses and review them often. You might even keep a notebook of words you read or hear and their pronunciations and definitions. You will end up with a larger and more varied vocabulary.

QUICK REVIEW

Circle the correct answer. Check your answers at the bottom of the page before reading the next section.

1. Decoding rules apply to all English words. T (F)

2. Words in English really come from many different languages. (T) F

3. Making a set of note cards for difficult words is a good way to learn the words. (T) F

Quick Review Answers: 1. F 2. T 3. T

WRITING CONNECTION

Respond to the following on a separate sheet of paper or in your notebook.

What part of decoding (e.g., consonant sounds, vowel rules, words that fail to follow the rules) is most difficult for you? Why?

EXERCISE 3.7   **Does English sometimes drive you crazy? You're not alone in feeling that way.** Read the following article from the book *Crazy English* and answer the questions that follow.

ENGLISH IS A CRAZY LANGUAGE

1 Let's face it—English is a crazy language. There is no *egg* in *eggplant* nor *ham* in *hamburger*. There's no *apple* nor *pine* in *pineapple*. English muffins weren't invented in England nor French fries in France. *Sweetmeats* are candies while *sweetbreads*, which aren't sweet, are meat.

2 We take English for granted. But if we explore its **paradoxes** (contradictions that are still true), we find that *quicksand* can work slowly, *boxing rings* are square and a *guinea pig* is neither from Guinea nor is it a pig.

3 And why is it that writers write but fingers don't *fing* and hammers don't *ham*? If the plural of *tooth* is *teeth*, why isn't the plural of *booth beeth*? One *goose*, 2 *geese*. So one *moose*, 2 *meese* . . . One *blouse*, 2 *blice*?

4 Doesn't it seem crazy that you can make *amends* (ask for forgiveness) but not one *amend*, that you comb through *annals* (records) of history but not a single *annal*? If you have a bunch of odds and ends and get rid of all but one of them, what do you call it?

5 If teachers taught, why didn't preachers praught? If a vegetarian eats vegetables, what does a humanitarian eat? If you wrote a letter, perhaps you bote your tongue?

6 Sometimes I think all the English speakers should be committed to a hospital for the verbally insane. In what language do people recite at a play and play at a *recital* (a musical performance)? Ship by truck and send *cargo* (goods) by ship? Have noses that run and feet that smell? Park on driveways and drive on **parkways?**

7 How can a "slim chance" and a "fat chance" be the same, while a "wise man" and "wise guy" are opposites? How can *overlook* and *oversee* be opposites, while "quite a lot" and "quite a few" are alike? How can the weather be "hot as hell" one day and "cold as hell" another?

8 You have to be impressed with the special madness of a language in which your house can burn up as it burns down. Then consider that you fill in a form by filling it out and an alarm clock goes off by going on.

9 English was invented by people, not computers. It shows the creativity of the human race (which, of course, isn't a race at all). That is why, when the stars are out, they are visible (seen), but when the lights are out, they are invisible (not seen). And why, when I wind up my watch, I start it, but when I wind up this essay, I end it?

Excerpted with permission of Atria Books, an imprint of Simon & Schuster Adult Publishing Group, from CRAZY ENGLISH by Richard Lederer. Copyright © 1989 by Richard Lederer.

VOCABULARY   Review the article you just read and fill in the answers below.

1. Find a word with a short vowel sound. _egg_

2. Find a word with a long vowel sound. _face_

3. Find two words in which the letter *y* has different sounds.

   you and _your_

4. Find three words with one syllable.
   A. _few_
   B. _ham_
   C. _day_

5. Find three words with two syllables.
   A. _impressed_
   B. _madness_
   C. _alike_

6. Find three words with three or more syllables.
   A. _visible_
   B. _invisible_
   C. _opposite_

7. Find one word with a silent consonant. _apples_

8. Find three words with consonant blends.
   A. _invented_
   B. _french_
   C. _fries_

9. Find three words with digraphs.
   A. _English_
   B. _French_
   C. _watch_

10. Find three words with a schwa sound.
   A. _invisible_
   B. _alarm_
   C. _alike_

VOCABULARY BUILDER

List five words from the article that are new to you. Look up each word and write its meaning based on how it is used in the sentence. Use the word in a sentence of your own.

1. _____

_____

_____

2. _____

_____

_____

3. _____

_____

_____

4. _____

_____

_____

5. _____

_____

_____

COMPREHENSION

How much did you understand in the reading? Read the questions below and circle the correct answer.

1. What is the shape of a boxing ring?
   A. circle
   B. square
   C. triangle
   D. rectangle

2. Complete the following:
   Sweetmeats are a kind of candy but sweetbreads are a kind of _____.
   A. candy
   B. bread
   C. meat
   D. vegetable

3. Who invented the English language?
   A. computers
   B. people

4. Which of the following pairs have the same meaning?
   A. slim chance; fat chance
   B. wise man; wise guy
   C. overlook; oversee
   D. annals, amends

5. What is a parkway?
   A. driveway
   B. highway
   C. sidewalk
   D. street corner

6. A paradox is probably _____.
   A. two dice
   B. something that isn't what it seems
   C. an obvious truth
   D. two physicians

7. Which of the following singular and plural forms are correctly matched?
   A. booth, beeth
   B. blouse, blice
   C. moose, mice
   D. mouse, mice

8. Which of the following would NOT be eaten by a vegetarian?
   A. sweetmeats
   B. sweetbreads
   C. eggplant
   D. English muffins

LEARNING TIP

Forming Study Groups

Most students find they get better grades when they study with others. Why? Learning is more active. Study groups let you see, hear, and talk about information. Study groups also show you how others think about a subject. This helps you think about a subject in new ways. Group members keep each other motivated and interested in learning. Group study also improves communication and helps you learn to work as a team. So, how do you form a study group?

First, you need to find study group members. Where will you find group members? You can ask people you know in your class. You can ask the instructor to announce that a group is forming. Students who are interested can meet you after class to choose a meeting time and place.

Second, limit the group's size. If the group is too large, members won't be able to contribute. The larger the group, the harder it will be to find a time when everyone can meet.

Third, decide what your goals will be. It's important that you choose members who have similar goals. Without a common goal, members will lose interest. They might get upset. As the group forms, decide what the group wants to get done. Will you review class or reading notes, answer review questions, or study for an exam?

Fourth, the group should agree on how many times it will meet. For instance, will the group meet weekly throughout the semester? Will it meet once before an exam? If the group wants to meet regularly, choose the same time and place for each meeting. Meetings should begin on time. In addition, set a purpose and time limit for each session. For instance, a group could meet for two hours to review for an exam. It could meet for one hour to work on problems.

Here are a few more tips about study groups:

1. Group learning doesn't replace your own studying. Group members should study alone before coming to the study group. Once together, you can discuss homework, class work, or tests.
2. Each member should come to the group prepared. Each member must take responsibility for what the group learns.
3. Choose a moderator (leader) for each study session. A leader can keep the group focused.
4. It is okay for members to talk about other topics, but only for a short time. As group members get to know each other, they will be interested in talking about things like friends, family, and activities. Set a time limit on chatting, then get to work.

CHAPTER SUMMARY

1. Your learning styles can help you decode words better.
2. Twenty-six letters are used to form words.
3. A dictionary pronunciation key helps you decode unfamiliar words.
4. Consonant sounds occur when the lips, teeth, or tongue stop the flow of air when forming a word.
5. Consonants can appear singly, in blends, as digraphs, and as silent letters.
6. Vowel sounds determine the number of syllables in a word.
7. Single vowels often form short vowel sounds.
8. Two vowels can combine in different ways to form long and other vowel sounds.

CHAPTER REVIEW

On a separate sheet of paper, answer briefly but completely.

1. Complete the following diagram by writing the letters of the alphabet in the correct part of the diagram:

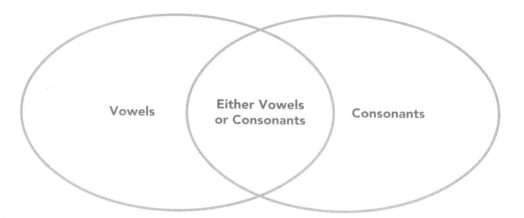

2. What is a dictionary pronunciation key? How can it help you decode words?
3. What's the difference between a blend and a digraph?
4. What is the biggest difference between vowel and consonant sounds in terms of the way you say words?
5. Why does chin movement show the number of syllables?
6. What are the rules for forming long vowel sounds?
7. How would you explain the schwa sound to someone? What is an example of a word with a schwa sound?

ACTION SUMMARY

- Which ideas from this chapter do I already use?

  _____

  _____

- Which ideas from this chapter are new to me?

  _____

  _____

- The best idea I learned from this chapter is . . . . Why?

  _____

  _____

- The ideas from this chapter I would like to try are . . . .

  _____

  _____

- How will I put the new ideas I've learned into action?

  _____

  _____

LEARNING ONLINE

Go to http://developmentalenglish.wadsworth.com/atkinson-longman to find the website for *Reading Strategies for Today's College Student.* This website is designed for students using this book. Here you will find:

- fun and interesting websites related to reading
- web exercises and reading quizzes that will help you become a better reader
- a list of chapter objectives
- a glossary of terms used in the chapter
- flashcards
- crossword puzzles

CHAPTER VOCABULARY REVIEW

Go back to the "Vocabulary Check" at the beginning of the chapter. Now that you've read this chapter, rate how well you understand the vocabulary words in the "After-Reading Ratings" column. If you rate any word less than a 3, read the information about that term again.

CHAPTER 4

Dictionary and Thesaurus

OBJECTIVES

After you finish this chapter, you should be able to

- Know what to look for when buying a dictionary or thesaurus
- Identify the parts of a print dictionary
- Identify the parts of a print thesaurus

CHAPTER OUTLINE

CHAPTER MAP

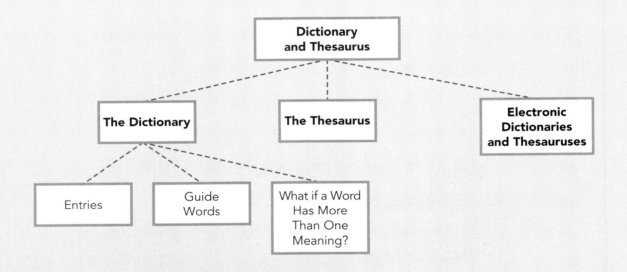

VOCABULARY CHECK

Below are the vocabulary words you will need to know in this chapter.

If you see a word that's brand-new to you, write a 0 in the "Before-Reading Ratings" column. If you have seen the word before but don't know what it means, write a 1. If you think you know what the word means, write a 2. If you know the word and can use it in a sentence, write a 3.

If you wrote a 0 or 1, look up the word in the Glossary at the back of the book. Then, after reading the chapter, look at these words again and rate them in the "After-Reading Ratings" column.

If you come across new words in the chapter that are not on this list, underline them or write them in your notebook, and look them up in your dictionary. Write down their meaning. This will help you increase your vocabulary.

Before-Reading Ratings	Vocabulary Words	Pronunciation Guide (How do I say this word?)	After-Reading Ratings
	dictionary	'dik-shə-ˌner-ē	
	thesaurus	thi-'sȯr-əs	
	entries	'en-trēz	
	part of speech	'pärt əv 'spēch	
	etymology	ˌe-tə-'mä-lə-jē	
	guide words	'gīd 'wərdz	
	context	'kän-ˌtekst	
	glossary	'glä-sə-rē	
	synonyms	'si-nə-ˌnimz	
	cross-reference	'krȯs-'re-fərn(t)s	
	antonyms	'an-tə-ˌnimz	
	unabridged dictionary	ˌən-ə-'brijd 'dik-shə-ˌner-ē	

*". . . the ability
to read awoke
in me some long
dormant craving
to be mentally
alive."*

Malcolm X

Civil Rights Leader

Sometimes strange events change lives. Malcolm X was a civil rights leader in the 1960s. He first learned about the power of words in prison. He could not say what he wanted to, so he began copying pages from the dictionary by hand. That led to his interest in words and grew into a love of reading and learning. Malcolm X never went to high school, but he became a powerful speaker and leader.

You might not think books can change your life, but they can. Two of the most important books you should know about are a **dictionary** and a **thesaurus.** These two books can put a world of words in your hands. They can help your vocabulary grow. They can help you better understand words. They can help you improve your speech and writing. They can help you to learn more quickly.

The Dictionary

Dictionaries are lists of words and meanings in alphabetical (*ABC*) order. They also help you decode or say words correctly, as you learned in Chapter 3. Understanding each part of a dictionary will help you use it better.

Entries

The words in a dictionary are called **entries.** Each word and the information about that word form one entry. Here is a dictionary entry for the word *education.*

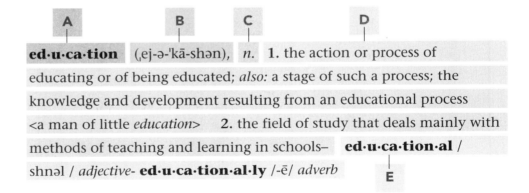

Look at **A. A** shows you the word with dots between letters to show the syllables in the word. Does **B** look familiar to you? **B** is the pronunciation guide. It's like the one you see at the beginning of every chapter and learned about in Chapter 3. The pronunciation guide helps you say the word correctly. Next look at **C. C** tells you the abbreviated (shortened) version of the word's **part**(s) **of speech.** This is how a word is used in a sentence. In this case, you see an *n,* which stands for *noun* (a person, place, or thing). For other words, you might see a *v* for *verb* (a word that shows action), an *adj* for *adjective* (a word that describes a person, place, or thing), or *adv* for *adverb* (a word that tells about verbs, adjectives, or other adverbs). There are other abbreviations, but these are the most common. Next look at **D. D** shows the meaning(s) of the word. Some words, like *education,* have more than one meaning. The different meanings are numbered. Some dictionaries give the most common meaning first. Now look at **E. E** shows other ways that the word can be used. For example, the ending *-al* could be added to *education* to make the adjective *educational*.

Some dictionaries show if a meaning has a special use. For example, the entry might say if a word is from a foreign country, if it is used in a special field like math, or if it is a slang word. A college dictionary also often gives a word's **etymology**, or history.

Guide Words

Another important part of a dictionary is the **guide words.** You see the guide words at the top of each dictionary page. They show which entries can be found on that page. For example, on the page with the entry for *education,* you might see the guide words *"Eden"* and *"educator."* That means the first word on the page is *Eden* and the last word on the page is *educator.* Since *education* comes after *Eden* and before *educator,* you know you can find it on that page, since only words that come between *Eden* and *educator* will be on these pages.

What if a Word Has More Than One Meaning?

Suppose you are looking up a word in the dictionary and find that it has more than one meaning. Often **context** (the meaning of a word as used in a sentence or paragraph) can help you choose the correct meaning. (Chapter 5 provides more information about using context.) For example, suppose you see this sentence: "The *set* is incomplete." If you are reading about tennis, *set* means a complete game. If you are reading about math, *set* means an exact amount of numbers. So, *set* means different things in different subjects. For this reason, the **glossary** in your textbook is a good first place to look for meanings. It will tell you the meaning needed for your text.

If you think you're ready to buy a dictionary, take a look at these questions below. They will help you decide what kind of dictionary might be best for you.

1. *What size is the dictionary?* If you plan to use the dictionary only at home, you might want to buy a larger dictionary. If you plan to carry it to classes, a smaller size might be better for you.

2. *How much does the dictionary cost?* The cost depends on how many pages it has and how it is made. A dictionary can be long

or somewhat short. It can be in hardcover or paperback. The amount of detail in the dictionary also affects cost.

3. *How many entries are included?* You should decide if you need a large dictionary with 150,000 entries or a smaller one with a few thousand entries.

4. *What is the focus of the dictionary?* Some dictionaries are for home or office use, and others are more general. Some dictionaries are written for elementary or secondary school students. They include fewer words and more basic meanings. Other dictionaries are for college use. The word *college* or *collegiate* in the title will tell you if it is written for college use.

5. *What is the copyright date of the dictionary?* The copyright date tells when the book was published. This information is found in the first few pages of the book. Since new words are always being added to our language, you should buy the most current dictionary you can find.

6. *What is the quality of the entries?* How much information about the word is given? You can find this by looking at the same word in several different dictionaries. How much information do you think you'll need?

7. *Is the type clear and easy to read?* Some dictionaries—like those that fit in your pocket—have very small print. Larger dictionaries have larger type. You'll have to decide which is best for you.

8. *Does the dictionary include a clear guide to help you use it?* The first few pages of the dictionary should tell how to read an entry in that dictionary. You can also skim the dictionary to see how easy it is to use.

9. *What other information does the dictionary include?* Many contain features such as sections on punctuation and language usage, lists of foreign words, and a table of weights and measures. The information you need depends on how you plan to use it.

10. *Do you want an electronic dictionary?* There are electronic versions of dictionaries that are small in size and easy to carry, but they can be costly.

QUICK REVIEW

Circle the correct answer. Check your answers at the bottom of the page before reading the next section.

1. Guide words tell about a word's history. **T** **F**

2. A word's part of speech is its use in a sentence. **T** **F**

3. A textbook's glossary includes all the meanings of a word. **T** **F**

Quick Review Answers: 1. F   2. T   3. F

EXERCISE 4.1   **Knowing how to use guide words helps you find the entry you need faster.** The words in the left and right columns are guide words that would be found at the top of a dictionary's pages. Look at the words in the middle column. Circle the words in that column that would be found on that page in a dictionary, between the two guide words. Cross out the words that would not be found on that page.

	Guide Word					Guide Word
1.	inject	injustice	insist	install	invention	instant
2.	path	patent	patrol	pest	piece	pie
3.	cent	century	chalk	change	charge	champion
4.	slick	silver	slide	slime	slip	sliver
5.	verb	verse	virtual	Virginia	violet	virus
6.	blister	blaster	bless	blue	boll	bolt
7.	acid	acrid	active	adapt	afternoon	after
8.	ego	egg	eight	elephant	eliminate	elegant
9.	there	thank	their	threw	thrift	throw
10.	story	steal	stole	store	summit	summer

EXERCISE 4.2   **The more you use a dictionary, the more your skills will improve.** Use the following dictionary entries to answer the questions that appear below them.

1. **sil·hou·ette** \ˌsi-lə-'wet\ n [French, from Étienne de *Silhouette,* died 1767, French controller general of finances] **1** : a likeness cut from dark material and placed on a light ground or one drawn in outline and solidly colored in like a shadow **2** : an outline of a person, usually in profile

   a. What is the etymology of the word? _from Etienne de Silhouette, a French controller general of finances_

   b. What part of speech is the word? _noun_

c. Look at the pronunciation guide. How would you say this word?

d. How many definitions does the word have? _2_

e. Use the word in a sentence. There was a carved silhoutte of my grandparents in my house.

2. **scu·ba** \'skü-bə\ n [acronym from *self-contained underwater breathing apparatus*] : equipment that provides oxygen and is used for breathing while swimming underwater

a. What is the etymology of the word? from self-contained underwater breathing apparatus.

b. What part of speech is the word? noun

c. Look at the pronunciation guide. How would you say this word?

d. How many definitions does the word have? 1

e. Use the word in a sentence. My scuba gear didn't work

3. **re·luc·tant** \ri-'lək-tənt\ adj [Latin *reluctant-, reluctari* to struggle against, from *re-* + *luctari* to struggle] : uncertain or unwilling <*reluctant* to get involved>; *also* : having or assuming a particular role against your better judgment <a *reluctant* hero> **re·luc·tant·ly** *adv*

a. What is the etymology of the word? latin reluctant, reluctari to struggle against.

b. What part of speech is the word? adjective

c. Look at the pronunciation guide. How would you say this word?

d. How many definitions does the word have? 2

e. Use the word in a sentence. I was reluctant to ride the horse

4. **zip·per** \'zi-pər\ n [from *Zipper,* a trademark] : two rows of metal or plastic teeth on strips of cloth and a sliding piece that closes an opening by pulling the teeth together

a. What is the etymology of the word? Zipper a trademark

b. What part of speech is the word? noun

c. Look at the pronunciation guide. How would you say this word?

d. How many definitions does the word have? 1

e. Use the word in a sentence. My zipper broke

5. **di·plo·ma** \də-ˈplō-mə\ n [Latin, passport, diploma, from Greek *diploma* folded paper, passport, from *diploun* to double, from *diploos*] **1** : an official or government document **2** : a document that gives some honor or privilege **3** : a record of graduation from or degree given by an educational institution

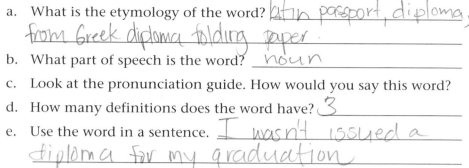

   a. What is the etymology of the word? *Latin passport, diploma, from Greek diploma folding paper.*

   b. What part of speech is the word? *noun*

   c. Look at the pronunciation guide. How would you say this word?

   d. How many definitions does the word have? *3*

   e. Use the word in a sentence. *I wasn't issued a diploma for my graduation.*

The Thesaurus

Think about the words *stone, rock,* and *pebble.* These words are **synonyms.** This means they are different words, but their meanings are about the same. The English language contains many synonyms, so a thesaurus can be helpful. Thesauruses are books that list synonyms. Why is it important to use a thesaurus?

Thesauruses give you new ways to say the same thing. They also help you think about words that are close in meaning. Words that are close in meaning are almost but not quite synonyms. For example, *jet, airplane, blimp,* and *balloon* are synonyms for *aircraft.* But they are different types of aircraft. Knowing these differences increases your vocabulary. They help you make a network (group of related words) of meanings.

Let's take a look at a sample entry from a thesaurus for the word *difficult.*

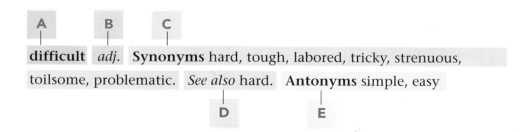

Like a dictionary, the words in a thesaurus are called *entries.* Most thesauruses list entries alphabetically. (Some list their words by subjects. These are harder to use. This textbook only describes those that use alphabetical order.) Look at **A. A** shows you the word. **B** is the word's part of speech. You can see that *difficult* is an adjective. Next look at **C. C** tells you synonyms for the word. Words like *hard, tough,* and *tricky* have similar meanings. **D** is a **cross-reference.** Cross-references tell you where to look for more information. In this case, you are asked to look at the word *hard.* **E** tells some **antonyms** for the word. Antonyms are words with opposite meanings. In this case, you can see that *simple* and *easy* are the opposite of *difficult.* If you're thinking about buying a thesaurus, take a look at these helpful hints.

1. *Are entries listed alphabetically or by subject?* Thesauruses in alphabetical order are easier to use than those listed by subject.
2. *How many entries are included?* In general, the more entries, the better.
3. *Are cross-references included?* Good cross-references will help your vocabulary grow if you use them. These are found at the end of an entry. They often start with the phrase *See also* or the word *See.* The word that follows sends you to other entries. These often help you find the exact synonym you need.
4. *Are antonyms included when possible?* Thesauruses with antonyms are helpful. Sometimes you need a word or phrase that means the opposite of the word you know.
5. *Is the type clear and easy to read?* Like with dictionaries, you need to find the thesaurus that will be easiest for you to use.
6. *Does the thesaurus include a clear guide to help you use it?* Skim to see how clear it is.
7. *Are you interested in an electronic thesaurus?* Just like with dictionaries, you can buy an electronic thesaurus. They are small and easy to carry, but they can be expensive.

QUICK REVIEW

Circle the correct answer. Check your answers at the bottom of the page before reading the next section.

1. The reference book you need depends on your purpose. **T** **F**
2. Dictionaries list words either in alphabetical order or by topic. **T** **F**
3. A thesaurus entry tells a word's definition. **T** **F**
4. A thesaurus gives you new ways to say the same things. **T** **F**
5. A thesaurus entry shows part of speech and synonyms. **T** **F**

WRITING CONNECTION

Respond to the following on a separate sheet of paper or in your notebook.

Which have you used more—a dictionary or a thesaurus? Why?

Quick Review Answers: 1. T   2. F   3. F   4. T   5. T

EXERCISE 4.3   **A thesaurus helps you build vocabulary quickly.** Use a thesaurus to look up each of the following words. List four synonyms for each on a separate sheet of paper or in your notebook.

1. instructor ~~teacher, educator, faculty~~
2. college - ~~~~, school
3. student - pupil
4. learning education, research
5. lecture lesson

Electronic Dictionaries and Thesauruses

Your college library contains a special print dictionary. It is called an **unabridged dictionary.** It contains all the known words in the English language. Such dictionaries are extremely large and cost a lot of money. They are too large and costly for most people to own. You can also find unabridged dictionaries online. (For more information about reading online, see Chapter 12.) To find one, use *online dictionary* as the keyword to search the Internet. Thesauruses can be found online as well. To find them, use *online thesaurus* as the keyword.

Online references have many advantages:

- They are quick and easy to use.

- They may be more up-to-date than print references. Some can play a word's pronunciation so you can hear how the word sounds.

- Some translate words into other languages.

You can also find a dictionary spell-check and thesaurus in your computer's word-processing program. These can be of great help when you are writing. The spell-check will show you when words are misspelled. Some programs will even correct misspellings for you. The thesaurus function isn't automatic like the dictionary spell-check is. You must use function keys to get synonyms.

QUICK REVIEW

Circle the correct answer. Check your answers at the bottom of the page before reading the next section.

1. Computer word processors include a dictionary and thesaurus. (T)   F

2. An unabridged dictionary is cheaper and often comes in paperback forms. T (F)

3. Unabridged dictionaries can be found online. (T)   F

Quick Review Answers: 1. T   2. F   3. T

WRITING CONNECTION

Respond to the following on a separate sheet of paper or in your notebook.

Which have you used—a print dictionary and thesaurus or online versions? Which do you prefer to use—print references or online references? Why?

EXERCISE 4.4   **Many people are interested in words. As a result, new versions of a dictionary can be big news.** Read the article below, then answer the questions that follow.

NEW WORDS FIND PLACE IN UPDATED WEBSTER'S

Now a home for "McJob," "headbanger," "Frankenfood"

1 **SPRINGFIELD, Massachusetts (AP)**—A former dot-commer working a McJob was listening to some headbangers while laying out the last of his dead presidents for longnecks and some less than heart-healthy Frankenfood.

2   Confused? Look at the new **edition** of the Collegiate Dictionary from the folks at Merriam-Webster.

3   Once a decade, Merriam-Webster redoes its best-selling dictionary. The 11th edition, available in bookstores Tuesday, includes 10,000 new words and more than 100,000 new meanings and revisions among its 225,000 definitions.

4   Some of the new words have been a long time getting the widespread use that calls for a move from the unabridged dictionary to the Collegiate. The file on the Yiddish exclamation "oy," for example, dates back to the immigrant (people who moved to the United States from other countries) groups of the 1890s. Others have zoomed into the language with the speed of the Internet.

5   The Web has had the biggest effect on the American language in the past decade both with the new words it has created and the speed with which they have been adopted by the general public, said John Morse, president and publisher of Merriam-Webster.

6   "Typically, it takes 10 to 20 years before a word moves out of usage by small groups into the larger population," Morse said. But *dot-commer*—someone who works for an online outfit—made it in a short five years.

7   That's not the only trend, he said.

8   "In new words for diseases and cures, we are clearly seeing the effect of aging on the baby boomers (people born from the late 1940s through the early 1960s)," he said.

9   "**Comb-over**" (an attempt to cover a bald spot), "**macular degeneration**" (an eye problem that mainly affects the elderly), and the adjective "**heart-healthy**" (good for the heart) are all new to the 11th edition. Along with them have come many new words dealing with how we pay for medical services, such as "primary care."

10   "It mirrors changes in society," Morse said.

Reprinted with permission of the Associated Press.

11   Pop culture still remains a source of new words, with such additions as "headbanger" (defined as both a hard-rock musician and a fan), "dead presidents" (paper currency), "McJob" (low-paying, dead-end work), and "Frankenfood" (genetically engineered food).

12   Over the past decade, Americans have also adopted more slang expressions—such as "bludge" (**goof off**)—from other English-speaking nations such as New Zealand and Australia, he said.

13   "We are coming around full circle," Morse said, pointing out that Noah Webster, America's first dictionary editor, had tried to make a uniquely American language, separate from British usage.

14   To find new words and usages, Merriam-Webster's editors spend much of their day reading newspapers, magazines and other popular publications.

15   Each new word and usage—along with a snippet from the publication showing how it was used—goes into an electronic database as well as the Springfield-based industry leader's huge card files. The files, started by Webster himself, now contain more than 75 million words and their usage dating to 1790.

16   *Merriam-Webster's Collegiate* is the bestselling hardcover dictionary on the market with more than 55 million copies sold since 1898, according to Arthur Bicknell, a spokesman for Merriam-Webster.

17   The privately held company does not give out sales figures, Bicknell said. However, he said, sales have set records for the past five years and the company was expecting to set a new mark this year.

Adding More Computer Presence

18   A decade is fairly typical for a complete overhaul of a collegiate dictionary, but, of course, the newer companies haven't been at it as long as Merriam-Webster. *Webster's New World* (published by Macmillan) released the 4th edition of its college dictionary in 1999, updating its 3rd edition published in 1988. *The American Heritage Dictionary* updated its 1994 edition in 2001.

19   All of the dictionary publishers, including Merriam-Webster, print smaller yearly updates of new words.

20   The computer age is also affecting how the 162-year-old publishing company is marketing (selling) the new edition of the *Collegiate*. The new book costs $25.95 and comes with a CD-ROM and a one-year subscription to a new Collegiate Web site.

21   For the past seven years, the 10th *Collegiate* has been available free on the company's Web site, Morse said. But readers who want to use the Web to read the 11th edition will have to subscribe (join for a fee), he said. The annual cost is $14.95 and also gives you online access to the *Collegiate Thesaurus, Collegiate Encyclopedia* and *Spanish-English Dictionary.*

22   "People were telling us they didn't want the dictionary in just one form," he said.

23   The book, at least for now, is still king (most important) in the dictionary business with the print volume getting the most use, he said.

24   "People love the **serendipity** (unexpected surprise) of what is put in front of them when they page through the book in search of a word," Morse said.

VOCABULARY

These vocabulary words are in the article you just read. Answer each question. For words you do not know, check your dictionary.

1. What is a *dot-commer*?
   A. a person who publishes books
   B. someone who works for an Internet company
   C. an online company
   D. The article does not say.

2. Who is a *baby boomer*?
   A. an infant
   B. someone born between the 1940s and 1960s
   C. a parent with a child under the age of 2
   D. The article does not say.

3. *Bludge* means to _____.
   A. goof off
   B. study
   C. eat Frankenfood

4. A *decade* is _____.
   A. ten years
   B. five years
   C. three years
   D. one year

5. Which word is most closely related to hair care?
   A. macular degeneration
   B. longnecks
   C. comb-over
   D. McJob

VOCABULARY BUILDER

List five words from the passage whose meanings you do not know. Look up each word and write its meaning based on how it is used in the sentence. Use the word in a sentence of your own.

1. _____

   _____

   _____

2. _____

   _____

   _____

3. _____

_____

_____

4. _____

_____

_____

5. _____

_____

_____

COMPREHENSION   How much did you understand in the reading? Read the questions below and circle the correct answer.

1. How often is the Merriam-Webster dictionary redone?
    A. every year
    B. every five years
    C. every ten years
    D. The article does not say.

2. Who is John Morse?
    A. president and publisher of Merriam-Webster
    B. a dot-commer
    C. a person with a McJob
    D. The article does not say.

3. America's first dictionary editor was _____.
    A. John Morse
    B. Noah Webster
    C. Merriam Webster
    D. The article does not say.

4. According to the article, what is an example of *dead presidents*?
    A. coins
    B. one-, five-, or ten-dollar bills
    C. governmental buildings
    D. laws passed by previous American presidents

5. How much is a print copy of the 10th edition of the Merriam-Webster dictionary?
    A. $14.95
    B. $25.95
    C. free
    D. The article does not say.

6. Which of the following is not available for subscription at the Merriam-Webster website?
    A. a collegiate encyclopedia
    B. a Spanish-English dictionary
    C. the 10th edition of the Merriam-Webster dictionary
    D. a collegiate thesaurus

7. What has been the greatest source of new words in the last ten years?
    A. the Internet
    B. television
    C. fast food
    D. The article does not say.

LEARNING TIP
Examining Returned Tests

Suppose you get a test back with a lower grade than you expected. What do you do? Your first reaction might be to look at the grade quickly, stuff the test in your backpack, and try to forget it ever happened.

That's understandable. But, it's not what you should do. Instead, you need to really look at that test. A careful study of the test can help you make a better grade on the next exam. This is because your exam is a kind of reference for future study. Figure 4.1 provides a form for looking at returned *objective exams*. Objective exams have either multiple choice, true/false, or matching questions.

Subjective exams are essay or short-answer exams. When you get back a subjective exam, you need to read your instructor's comments. If you agree with the comments, highlight them. If you disagree, write polite questions beside the comments. Even if your instructor does not allow you to keep your exam, take time to look at it carefully during class. Make notes about what you did well and how you could improve.

Test Item Missed	Insufficient Information						Test Anxiety							Lack of Test-Wisdom			Test Skills							Other	
	I did not read the text thoroughly.	The information was not in my notes.	I studied the information but could not remember it.	I knew the main ideas but needed details.	I knew the information but could not apply it.	I studied the wrong information.	I experienced mental block.	I spent too much time daydreaming.	I was so tired I could not concentrate.	I was so hungry I could not concentrate.	I panicked.	I carelessly marked a wrong choice.	I did not eliminate grammatically incorrect choices.	I did not choose the best choice.	I did not notice limiting words.	I did not notice a double negative.	I changed a correct answer to a wrong one.	I misread the directions.	I misread the question.	I made poor use of the time provided.	I wrote poorly organized responses.	I wrote incomplete responses.		
Number of Items Missed																								

Figure 4.1   Examining a Returned Test

If you need more time to look at your exam, make an appointment to see your instructor in his or her office. Next, you need to think about how you can make the most of your strengths and reduce your weaknesses before the next exam. Ask yourself what you could have done to get a higher grade. Then make a plan to put these ideas to work.

Whether your exam is objective or subjective, the next step is the same. If you need help, get it. Help comes from many places. Your instructor keeps office hours and wants to help you. Consider visiting a campus writing or learning center or joining a study group. Hiring a tutor is another option, although it might cost money. Whatever choice you make, make it and act upon it. All exams require the best efforts you have to give at that particular time. All you need to do is find your best and give it.

CHAPTER SUMMARY

1. Basic vocabulary reference books include a dictionary and a thesaurus.
2. When buying a dictionary, you should look at size, cost, number of entries, focus, copyright date, quality of entries, clearness of type, guide to use, and other features.
3. When buying a thesaurus, you should look at format, number of entries, cross-references, possible antonyms, clearness of type, and guide to use.
4. The format of an entry in a print dictionary includes syllables, pronunciation, part of speech, meaning(s), and, sometimes, etymology.
5. Although a dictionary helps you build vocabulary, the glossary in your textbook or looking at a word's context often are better for finding content-specific meanings.
6. The format of an entry in a thesaurus includes part of speech, synonyms, and antonyms. Entries use cross-references to show entries with more synonyms.
7. Thesauruses build vocabulary by helping you make networks of related meanings.
8. Online and electronic forms of dictionaries and thesauruses can also aid vocabulary development.

CHAPTER REVIEW

On a separate sheet of paper, answer briefly but completely.

1. How are a dictionary and a thesaurus different? How are they alike?
2. How is a collegiate dictionary different from other dictionaries?
3. List two ways in which a thesaurus may be organized.
4. What is the purpose of guide words?
5. What is etymology?
6. What is the purpose of cross-references in a thesaurus?
7. Explain why most people do not own an unabridged dictionary.
8. What vocabulary tools are found in word-processing software?

ACTION SUMMARY

• Which ideas from this chapter do I already use?

Dictionary

• Which ideas from this chapter are new to me?

• The best idea I learned from this chapter is . . . . Why?

• Ideas from this chapter I would like to try are . . . .

• How will I put the new ideas I've learned into action?

LEARNING ONLINE

Go to http://developmentalenglish.wadsworth.com/atkinson-longman to find the website for *Reading Strategies for Today's College Student*. This website is designed for students using this book. Here you will find:

- fun and interesting websites related to reading
- web exercises and reading quizzes that will help you become a better reader
- a list of chapter objectives
- a glossary of terms used in the chapter
- flashcards
- crossword puzzles

CHAPTER VOCABULARY REVIEW

Go back to the "Vocabulary Check" at the beginning of the chapter. Now that you've read this chapter, rate how well you understand the vocabulary words in the "After-Reading Ratings" column. If you rate any word less than a 3, read the information about that term again.

CHAPTER 5

Using Context

OBJECTIVES

After you finish this chapter, you should be able to

- Use context to identify parts of speech
- Get meaning from different kinds of context clues

CHAPTER OUTLINE

CHAPTER MAP

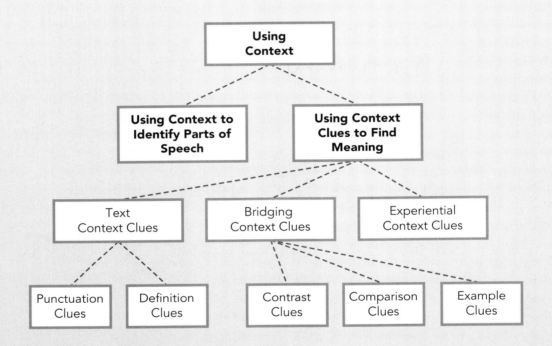

VOCABULARY CHECK

Below are the vocabulary words you will need to know in this chapter.

If you see a word that's brand-new to you, write a 0 in the "Before-Reading Ratings" column. If you have seen the word before but don't know what it means, write a 1. If you think you know what the word means, write a 2. If you know the word and can use it in a sentence, write a 3.

If you wrote a 0 or 1, look up the word in the Glossary at the back of the book. Then, after reading the chapter, look at these words again and rate them in the "After-Reading Ratings" column.

If you come across new words in the chapter that are not on this list, underline them or write them in your notebook, and look them up in your dictionary. Write down their meaning. This will help you increase your vocabulary.

Before-Reading Ratings	Vocabulary Words	Pronunciation Guide (How do I say this word?)	After-Reading Ratings
	literal	ˈli-t(ə-)rəl	
	text context clues	ˌtekst ˈkän-ˌtekst ˈklüz	
	denotation	ˌdē-nō-ˈtā-shən	
	punctuation clues	ˌpəŋk-chə-ˈwā-shən ˈklüz	
	definition clues	ˌde-fə-ˈni-shən ˈklüz	
	linking verbs	ˈliŋ-kiŋ ˈvərbz	
	bridging context clues	ˈbri-jiŋ ˈkän-ˌtekst ˈklüz	
	connotation	ˌkä-nə-ˈtā-shən	
	contrast clues	ˈkän-ˌtrast ˈklüz	
	comparison clues	kəm-ˈpa-rə-sən ˈklüz	
	example clues	ig-ˈzam-pəl ˈklüz	
	experiential context clues	ik-ˌspir-ē-ˈen(t)-shəl ˈkän-ˌtekst ˈklüz	

> **Time flies like an arrow.**
> **Fruit flies like a banana.**
>
> *Groucho Marx*
>
> Comedian, Actor, and Television Host

Think about the different meanings of *flies* in Marx's quote. In the first, *flies* is a verb. It means to go fast. In the second, it is a noun. It names a kind of insect. Both are **literal** (exact or factual) meanings of the word *flies*. So when you see the word *flies* in a sentence, how do you know what it means? You look at the way the word is used. The words around a word are its *context*. Using context is one way to define words. In this chapter, we will discuss how to figure out a word's meaning by using context clues.

Using Context to Identify Parts of Speech

Parts of speech help you know the meaning of a word. For example, look at the word *back* in these sentences:

a. I hurt my *back* at work today.
b. Move *back* three spaces.
c. The *back* room needs painting.
d. Can you *back* your car out of the driveway?

The meaning of *back* changes in each sentence. Why? It is used differently in each sentence. In the first sentence, it is a noun. It refers to a body part. In the second sentence, *back* is an adverb. It shows how movement should take place. In the third sentence, *back* is an adjective. It tells which room to paint. In the fourth sentence, *back* is a verb. It shows action. Thus, *back*'s meaning depends on its part of speech. Not all words can be used as different parts of speech, however. Many words are only one part of speech.

Nouns, pronouns, verbs, adjectives, articles, adverbs, prepositions, conjunctions, and interjections are all parts of speech. Look at Table 5.1. Here you'll find definitions, examples, and sample sentences for the parts of speech.

QUICK REVIEW

Circle the correct answer. Check your answers at the bottom of the page before reading the next section.

1. Few words have more than one meaning.   T   (F)

2. What surrounds a word is called the context.   (T)   F

3. How a word is used in a sentence shows its part of speech.   (T)   F

Quick Review Answers: 1. F   2. T   3. T

Table 5.1   Parts of Speech, Definitions, and Examples

Part of Speech	Definition	Examples	Sample Sentence
noun (n.)	names, people, places, things; qualities or conditions	*Names*: Joe, Selena, Ming-na; *People*: teacher, Democrats, family; *Places*: Maine, college, England; *Things*: book, thoughts, rocks; *Qualities or Conditions*: love, darkness, prettiness, happiness, sadness, light	*Sam* lost the *book.* *Sam* and *book* are nouns.
verb (v.)	shows action or being	run, sit, swim, go, is, are, am, was, were, have, had, do, does, did	Sam *lost* the book. *Lost* is the verb. It tells what happened to the book.
pronoun (p.)	replaces a noun	he, she, it, they, I, me, my, his, her, hers, their, theirs, you, your, yours, yourself, themselves, himself, itself, herself	*He* lost *it.* The pronoun *He* replaces the word *Sam.* The pronoun *it* replaces the word *book.*
adjective (adj.)	describes a noun	big, young, smart, difficult, red, hot, small	Sam lost the *old, expensive* book. *Old* and *expensive* are adjectives that describe the book.
article (art.)	articles are part of adjectives—they tell which one	a, an, the	Sam lost *the* old, red book he bought last week. *The* is an article that describes which book Sam lost. It was the old, red book.
adverb (adv.)	describes a verb, adjective, or other adverb; answers the questions *how, where, when* and *why*	quickly, too, very, soon, here, there, tomorrow, sadly, great	*Today,* Sam *carelessly* lost the old, expensive book. *Today* is an adverb that describes when Sam lost the book. *Carelessly* is the adverb that describes how he lost it.

(*continued*)

Table 5.1   Parts of Speech, Definitions, and Examples (*continued*)

Part of Speech	Definition	Examples	Sample Sentence
preposition (prep.)	connects the noun or pronoun following it to another word in the sentence	aboard, about, above, across, after, against, along, among, around, as, at, before, behind, below, beneath, beside, besides, between, beyond, by, down, during, except, for, from, in, into, inside, like, near, of, off, on, over, past, since, through, than, to, under, unlike, until, up	Sam lost the old, red book *in* the student center. *In* is a preposition that connects the book to the student center.
conjunction (conj.)	joins words or groups of words	and, but, or, after, because, although, even if, since, until, while	Sam lost the old, red book *and* a backpack. *And* is the conjunction that joins *book* and *backpack*.
interjection (intj.)	shows strong emotion	Oh! Oops! Wow! No!	*Oh, no!* Sam lost the old, red book and a backpack. *Oh, no!* is the interjection that shows deep feeling.

EXERCISE 5.1   **Sometimes words have more than one meaning. That can make learning new words a challenge.** For example, the three words below (*cap*, *fix*, and *down*) each have many meanings. Look at their meanings, then read the sentences that follow. Decide which meaning best fits each sentence. Write in the letter of the correct meaning next to each sentence. Use parts of speech to help you find the correct meaning.

1. cap
   a. limit (n)
   b. cover (v)
   c. hat (n)

   ___c___ He purchased his new *cap* at a baseball game.
   ___a___ The credit bureau put a *cap* on my credit card.
   ___b___ The university *capped* the swimming pool with a hard rubber top.

2. fix
   a. solution (n)
   b. repair (v)
   c. problem (n)
   d. arrange (v)

   __b__ Please call the plumber to *fix* the leaky faucet.
   __c__ When my tuition check bounced, I was in a financial *fix*.
   __d__ Can you *fix* it so that I don't have classes on Tuesdays?
   __a__ Good time management is the *fix* for balancing work and school.

3. down
   a. sad (adj)
   b. scheduled (adj)
   c. feathers (n)
   d. downward (adv)
   e. nonproductive/not working (adj)

   __d__ The team marched *down* the hill toward the field.
   __a__ She's *down* after failing her exam—I saw her crying yesterday.
   __b__ The secretary made sure I was *down* on my advisor's calendar.
   __c__ My jacket is filled with *down* and keeps me warm all winter.
   __e__ The printer is *down* today, so I can't print out my essay.

WRITING CONNECTION

Respond to the following on a separate sheet of paper or in your notebook.

How well do you understand parts of speech? How would you rate your understanding of them? If you rate your understanding high, explain why. If you rate your understanding low, explain how you might improve it.

Using Context Clues to Find Meaning

Police search for clues at a crime scene. First, they look for clues in plain sight. They might find a gun or a knife. They might see a broken lock. Then they search for clues that are not in plain sight. These might be fingerprints or a strand of hair. Finally, they look for a motive. This is another type of clue. Why did the crime happen? Maybe greed. Maybe anger. Looking at clues helps police solve crimes.

Just as police use clues to solve crimes, you use context clues to find meanings. Some clues are like the clues in plain sight. They are stated in the sentence. Others are like clues that are not in plain sight. They are there but you must look for them. Finally, sometimes you use only your background knowledge to find meaning. The context clues we will be learning are text, bridging, and experiential context clues.

Text Context Clues

Text context clues are written clues to a word's meaning. There are two kinds: punctuation clues and definition clues. These types of context clues help you to find a word's **denotation**, or exact meaning. Often, this meaning is found in a dictionary or glossary. But using text context clues can be faster. It saves you the step of looking up the word. Let's take a closer look at each type.

Punctuation Clues

Punctuation clues consist of commas, parentheses, brackets, or dashes. Sometimes, the words within the punctuation marks tell you the meaning of the new term. Other times, the word within the punctuation marks is unknown. If so, the words before or after the punctuation marks define the new word or give examples of it. Let's look at some examples.

Commas

Sentence 1: A *dissertation,* a long research paper, may take years to write.

Sentence 2: A long research paper, a *dissertation,* may take years to write.

In the first sentence, *dissertation* is defined by the words between the commas. In the second sentence, the unknown word is between the commas. By using these punctuation clues, you learn that a *dissertation* is a long research paper.

Parentheses

Sentence 1: Some students resort to *plagiarism* (copying the work of others) to make good grades.

Sentence 2: Some students copy other's work as their own (*plagiarism*) to make good grades.

In the first sentence, the definition of *plagiarism* is in parentheses. In the second sentence, you can see that the sentence defines the word, and the word itself is in parentheses.

Brackets

Sentence 1: Students must show *competency in language* [skill in reading and writing].

Sentence 2: Students must show skills in reading and writing [*competency in language*].

In the first sentence, *competency in language* is defined by the words within the brackets. In the second sentence it is defined in the sentence itself, and the term is in the brackets.

Dashes

Sentence 1: The development of *ethical standards*—high values—is expected of all students.

Sentence 2: The development of high values—*ethical standards*—is expected of all students.

The definition of *ethical standards* is set apart by dashes in the first sentence. In the second sentence, the meaning is stated in the sentence itself and the term *ethical standards* is set off by dashes.

Definition Clues

Definition clues are a second kind of context clue. They join the new word with the word or words that rename it or tell its meaning. Definition clues are also called **linking verbs.** A linking verb shows no action. Rather, it shows what something is or defines something. Some of these clues include *is, was, are, am, seems, feels, means, involves, is called,* and *resembles.* For instance:

The art, science, or work of teaching *is called* pedagogy.

The linking verb *is called* shows that *pedagogy* means "the art, science, or work of teaching."
Here's another example:

Interlibrary loans *are* transactions in which books from one library are made available to another library.

The word *are* signals that the definition of *interlibrary loans* is to follow.

EXERCISE 5.2 **Punctuation can help you find the meanings of new words.** Use punctuation clues to find the meanings of the words below in italics. Circle the word or words that tell you the meaning.

1. A *baccalaureate* (Bachelor of Arts or Science) degree involves at least 124 hours of credit.
2. The nursing program is *accredited*—approved—by the National League for Nursing.
3. *Web-based classes,* courses taught through the Internet, can be taken anytime and anywhere.
4. Art majors need a *portfolio* (collection) of all work.
5. The financial aid office mailed *award letters*—official notice of all money given to a student.

EXERCISE 5.3 **Sometimes you find definitions in obvious places. In these sentences, the meanings of new words are in the sentences themselves.** Use definition clues to find the meaning of the words in italics. Circle the word or words that tell you the meaning.

1. My *cumulative* GPA is the average of my grades from all the courses I've taken.
2. *Consolidation* means several small loans combined into one loan.
3. *Fellows* are freshmen advisors.
4. In *pass/no credit courses*, grades of *A, B,* or *C* show as a *P* on your transcript.
5. The *cost of attendance* involves tuition, fees, living costs, and other costs for going to college.

Bridging Context Clues

Bridging context clues use words in the text to help you find meaning. They show the kinds of conclusions to draw. Bridging context clues help you find a word's **connotation**. A *connotation* is the meaning of a word based on your feelings. For example, the denotation, or dictionary definition, of *home* is "a place where people live." The connotation of *home* might be a warm, safe place with people you love. Because your connotation of a word has a personal meaning for you, it may help you understand how others define this same word. There are three types of bridging context clues: contrast, comparison, and example.

Contrast Clues

Contrast clues point to opposite meanings. Examples of these words are *however, on the other hand, instead of, but, while, on the contrary, nevertheless, yet,* and *although*. Look at this example:

> Some problems among students can be solved without campus police, *but* others need criminal inquiry.

The word *but* signals that *without campus police* is the opposite of *criminal inquiry*. This tells you that *criminal inquiry* means police involvement. Here's another example:

> *While* students often cram at the last minute, paced study proves more effective.

The word *while* signals that a new idea, different from cramming at the last minute, is coming.

Comparison Clues

Comparison clues show how two or more things are alike. Such words as *similarly, as well as, both,* and *likewise* show likenesses. For instance:

> Periodicals *as well as* other reading materials are often used in research.

The comparison clue *as well as* tells you that *periodicals* are a kind of reading material.

Another example is:

> *Both* psychology and sociology study human beings.

The word *both* signals that the two courses mentioned have something in common: Both involve studying people.

Example Clues

Example clues tell you that an example, or explanation, of a new word or words is to follow. You see what features the examples share and use background knowledge to find meaning. Words and phrases that introduce example clues include *such as, such, and other, for instance, for example*, and *like*. For instance:

> Students use bikes, motorcycles, cars, *and other* means of conveyance to come to campus each day.

Bikes, motorcycles, and *cars* are all types of vehicles. The words *and other* show that they are examples of *means of conveyance*. Therefore, *means of conveyance* must be ways of getting around. Here's another sentence:

> This class will have regular assessments—quizzes and presentations, *for example*—throughout the semester.

Using your background knowledge, you know that how you do on quizzes and presentations makes up part of your grade for a course. *For example* shows that these two things are examples of *assessments*. The word *assessments*, therefore, must mean ways to evaluate students.

QUICK REVIEW

Circle the correct answer. Check your answers at the bottom of the page before reading the next section.

1. Punctuation and linking verbs are examples of bridging context clues. **T** **(F)**

2. Context clues in the text help you find a word's connotation. **T** **(F)**

3. Text context clues help you find a word's denotation. **(T)** **F**

EXERCISE 5.4   **Using the opposite of what you know can help you define new words.**
Use contrast clues to figure out the meaning of the italicized word or phrase in the sentences that follow. Write your answers on the lines below.

1. ROTC was once only for male students; however, now it is *coed*.

   Coed- both males and females
   _____

   _____

Quick Review Answers: 1. F   2. F   3. T

2. Education is no longer a 4-year program; on the contrary, today's careers require *lifelong learners*.

Lifelong learners-no limit to any specific time

3. Although many students *default* on them, I plan to repay my student loans.

default- lack fall back on

4. While the *principal* of my school loan was $3000, interest raised the total I need to repay to $3600.

Principal - amount borrowed

5. My adviser asked me if I had *transfer credit,* but I had not attended any other college.

transfer credit - credit from other colleges

EXERCISE 5.5   **Using comparison clues lets you see how items are alike.** Use comparison clues to figure out the meaning of the italicized word or phrase in the sentences below. Write your answers on the lines below.

1. Students need to know the meaning of CLEP and TOEFL, as well as other *acronyms*.

letters used as word instead of a phrase

2. He is very *fickle* with his friends; similarly, he keeps changing his mind about what to major in.

Changeable

3. Both dogs and wolves are *canines,* but cats are not sea lions.

animal in the dog family.

4. She painted her house *chartreuse;* likewise, her car is bright green.

Bright green color

EXERCISE 5.6   **Sometimes a clear example provides the best definition of a new word.** Use example clues to figure out the meaning of the italicized word or phrase in the sentences below. Write your answers on the lines below.

1. Student teaching and internships in the senior year are examples of *capstone courses*.

   Course taken at last school year

2. Frisbee teams, political groups, chess clubs, community service, and other *extracurricular* activities add to a well-rounded college experience.

   Not part of the curriculum; non-credit

3. Students with physical disabilities often need various *academic accommodations* like extended test time, readers, and note takers.

   Classroom adaptations

4. Students who have broken major campus rules may be punished with *sanctions* such as suspension, expulsion, or dismissal from college.

   Penalties

5. Students who live with *close relatives*—for instance, parents, legal guardians, or grandparents—do not have to stay on campus.

   family members

Experiential Context Clues

Experiential context clues are harder to use than other context clues. You use them when the text gives no written clues. You have only your experience and background knowledge to help you. So what do you do? You must look at the sentence. Then you use the word's context and your background knowledge. Common sense and your knowledge of parts of speech will also help. For instance:

> The angry student argued *vehemently* with her instructor about her test grade.

What does *vehemently* mean? Let's see. You know what *angry* means. You know why people *argue*. From this, you can figure out what *vehemently* means. It concerns strong emotions or feelings.

WRITING CONNECTION

Respond to the following on a separate sheet of paper or in your notebook.

Which is more difficult for you to use: definition, bridging, or experiential context clues? Why?

EXERCISE 5.7   **What you know about the world around you is your most valuable tool in defining new words.** Use experiential context clues to figure out the meaning of the italicized word or phrase in the sentences below. Write your answers on the lines below.

1. My meal ticket allows me to eat in the college *commons* any time.

   dinning arear

2. The weather is nice enough for us to meet in the *quad* between the buildings.

   outside areas

3. My online course was *asynchronous,* so I could participate in it any time I wanted to.

   not a specific time

4. *Articulation agreements* between colleges help with the transfer of credits from one college to another.

   contract thrt state course work

5. The campus library is a *depository* for both federal and state publications.

   Storage place

EXERCISE 5.8   **Clues to meanings of new words come from many places.** Use context clues to figure out the meaning of each of the boldfaced terms from the passage in Exercise 4.4 on pages 88–89. Identify each word's part of speech. Write your answers in your notebook or on a separate sheet of paper.

EXERCISE 5.9   **College newspapers often provide contexts for new words.** Use context clues to figure out the meaning of each of the boldfaced terms from the article below. Then identify each word's part of speech. Write your answers in your notebook or on a separate sheet of paper.

PHOBIAS PLAGUE MANY COLLEGE STUDENTS
by Bonnie Allen, *News reporter*

1 Imagine being afraid of noise, crowds, beautiful women, or germs. Believe it or not, these fears are among some of those faced by college students.

2 There are hundreds of phobias. Fear of heights (**acrophobia**) is a common one. Some people even fear peanut butter sticking to the roof of the mouth (**arachi-butyrophobia**).

3 "Other than alcohol *dependency*, phobias are the most common *psychological* disorder college students have," said David Carpenter, a psychology department lecturer.

4 According to the U.S. Food and Drug Administration, about 18 percent of all Americans have a phobia.

5 But, a phobia is not the same thing as being afraid.

6 The FDA reports that a **phobia** is "an *intense unrealistic* fear of an object, an event, or a feeling."

7 Anyone can develop a fear of something. Contact with the object associated with the phobia often *triggers* rapid heart rate and breathing. Sweating and overall feelings of **panic** also occur.

8 A phobia is an irrational fear.

9 For instance, someone could have a phobia of cats, even though most cats are harmless.

10 "A phobia goes beyond a normal fear," Carpenter said. "If you have a phobia of snakes and you see one, you will really *freak* out."

11 According to the National Mental Health Association (NMHA), phobias are classified into three groups: specific phobias, social phobias, and agoraphobia.

12 The most common type of phobias is **specific phobias.** These are *irrational* fears of certain objects, ideas, or situations. Some of the stranger phobias in this group include fear of the color purple or the fear of looking up.

13 The American Psychiatric Association (APA) reports that most specific phobias involve animals. These include the fear of wild animals, chickens, birds, and worms.

14 Most simple phobias surface and disappear during childhood. If a phobia continues into adulthood, medical treatment is most likely needed to manage it.

15 **Social phobias** are a little easier to understand than most specific phobias. The

(continued)

Reprinted with the permission of Texas State University, San Marcos, TX. Originally published by *The Daily University* on March 19, 2003. Written by Bonnie Allen.

NMHA explains that a social phobia is the fear of "being humiliated or embarrassed in front of others."

16   This may be confused with shyness, but social phobias cause extreme anxiety and even panic, just like specific phobias.

17   Social phobia symptoms include fear of blushing, fear of public speaking, fear of dating, fear of public places, and fear of being watched. According to the APA, these types of phobias usually develop after *puberty*.

18   The third type of phobia is **agoraphobia.** This is the fear of being in a situation or place where escape would be embarrassing or challenging. People who suffer from agoraphobia are likely to avoid crowded places such as elevators [and] stores. . . .

19   The APA explains that people with the disorder experience **panic attacks.** Panic attack symptoms include sweating, rapid breathing and heart rate, and intense fear. This might progress to the level of not being able to leave the house for fear of an attack or a panic-triggering situation.

20   All three types of phobias can affect anyone, including college students.

21   "The most common phobia is the fear of public speaking, especially among college students," Carpenter said. "That's why so many students put off taking speech classes."

22   The fear of public speaking, **glossophobia,** is a social phobia. The fear itself is public in nature. Those who suffer from this phobia are afraid of embarrassment and humiliation in front of a group of people, Carpenter said.

23   Andrew Carr, a public relations senior, has experienced public speaking anxiety first hand.

24   "Initially, I'm nervous. I have sweaty palms, and I blush," he said. "But once I get going, it gets better. It depends on what I am talking about and if I know what I'm talking about. I think it has more to do with preparation."

25   But some people can ease through a speech like it's nothing to worry about. For example, Chris Cumby, a math freshman, is confident in his public speaking abilities.

26   "I've given speeches before in high school for a public speaking class and a school club," he said.

27   Cumby is enrolled in a speech communication class. He must give a persuasive speech at the end of the semester. He believes the class atmosphere is a healthy, accepting one. He hopes his classmates will enjoy his speech.

28   Cumby also has advice for those who fear getting up in front of a group.

29   "Try to get **familiar** with the class so you don't feel like you're talking to strangers," he said. "Picture it like you're talking to a group of your friends."

30   Not every fear a student has is a phobia. If it is someone's first shot at public speaking and he's a little nervous about it, that doesn't necessarily mean his anxiety and nervousness **constitutes** a phobia or anxiety disorder.

31   "College students have lots of anxieties that are probably not extreme enough to be considered phobias, such as math anxiety," Carpenter said. "If a person's reaction to (math tests) is **extreme,** then it might be considered a phobia, which is an irrational fear of rather serious proportions."

VOCABULARY

These vocabulary words are in the article you just read. Answer each question. For words you do not know, check your dictionary.

1. *Blush* means to _____.
   A. feel ill
   B. turn red
   C. have a fever
   D. get a chill

2. *Intense* means _____.
   A. strong
   B. weak
   C. complete
   D. concerned

3. *Specific* means _____
   A. particular
   B. diagnosed
   C. hidden
   D. group

VOCABULARY BUILDER

List three words from the passage whose meanings you do not know. Look up each word and write its meaning based on how it is used in the sentence. Use the word in a sentence of your own.

1. _____

   _____

   _____

2. _____

   _____

   _____

3. _____

   _____

   _____

VOCABULARY BUILDER

Use a dictionary to find the pronunciations and meanings of the following italicized words from the reading. Use context clues to be sure you have the correct definition. Next write the definitions in your own words. Then, on a separate sheet of paper or in your notebook, write a sentence with each word.

Word	Pronunciation	Definition from Dictionary	Definition in Your Own Words
dependency			
psychological			
intense			
unrealistic			
triggers			
freak			
irrational			
puberty			

COMPREHENSION   How much did you understand in the reading? Read the questions below and circle the correct answer.

1. What fraction of Americans have a phobia?
   - A. about ⅕
   - B. about ⅓
   - C. about ½
   - D. about ¾

2. What is the most common phobia?
   - A. flying
   - B. giving a speech
   - C. spiders
   - D. snakes

3. What is the FDA?
   - A. a kind of phobia
   - B. a treatment for phobia
   - C. a psychiatric association
   - D. a government agency

4. What is the most common psychological disorder faced by college students?

    Ⓐ dependency on alcohol

    B. phobias

    C. mental illness

    D. intense fears

5. According to the article, which is NOT a physical symptom caused from contact with the object associated with a phobia?

    A. sweating

    B. rapid heart rate

    C. headache

    Ⓓ rapid breathing

6. The most common kinds of phobias are _____.

    A. social phobias

    Ⓑ specific phobias

    C. agoraphobias

    D. glossophobias

LEARNING TIP

Interacting with Instructors in the Classroom

(*Hint: As you read this Learning Tip, use what you've learned about context clues to figure out new words.*)

Think about people you've met. Some were people you wanted to know better. Some were people you didn't want to know better. Instructors feel the same way about students. Each term, they meet many new students. You should try to make a good impression on your instructors. Your behavior (how you act) will help your instructors decide whether or not you are a student they want to know better.

Why does making a good impression matter? Because they are part of your network of support at your college. They can advise you on course choices. They can refer you to other resources. They can write letters of recommendation for you. They can suggest you for awards. They can help you get jobs after graduation.

To get and keep an instructor's goodwill, you need to be polite and interested. Getting to class on time is a good first step. Being properly dressed also makes a good impression. Going to class without fail shows

(*continued*)

you want to work hard. It shows that you're serious about learning. Your work reflects you. Thus, the quality of your work shows your respect for the instructor and the course. Only your best work should be turned in to your instructors.

Sitting near the front of the room is always a good idea. Sitting in about the same seat lets the instructor know where you are. Your instructor may or may not keep attendance records. Even so, he or she may look for you and know you are there regularly. Sitting near the front of the room also helps you keep eye contact with the instructor. This eye contact shows your interest in the topic.

Some students act as if the instructor doesn't see them. They look bored. They sleep. They read the newspaper. They may even talk to others. But instructors notice body language—both bad and good. Positive facial expressions (smiling, nodding your head, raising your eyebrows) are important. Body language (sitting straight, facing the instructor, arms uncrossed) shows your desire to learn. Body language is very important when you read your instructor's comments on returned assignments or tests. Constructive criticism (comments meant to help you improve) is part of the learning process. Such comments are not a personal attack. Your body language should show that you accept these comments in the spirit in which they are given.

Instructors welcome questions that are related to the topic. But asking rude questions, unrelated questions, or questions whose answers were just discussed often annoys them. If you tell the instructor what you do understand before asking a question, your instructor will be better able to answer you. Briefly stating what you think was just said helps the instructor find gaps in your knowledge. You can also help an instructor help you by clearly stating the information you need.

Active participation in class discussions shows your interest. If you ask questions or make comments about the lecture topic, you show your desire to learn. If you have a question you do not want to ask in class, see your instructor before or after class or make an appointment.

You'll see your instructor most often in class. But you can also see your instructor during office hours. Faculty schedule these so students can contact them. However, instructors also use that time to grade papers. They use that time to do research. Although you can stop in to say hello or ask for help, you should avoid spending long periods of time visiting faculty.

There are many good reasons for an office visit. You may have questions about course content. You may have questions about university policies. Questioning a grade or asking for extra time on assignments are also good reasons to see an instructor. Offering options strengthens your case if you question a grade or ask for more time. For instance, you could write a research paper, take a make-up exam, do extra problems, or state an alternative due date for finishing an assignment. This proves you know your grade is your responsibility. Whether or not you get to make up work or get more time for an assignment is the instructor's choice.

Instructors will often take a greater interest in you if you are a student who has made an effort to get to know them. This is true, however, only if you're a person they'd want to know.

CHAPTER SUMMARY

1. Using the context involves finding the connection between a word and its surroundings.
2. Context helps identify parts of speech.
3. Context involves finding meaning through text, bridging, and experiential clues.

CHAPTER REVIEW

On a separate sheet of paper, answer briefly but completely.

1. Explain how the wrong meaning of a word in context can cause confusion. Write an example.
2. Why would using context to define words be harder for ESL (English as a Second Language) speakers?
3. Write one or more sentences, and label any five parts of speech in the sentences.
4. How are adjectives and adverbs alike? How are they different?
5. What type of context is hardest for you to use? Why?
6. What forms the "bridge" in bridging context clues?
7. What is the difference between denotation and connotation?
8. How does knowing parts of speech affect your skill in using context?

ACTION SUMMARY

• Which ideas from this chapter do I already use?

_____

_____

- Which ideas from this chapter are new to me?

  _____

  _____

- The best idea I learned from this chapter is . . . . Why?

  _____

  _____

- The ideas from this chapter I would like to try are . . . .

  _____

  _____

- How will I put the new ideas I've learned in action?

  _____

  _____

LEARNING ONLINE

Go to http://developmentalenglish.wadsworth.com/atkinson-longman to find the website for *Reading Strategies for Today's College Student*. This website is designed for students using this book. Here you will find:

- fun and interesting websites related to reading
- web exercises and reading quizzes that will help you become a better reader
- a list of chapter objectives
- a glossary of terms used in the chapter
- flashcards
- crossword puzzles

CHAPTER VOCABULARY REVIEW

Go back to the "Vocabulary Check" at the beginning of the chapter. Now that you've read this chapter, rate how well you understand the vocabulary words in the "After-Reading Ratings" column. If you rate any word less than a 3, read the information about that term again.

CHAPTER 6

The Structure of Words

OBJECTIVES

After you finish this chapter, you should be able to

- Talk about different word parts
- List common roots, prefixes, and suffixes
- Identify the limits of using word parts to define words

CHAPTER OUTLINE

CHAPTER MAP

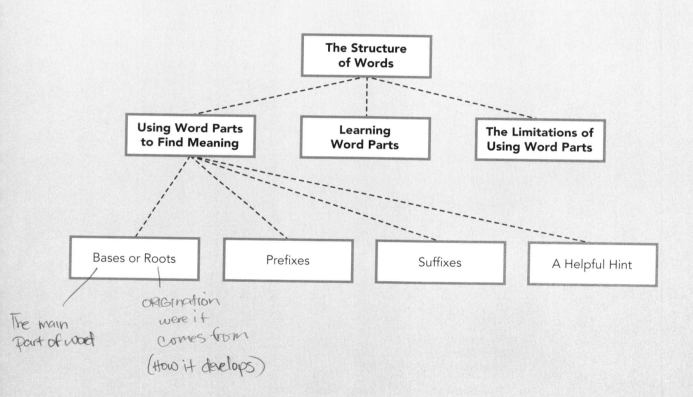

The Structure
of Words

Using Word Parts
to Find Meaning

Learning
Word Parts

The Limitations of
Using Word Parts

Bases or Roots

Prefixes

Suffixes

A Helpful Hint

The main
Part of word

ORIGInation
were it
comes from

(How it develops)

VOCABULARY CHECK

Below are the vocabulary words you will need to know in this chapter.

If you see a word that's brand-new to you, write a 0 in the "Before-Reading Ratings" column. If you have seen the word before but don't know what it means, write a 1. If you think you know what the word means, write a 2. If you know the word and can use it in a sentence, write a 3.

If you wrote a 0 or 1, look up the word in the Glossary at the back of the book. Then, after reading the chapter, look at these words again and rate them in the "After-Reading Ratings" column.

If you come across new words in the chapter that are not on this list, underline them or write them in your notebook, and look them up in your dictionary. Write down their meaning. This will help you increase your vocabulary.

Before-Reading Ratings	Vocabulary Words	Pronunciation Guide (How do I say this word?)	After-Reading Ratings
	base	'bās	
	root	'rüt	
	prefixes	'prē-ˌfiks-z	
	suffixes	'sə-fiks-z	
	term planner	'tərm 'plan-nər	
	syllabus	'si-lə-bəs	
	weekly schedule	'wē-klē 'ske-(ˌ)jül	
	to-do list	tə-'dü 'list	

> **Colors fade, temples crumble, empires fall, but wise words endure.**
>
> *Edward Thorndike*
>
> Twentieth-century American psychologist

In Chapter 5 you learned about words in context and parts of speech. You learned you could sometimes figure out what a word means by how it is used in a sentence. In this chapter, you will see how knowing the meanings of parts of words can help you learn the meanings of entire words.

In college, you have to take many different courses. Maybe you will take *geology, sociology,* or *theology.* These are very different classes, but they have one thing in common—they each end in *-ology,* which comes from the Greek word *logos.* It means *the study of.* So *geology, sociology,* and *theology* all involve the study of something.

Now look at what makes these words different. The *geo* in *geology* is a Greek word that means *earth.* So *geology* is the study of the earth. The *socio* in *sociology* comes from the Latin word *socius.* This word means *companion,* so *sociology* is the study of society (groups of people, or companions). The *theo* in theology comes from Greek. It means *God.* So, theology is the study of God or religions.

Many words in the English language are made up of parts of Greek or Latin words. Once you learn some of these, you'll be able to find the meanings of many words.

Using Word Parts to Find Meaning

Many words can be broken down into three parts: the base or root, the prefix, and the suffix. A **base** or **root** gives a word's basic meaning. It helps you find the subject of an unknown word. Some roots may be used alone. Others must be used with other roots, **prefixes,** or **suffixes.** A prefix comes at the beginning of a word—like *un* in *unhappy.* A suffix comes at the end of a word—like *ful* in *careful.*

Look at the following sentence:

The instructor's voice was *inaudible* most of the time.

Inaudible contains three word parts: *in, aud,* and *ible. In* is a prefix that means *not.* The root *aud* means *heard.* The suffix *ible* means *able to.* It makes the word an adjective, because it describes the instructor's voice. Together, *inaudible* means *not able to be heard.* Let's take a closer look at bases or roots, prefixes, and suffixes.

Bases or Roots

Bases or roots give words their basic meaning. Think about the roots of a plant. The leaves and flowers of a plant grow from the roots. With words, the meaning also "grows" from its root. Table 6.1 lists common roots and bases of words you will find in college or on campus, along with some examples. The meanings are in parentheses.

Table 6.1   Common Bases, Meanings, and Examples

Base (Meaning)	Example	Definition of Example
astr (star)	*astronomy* professor	science or study of stars
aud (hear)	lecture *auditorium*	a place to hear
biblio (book)	*bibiliography* for the paper	a written list of books
bio (life)	*biology* lab	the study of life
congn (know)	*recognize* the answer	to know
cred (believe)	a *credible* answer	believe the answer to be true
doc (lesson/teach)	*indoctrinate* new students	teach
fract (break/broken)	*infraction* of the rules	breaking
gam (mate/marry)	*monogamous* relationships	one mate
geo (earth)	*geology* class	study of the earth

(*continued*)

Table 6.1 Common Bases, Meanings, and Examples (*continued*)

Base (Meaning)	Example	Definition of Example
grad/gress (move by steps)	academic *progress*	step to next level
junct (join)	*adjunct* faculty	joined to (part-time)
kinesi (movement)	*kinesiology* requirement	study of movement
lect/leg (read)	*legible* handwriting	able to be read
manu (hand)	chemistry *manual*	handbook
mem (mind)	*memorize* information	keep in the mind
ology (study of)	*archeology* notes	study of past life
onomy (science of)	*astronomy* class	science or study of stars
onym (name)	*synonym* for the term	same name
phil (love)	*philanthropic* donor	one who loves humankind

Base (Meaning)	Example	Definition of Example
photo (light)	*photosynthesis* in plants	energy from light
psych (soul; mind)	*psychological* experiment	study of the mind
scope (see)	electron *microscope*	instrument for seeing small things
script (write)	English *manuscript*	something written by hand
soph (wisdom)	*sophomore* student	"wise and foolish"; second year
tele (far from)	*telelearning* class	learning far from the campus
text (weave)	a new *textbook*	words woven together to create a book
vice (second in command)	*vice-president* of the college	person just below the president
voc/vok (call)	*revoked* the scholarship	recalled

WRITING CONNECTION

Respond to the following on a separate sheet of paper or in your notebook.

Explain how understanding the meaning of bases or roots helps you develop your vocabulary.

Prefixes

Prefixes appear at the beginnings of words. They change the meaning of the base or root in different ways. For instance, some prefixes, such as *un-*, *in-*, *a-*, and *anti-*, cancel or negate meaning. They change the meaning of the base word into its opposite. So, *untrue* means *not true*. *Incomplete* means *not complete*. *Atypical* means *not typical*. *Antisocial* means *not social*. Other common prefixes that cancel or negate meaning include *contra-*, *il-*, *ir-*, *mis-*, and *non-*. Table 6.2 provides examples for each of these. Their meanings are in parentheses.

Prefixes also can show numbers or quantities. For instance, suppose you know that *uni* means *one*. Then you know that a Student *Union* is *a place where all gather as one group*. Knowing that *dec* means *ten* will help you remember that a *decade* is ten years. Table 6.3 on pages 127–128 gives you a list of prefixes that show number with an example for each. The meaning of the prefix is in parentheses.

Table 6.2 Prefixes That Show Negative or Opposite Meanings

Prefix	Example	Definition of Example
un (not)	*uneaten* food	not eaten
in (not)	*incorrect* response	not correct; wrong
a (not)	*asocial* behavior	not sociable
anti (against)	*antigovernment*	against the government

Prefix	Example	Definition of Example
contra (against)	*contradiction*	against what was said
il (not)	*illogical* argument	not logical
ir (not)	*irresponsible* act	not responsible
mis (bad)	*misinformation*	bad information
non (not)	*nonequivalent* course	not equivalent

Table 6.3   Prefixes That Show Number

Prefix	Example	Definition of Example
bi (two)	*bisect* an angle	cut in two parts
cent (100)	college *centennial*	100 years
dec (10)	sports *decathalon*	10 events
kilo (one thousand)	distance of one *kilometer*	1000 meters
milli (1/1000)	a *millisecond* in time	1/1000th of a second

(*continued*)

Table 6.3   Prefixes That Show Number (*continued*)

Prefix	Example	Definition of Example
multi (many)	*multilingual* students	able to speak many languages
quad (four)	campus *quadrangle*	four-sided area
tri (three)	musical *trio*	group of three
uni (one)	*universal* agreement	as one group

Some prefixes are like adverbs (a word that describes a verb, adjective, or other adverb) attached to a base. They show position. For instance, an *inter*library loan is a loan *between* libraries. Course *pre*requisites are classes that come *before* other courses. *Ad*junct faculty are joined *to* the college but are not a part of it like full-time faculty are. *Extra*curricular activities are done *outside* of the classroom. Table 6.4 lists such prefixes with their meanings in parentheses. The table also gives examples and tells what the examples mean.

Table 6.4   Prefixes That Show Position

Prefix	Example	Definition of Example
ad (to, toward)	*advance* in ability	move toward or ahead
circa/circum (around/round)	*circumvent* a rule	get around

Prefix	Example	Definition of Example
co/com/con/cor (with)	*coauthored* by	written with
di (apart)	college *division*	apart from other areas
e/ex/exo (out)	text *excerpt*	taken out of a book
extra (beyond)	*extraordinary* speaker	beyond what is usual or normal
hyper (over)	*hyperactive* behavior	overactive
hypo (under)	scientific *hypothesis*	idea under investigation
inter (between)	*interlibrary* loan	between libraries
intra (within)	*intramural* sports	within the community or organization
para (beside or equal)	*paralegal* studies	beside the law (the person who helps a lawyer do his/her job)
post (after/ later than)	*postsecondary* education	education after high school

(*continued*)

Table 6.4   Prefixes That Show Position (*continued*)

Prefix	Example	Definition of Example
pre (before)	*preregister* for classes	register before classes begin
pro (in front/ favor of)	graduation *processional*	to walk in front, as in a parade
re (back/again)	*readmit* a student	admit again
sub (under/below)	*substandard* work	below standard
super (above/ greater than)	political *superpower*	having power greater than others
tele (far away)	*telecommunications* office	communications from far away
trans (across/ through)	*transfer* coursework	move from one institution to another
under (below)	*undergraduate* education	below graduate level

Suffixes

Suffixes are found at the end of words. Like prefixes, they add to the meaning of a root word. They can also change how a word is used in a sentence by changing its part of speech. Certain suffixes turn the root word into a noun. Others turn it into an adjective. Still others turn the root into an adjective. Consider the verb *excel*. Adding the suffix *-ence* makes *excellence*, which is a noun. Changing the suffix to *-ent* makes *excellent*, an adjective. Adding another suffix (*-ly*) to *excellent* forms the adverb *excellently*. Table 6.5 lists suffixes by the part of speech they turn the root word into. It also provides meanings and examples.

Table 6.5   Suffixes by Part of Speech

Noun	Example	Definition of Example
ance/ence (state of being)	financial *assistance*	state of being assisted
ation (act of)	college *certification*	act of being certified
hood (state of being)	*adulthood* status	state of being an adult
cy (state of being)	on-campus *residency*	state of being a resident
ism (state of being)	collegiate *athleticism*	state of being an athlete
ist (one who does)	*chemist*	one who does chemistry

(*continued*)

Table 6.5   Suffixes by Part of Speech (*continued*)

Noun	Example	Definition of Example
ity/ty (state/ condition)	student *responsibility*	state of being responsible
ment (action or state of)	student *government*	state of being governed
ness (state or quality of)	complete *happiness*	state of being happy
or/er (that/one who does/is)	college *advisor*	one who advises
ory (place or thing for)	campus *directory*	place for directions
ship (state of being)	full *scholarship*	state of being a scholar
sion (act or state of)	college *admission*	act of admitting
sis (process or action)	structural *analysis*	process of analyzing
tion (state of)	freshman *orientation*	state of orienting
Adjective	Example	Definition of Example
able/ible (able to/ capable of)	*solvable* equation	able to be solved

Adjective	Example	Definition of Example
al (pertaining to)	*instructional* television	pertaining to instruction
ful (full of)	*beautiful* sunset	full of beauty
ic (pertaining to)	*academic* requirements	pertaining to the academy
ive (having the quality of)	*creative* expression	having the quality of creativity
ous (having)	*rigorous* schedule	having rigor
Adverb	Example	Definition of Example
ly (in the manner of)	*academically* ineligible	in the manner of academics

A Helpful Hint: Keeping Prefixes, Roots, and Suffixes Straight

Are you having trouble remembering the differences between prefixes, suffixes, and roots? Here's a hint to help you. Bases, or roots, come *after* prefixes. They come *before* suffixes. They come *between* prefixes and suffixes. To recall where each word part occurs, use this trick. Think of where the letters *P, R,* and *S* are in the alphabet. **Prefix, Root,** and **Suffix** follow this same order, as you see below:

A B C D E F G H I J K L M N O **P** Q **R** **S** T U V W X Y Z

QUICK REVIEW

Circle the correct answer. Check your answers at the bottom of the page before reading the next section.

1. A base is the opposite of a root. **T   F**

2. A prefix comes at the beginning of a word. **T   F**

3. A prefix determines a word's part of speech. **T   F**

4. A suffix comes at the end of a word. **T   F**

EXERCISE 6.1   **Coming up with your own examples increases your recall.** Add an example of your own in the blank space for each word part in Tables 6.1, 6.2, 6.3, 6.4, and 6.5. Use prefixes, suffixes, and roots to explain the meaning of each example. If you can't think of an example, use a dictionary to look up words that begin with the letters in the prefix or root. You can also use a dictionary to look up a suffix. The suffix entry generally gives examples.

EXERCISE 6.2   **Suffix clues help you know the part of the speech of new words.** Using the suffix clues from Table 6.5, identify the part of the speech (*noun, adverb, adjective*) for each word. Write your answer in the blank beside each word.

1. suspension *noun*
2. hypothesis *noun*
3. absence *noun*
4. accreditation *noun*
5. agricultural *adjective*
6. exemption *noun*
7. professionalism *noun*
8. elective *adjective*
9. scholastically *adverb*
10. lecturer *noun*

EXERCISE 6.3   **Your knowledge of prefixes, roots or bases, and suffixes helps you understand more when you read.** Read each of the paragraphs on the following pages. Use your knowledge of prefixes, roots or bases, and suffixes to circle your answers in the questions that follow.

Quick Review Answers: 1. F   2. T   3. F   4. T

1. Colleges must be *accredited*. There are special groups that *accredit* colleges. The group makes sure the college has clear goals. These groups look at the campus library. They check the degree programs offered by the college. They look at the college's mission, its purposes for being. They make sure these purposes are accomplished. They check to see how and if the college is organized. This means they look at the administration and faculty. They seek answers to questions. For instance, are there enough instructors? How many students are in each class? How are the classes taught? If these are done, the college gains *accreditation*.

   What is the purpose of accreditation?

   A. to give a college enough money to operate
   B. to decide if a college is meeting its goals
   C. to advertise college degrees
   D. to let students enroll

2. *Nontraditional* students are those students who have been out of school for a while. Some have only been out of school for four or five years. Some have been out of school for decades. They may be working or they could be retired. Some have children. They may be part-time or full-time students. They come to college for different reasons.

   Which of the following is NOT a nontraditional student?

   A. a member of a fraternity who wants to major in art
   B. a single father who works full-time and attends college part-time
   C. a retired woman with a GED who wants to get an associate's degree
   D. a mom who decided to attend college because her children are now in school

3. Many colleges offer *preprofessional* programs. For instance, the program might let a student complete the first two years of a dental assistant program on campus. The last two years would be completed in a dental school.

   Which of the following is LEAST likely to be a preprofessional program on a two-year campus?

   A. medicine
   B. law
   C. veterinary
   D. history

4. When choosing a career, some students try to make their *avocations* their *vocations*. For example, perhaps they like cars. So, they major in automotive technology. However, they learn that designing cars is different from driving or liking cars. Or, maybe they like cooking. They decide to get a degree in nutrition. But they find they are learning about the chemical content of food rather than ways to prepare it.

Vocation is to an *avocation* as _____ is to _____.

A. interest; hobby
B. hobby; job
C. job; hobby
D. job; career

5. Most students are familiar with the *Internet.* It is an information superhighway that lets people access the world from their computers. Anything—and everything—seems to be on the Internet. Some campuses also have an *Intranet.* It is more like a local road on a small island. It takes you around the island, but that is the only place to go.

Internet is to *Intranet* as _____ is to _____.

A. unlimited; limited
B. limiting; limited
C. limited; unlimited
D. limited; limitless

WRITING CONNECTION

Respond to the following on a separate sheet of paper or in your notebook.

How does identifying the part of speech of a word help you understand its meaning?

Learning Word Parts

Learning word parts takes study and practice, but it is worth it. You can learn word parts in many ways. Here are some hints to help make this easier. One way is to memorize word parts. Another way is to use the words you already know as keys to other words. For instance, suppose you need to know the meaning of *genocide* for a history class. You may already know the words *suicide* (to kill oneself), *homicide* (to kill another person), and *pesticide* (chemicals that kill bugs). They all have to do with *killing*. Now look at what these words have in common: the word part *cide.* You can figure out that *cide* must mean *to kill,* so the word *genocide* must also have to do with killing. (You should then look up the word in the dictionary to find the exact meaning. Here, *genocide* means to kill an entire race or culture.)

The Limitations of Using Word Parts

Does using word parts to find meaning always work? No. While many words have Greek or Latin backgrounds, some words come from other languages. So, what looks like a prefix, root/base, or suffix may not be one. For instance, the word *colt* (a young male horse) comes from a Middle English word. Middle English is a type of English that was spoken from about 1150 to 1475. In *colt, co* is not a word part. *Bitten* is another Middle English word that looks like it begins with a prefix. It means that something has had a bite taken from it. In this case, it looks like it has the prefix *bi*. However, *tten* isn't a real word. So, you cannot use word parts to define *bitten*.

How can you tell the difference? Sometimes you find meaning by splitting the word into parts. Then, you look for prefixes, suffixes, or roots that you know. Next, you try your meaning in context. Does it make sense? If not, then you may not be able to use word parts to define the word. Your skill in knowing when to use word parts will improve as you practice.

QUICK REVIEW

Circle the correct answer. Check your answers at the bottom of the page before reading the next section.

1. Using word parts is a foolproof way to determine word meaning. T (F)

2. All words have Greek or Latin backgrounds. T (F)

3. Word parts have the same meaning in all English words. T (F)

EXERCISE 6.4

Word parts help you find the meanings of new words. Each set of words below contains three words from the same prefixes, roots/bases, or suffixes. The common word part is italicized. The definition of each word is also given. Use the definitions of the words and the sentences they are in to define the common word part in each set.

1. a. The *med*ian (*average*) score for the class test was 84.
   b. The *med*iator (*third party*) helped the arguing couple.
   c. I like to buy a *med*ium (*middle*) sized drink.

   Common word part: *med*
   Definition: ___middle___

Quick Review Answers: 1. F   2. F   3. F

2. a. I paid the tele*phone* (*device for sending and receiving sound*) bill.
   b. What is the *phone*tic (*sounds of speech*) spelling of the word?
   c. Please play the old record on the *phono*graph (*machine that makes sound by having a needle move across it*).

   Common word part: *phone*

   Definition: Sound

3. a. She bought a used *auto*mobile (*car driven by one person*).
   b. I received my best score on the *auto*biography (*document written about one's self*) assignment.
   c. My classes were *auto*matically (*happened without anyone's direct action*) dropped for nonpayment of fees.

   Common word part: *auto*

   Definition: Self

4. a. Guam is an American *terr*itory (*a land supported or governed by another country*).
   b. The earthworm is a *terr*estrial (*lives in the earth*) animal.
   c. The physical *terr*ain (*earth form*) of the mountain made it difficult to climb.

   Common word part: *terr*

   Definition: earth / land

5. a. Use the soft *graph*ite (*type of lead used in pencils and other writing tools*) to draw this picture.
   b. The *graph*ic (*picture drawn for a specific purpose*) showed how to put the model together.
   c. A *graph*eme (*a written letter of the alphabet*) is the smallest unit of written language.

   Common word part: *graph*

   Definition: written / writing

EXERCISE 6.5   **Knowing word parts makes finding the meanings of new words easier.**
Using your knowledge of word parts, match the following words to their meanings. Write the letter of the definition next to the word. Use the italicized part of the word as a clue. Do not use a dictionary.

1. philosopher __D__
2. lectern __I__
3. subway __A__
4. bibliomania __J__
5. misnomer __B__
6. geography __H__
7. subscript __E__
8. audience __C__
9. percentage __F__
10. photograph __G__

A. passage below ground
B. a bad or wrong name
C. those who hear
D. lover of wisdom
E. written below
F. part of 100
G. a picture made with light
H. study of the earth
I. a stand that holds books so they can be read aloud
J. literally, crazy about books

LEARNING TIP
Time Management

College life may look easy. A full-time load is often only 12 hours. That should leave lots of time to do everything else. So why can college be so hard? Where does the time go? Time management means using time effectively for what you want to do. Three time management tools that can help you succeed are a term planner, a weekly schedule, and a to-do list.

First, a **term planner** shows what you need or want to do each term. You use it to plan for busier and less busy weeks. To make one, you'll need a calendar that shows a whole month on each page. Start by tearing out the pages for the months of the term. Or you can print out the pages for each month using a computer software program. (See Figure 6.1.) If your school is on a semester schedule, August through December will cover the fall term, and January through May will cover the spring term. Next, get the **syllabus** (outline of content) for each of your courses. Write all the dates for projects and tests on the calendar. Then, you can add other dates or appointments. These might include family visits or special events like sports or social activities. Post the term planner where you can see all the pages at once. Now you can see everything that is coming up for the whole term. Use it to plan ahead.

Your second tool is a **weekly schedule.** (See Figure 6.2.) This is one or two pages that shows all the days of the week. It should be divided into hours. You can buy these at office supply stores, or make your own. Start by marking the events that happen each day. This might include class time, work, commuting, family duties, or other regular events.

Sunday	Monday	Tuesday	Wednesday	Thursday	Friday	Saturday
						1 Volunteer at Humane Society—9-3
2 Do final review of biology notes—test tomorrow!	**3** Biology Test on Chapters 1-5 Reading—start chapt. exercises (due on Friday)	**4** Student Health Center appointment @ 2:30	**5** Biology Lab 3-5pm	**6** Reading—Finish all chapter exercises Math Quiz	**7** Reading chapter exercises due Chandra's Birthday Party @ 7pm	**8** Jazz Concert @ 8pm
9 Football Game vs. Ohio! 1:30	**10** Reading— Start chapter exercises (due on Friday)	**11**	**12** Biology Lab 3-5pm	**13** Reading— Finish all chapter exercises	**14** Reading chapter exercises due	**15** Volunteer at Humane Society—9-3
16 Date with Lynn	**17** Start studying for Hist. test Nov. 3rd Reading—Start chapt. exercises (due on Friday)	**18**	**19** Biology Lab 3-5pm College Nursing Student Assoc. Meeting @7pm	**20** Reading—Finish all reading chapt. exercises Math Quiz	**21** Reading chapter exercises due	**22**
23 History study group 7pm	**24**	**25**	**26**	**27** Math quiz	**28**	**29** Volunteer at Humane Society—9-3
30 Study for History test	**31** Study for History test	History test Nov. 3!				

Figure 6.1 Term Planner

Sunday	Monday	Tuesday	Wednesday	Thursday	Friday	Saturday
			Morning			
8:00	8:00	8:00 Reading	8:00	8:00 Reading	8:00	8:00
9:00	9:00 Biology	9:00	9:00 Biology	9:00	9:00 Biology	9:00 Humane Society
10:00	10:00	10:00 Math	10:00	10:00 Math	10:00	10:00
11:00	11:00	11:00	11:00	11:00	11:00	11:00
		11:30		11:30		
			Afternoon			
12:00	12:00 Lunch	12:00 Lunch	12:00 Lunch	12:00 Lunch	12:00 Lunch	12:00 Humane Society
1:00	1:00 History	1:00	1:00 History	1:00	1:00 History	1:00
2:00	2:00	2:00	2:00	2:00	2:00	2:00
3:00	3:00	3:00	3:00 Biology Lab	3:00	3:00	3:00
4:00	4:00	4:00	4:00	4:00	4:00	4:00
5:00	5:00 Dinner	5:00 Dinner	5:00 Dinner	5:00 Dinner	5:00	5:00

Figure 6.2   Weekly Schedule

(continued)

Sunday	Monday	Tuesday	Wednesday	Thursday	Friday	Saturday
Evening						
6:00	6:00 Work	6:00 Work	6:00 Work	6:00 Work	6:00	6:00
7:00 History Study Group	7:00	7:00	7:00	7:00	7:00	7:00
8:00	8:00	8:00	8:00	8:00	8:00	8:00
9:00	9:00	9:00	9:00	9:00	9:00	9:00
10:00	10:00	10:00	10:00	10:00	10:00	10:00

Figure 6.2   Weekly Schedule (*continued*)

If you wish, you can use different colors for different types of tasks. Your weekly schedule shows your ongoing responsibilities. Blank spaces show times when you're free for other things.

A **to-do list** is the third tool. (See Figure 6.3.) This is a list of the events and tasks you need to complete. You can write these on a piece of paper. Reviewing your term planner will help you see what you need to do. Next, put the list in order of importance. For instance, you could put #1 by the most important items. Your #2 items are those that can wait. Your #3 items are those you want to do but don't need to do. It's a good idea to estimate the time you need to complete each item. For instance, perhaps making note cards is a #1 item. You might judge that you can complete 20 cards in an hour.

Then, look at your weekly calendar. Write the #1 items from your to-do list in the spaces first. Add the #2 items. If you still have room in your schedule, add the #3 items. You can cross items off the list as you finish them. It's a good idea to adjust your to-do list and weekly calendar each week.

This Week's To-Do List

#1 — Review biology notes for tomorrow's test

#2 — Get Chandra's birthday present

#1 — Ask Lawanda for help with math problem for
      Thursday's quiz!

#3 — Start work on Humane Society posters

#2 — Call history study group to set up meeting time—
      Oct 23rd, 7 pm?

#2 — Buy get well-card for Grandma

#1 — E-mail reading instructor about assignment

#2 — Balance checkbook

#3 — Make appointment at writing center about history
      research paper

#3 — Get notes together for history test.

#1 — Send in tuition payment for next month

#1 — Pick up paycheck!

Figure 6.3   To-Do List

EXERCISE   Using Figures 6.1, 6.2, and 6.3 as examples, create a term planner for this term, a weekly schedule, and a to-do list.

CHAPTER SUMMARY

1. Using word parts is a way to figure out the meaning of words you don't know.
2. Roots (or bases) and prefixes or suffixes are word parts that can help you find a word's meaning.
3. A root or base provides the key meaning of a word.
4. Prefixes come at the beginning of words and change the meaning of the root.
5. Suffixes come at the end of a word and affect its part of speech.
6. Although knowing word parts is a good tool for finding meaning, it has some limits.

CHAPTER REVIEW

On a separate sheet of paper, answer briefly but completely.

1. How are bases (roots), prefixes, and suffixes different? How are they alike?
2. What information can word parts give you?
3. Which word part affects part of speech?
4. What are the limitations of using word parts to find a word's meaning?
5. What trick can help you remember the order in which word parts occur?
6. How does using word parts help you determine the meanings of words?
7. How can context and using word parts improve your understanding and recall of terms in a course?

ACTION SUMMARY

• Which ideas from this chapter do I already use?

_____

_____

• Which ideas from this chapter are new to me?

_____

_____

- The best idea I learned from this chapter is . . . . Why?

  _____

  _____

- The ideas from this chapter I would like to try are . . . .

  _____

  _____

- How will I put the new ideas I've learned in action?

  _____

  _____

LEARNING ONLINE

Go to http://developmentalenglish.wadsworth.com/atkinson-longman to find the website for *Reading Strategies for Today's College Student*. This website is designed for students using this book. Here you will find:

- fun and interesting websites related to reading
- web exercises and reading quizzes that will help you become a better reader
- a list of chapter objectives
- a glossary of terms used in the chapter
- flashcards
- crossword puzzles

CHAPTER VOCABULARY REVIEW

Go back to the "Vocabulary Check" at the beginning of the chapter. Now that you've read this chapter, rate how well you understand the vocabulary words in the "After-Reading Ratings" column. If you rate any word less than a 3, read the information about that term again.

CHAPTER 7

Developing a College Vocabulary

OBJECTIVES

After you finish this chapter, you should be able to

- Find sources of new words on a college campus
- Tell the difference between types of vocabulary words
- Use word cards and word maps to learn new words

CHAPTER OUTLINE

CHAPTER MAP

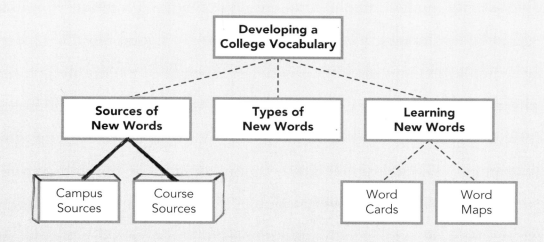

VOCABULARY CHECK

Below are the vocabulary words you will need to know in this chapter.

If you see a word that's brand-new to you, write a 0 in the "Before-Reading Ratings" column. If you have seen the word before but don't know what it means, write a 1. If you think you know what the word means, write a 2. If you know the word and can use it in a sentence, write a 3.

If you wrote a 0 or 1, look up the word in the Glossary at the back of the book. Then, after reading the chapter, look at these words again and rate them in the "After-Reading Ratings" column.

If you come across new words in the chapter that are not on this list, underline them or write them in your notebook, and look them up in your dictionary. This will help you increase your vocabulary.

Before-Reading Ratings	Vocabulary Words	Pronunciation Guide (How do I say this word?)	After-Reading Ratings
	general vocabulary words	'jen-rəl vō-'ka-byə-ˌler-ē 'wərdz	
	technical vocabulary words	'tek-ni-kəl vō-'ka-byə-ˌler-ē 'wərdz	
	specialized vocabulary words	'spe-shə-ˌlīzd vō-'ka-byə-ˌler-ē 'wərdz	
	synonyms	'si-nə-ˌnimz	
	antonym	'an-tə-ˌnim	
	homonyms	'hä-mə-ˌnimz	
	academic standing	ˌa-kə-'de-mik 'stan-diŋ	
	satisfactory progress	ˌsa-təs-'fak-t(ə-)rē 'prä-grəs	

> **The world occurs through language.**
> *Mal Pancoast*
> Author

. . . **A**udit. Bookstore. Catalog. Drop. Electives. Fees. GPA. Humanities. ID. Junior. Kinesiology. Load. Majors. Non-credit. Office hours. Part-time. Quality points. Register. Syllabus. Transcript. Undecided. Visual arts. Withdraw. eXams. Yearbook. Zoology. . . .

From **A** to **Z**, college has its own language. Each course you take has its own language, too. In this chapter, we'll look at ways to help you expand your college vocabulary. This will help you become both a better reader and student.

Sources of New Words

The world is full of new words! As you already know, college has its own vocabulary. Your skill in learning new words in college will help you after college, too. That's because as your life changes, your vocabulary will also change. You'll need new words for new interests, places, or jobs. Even people with large vocabularies have new words to learn. New words are all around. They come and will continue to come from what you see and hear.

Campus Sources

Each place has its own vocabulary. For instance, every campus has buildings. The buildings' names are part of the campus vocabulary. Some will have names specific to your campus, such as *Smith Hall* or *Jones Fieldhouse*. Some have general names such as the *student center, library, residence halls,* and *dining facililties*. The names of the courses are part of the campus vocabulary, too. They may include subjects like *earth science, algebra, history,* and *French*. Your orientation (introduction to campus) program was a crash course in the vocabulary of your campus. You may have learned new words such as *registration, curriculum,* and *advisor*. Now that you're part of the campus community, you'll learn more new words. So where will you find these words?

First, your campus newspaper reports on campus news. It lists events and activities like meetings, athletic events, art shows, or musical programs. If you attend these, you'll find more words to add to your vocabulary. For example, if you go to a meeting of a student organization, you might hear words like *minutes* (of the meeting) or *agenda*. You would hear words like *referee, penalty,* or *quarter* at many sports events. An art show provides words such as *sculpture, realism,* or *cubism*. Musical programs use words such as *concerto, tenor,* or *conductor*. Second, bulletin boards across campus are also places to find new words. They often tell about campus speakers, events, and meetings. You might find such words as *political, advocate,* or *rally*. Third, your campus catalog provides information. It tells about courses, majors, faculty, and policies. Most campus catalogs contain a brief glossary that defines key terms. Fourth, your campus website is another good source for new words. You'll find words such as *quick links, online enrollment,* or *faculty/staff directory*. It also shows words and pictures about your campus, tells about events and activities, and lists courses and departments. Last, your campus phone book can help you develop a campus vocabulary. It lists key offices and services like *provost* or *registrar.*

Course Sources

Each course you take has its own vocabulary. It's almost like using a new language for each course. People who know a certain language think in that language. Your goal is to know the vocabulary, or language, of each course you take. In other words, in an art course, you think and speak like an artist. In a science course, you think and speak like a scientist. If you don't know the language, you may have difficulties in the class. So you need to learn course terms quickly. How do you do this?

If you were going to another country, you would get a guidebook. The guidebook would tell you about the country and about common words you should know. Your textbooks are like guidebooks for your classes. They tell you about the classes you are taking and the words you need to know, so that you'll understand the chapter content in your textbooks. The terms may be in a list at the start of a chapter (like in this book) or at the end of a chapter. They might appear in boldface type within the chapter (like in this book). The definitions may be in the white space of the margins. Some words may be not defined, so you should look to see if the book has a glossary. This mini-dictionary defines key terms for the whole text. Previewing terms before class gets you ready to think in the language of the course. (See Chapter 2 if you want to review this strategy.) This prepares you for lectures. Lectures provide more new words. As you take notes, you need to mark key terms. Later, look up words you do not know. If you still have problems with a term, ask your instructor for help.

QUICK REVIEW

Circle the correct answer. Check your answers at the bottom of the page before reading the next section.

1. A college catalog reports on current campus news. **T**   **F**

2. A text glossary defines key words. **T**   **F**

3. Campus bulletin boards and the campus phone book can be sources of new words. **T**   **F**

Quick Review Answers: 1. F   2. T   3. T

WRITING CONNECTION

Respond to the following on a separate sheet of paper or in your notebook.

What new words have you learned in the last two weeks on your campus? Where did you first see or hear these words?

EXERCISE 7.1   **Many college catalogs include a glossary of terms and meanings specific to their campus.** Use the catalog glossary below to answer the questions that follow:

GLOSSARY

1   **A.A.** Associate in arts degree. A two-year degree designed to transfer to a four-year college.

2   **A.S.** Associate in science degree. A two-year degree for students who want technical or occupational training.

3   **Academic Average** Total average of grades on all college courses taken.

4   **Academic Calendar** A calendar covering the days in the school term. Shows important dates such as enrollment period, last dates to add or drop, and final exam periods.

5   **Academic Dismissal** An academic status or standing where a student is stopped from going to classes for one calendar year. This happens if a student returns from academic suspension and fails to earn at least a 2.00 (C) GPA (grade point average).

6   **Academic Probation** An academic standing given to a student who has less than a 2.00 (C) GPA. Students on academic probation may be asked to take less hours or may be required to take certain courses.

7   **Academic Suspension** An academic standing given to a student who has less than a 2.00 (C) GPA with a grade point deficit of 20 or more points.

8   **Academic Warning** An academic standing given to a student who has less than a 2.00 (C) GPA. Students are warned before being put on Academic Probation or Academic Suspension.

9   **Add/Drop** A period of time in which students may change schedules by adding or dropping classes without penalty.

10   **Audit** To take regular college credit courses for non-credit.

11   **Cancelled Class** A class that is dropped from the schedule due to not enough students enrolling in it or for other reasons.

12   **Catalog** Basic print or online reference for a college. Includes curricula, course descriptions, policies, academic calendars, and other information.

13   **Closed Class** A class that has no more available seats.

14   **Co-requisite** A course that must be taken during the same term as another course.

15   **Credit Hour** A semester hour of credit, usually consisting of the learning equal to 15 50-minute periods.

16   **Curricula** A planned group of courses aimed at an academic or occupational goal. May also be referred to as a program of study.

(continued)

17 **Drop Date** The last date on which a student may drop a class and receive money back.

18 **Electives** Nonrequired courses that students may choose to complete during their program of study.

19 **Faculty** Teaching employees at a college. Includes professors, associate professors, assistant professors, and instructors.

20 **Fee(s)** A charge for a class or laboratory.

21 **Freshman** A degree-seeking student with less than 30 earned credit hours.

22 **Full-time** Enrollment in 12 or more credit hours for fall or spring terms or enrollment of 6 or more credit hours in each summer term.

23 **General Education** Basic courses, including communication, math, science, social studies, and humanities.

24 **Grade** A letter showing measure of success in a course (A = excellent; B = above average; C = average; D = below average; F = failing). Each letter grade has a number value (A = 4; B = 3; C = 2; D = 1; F = 0).

25 **Grade Point Average** The decimal figure that results from the total number of credit hours in a semester divided by the number of quality points earned. This is a measure of academic success, which begins at a high of 4.00 (A) and goes downward.

26 **Grant** Financial aid to students that does not need to be repaid.

27 **Humanities** Courses in literature, philosophy, fine arts, and history.

28 **Independent Study** Learning in which a student enrolls in individualized non-classroom instruction in consultation with a faculty member.

29 **Interdisciplinary** Program or course using knowledge from two academic areas.

30 **Load** Also called academic load. The total number of credit hours taken in a term. A full-time load equals 12 credit hours.

31 **Major** Area of study for a specific degree or career.

32 **Multidisciplinary** Program or course using knowledge from more than two academic areas.

33 **Non-credit** A course that earns no credit for graduation.

34 **Part-time** Enrollment in less than 12 credit hours for fall or spring terms.

35 **Prerequisite** A requirement that must be met before enrolling in a specific course.

36 **Probation** A warning that a student is not in good academic standing. May come with limitations in credit hour enrollment.

37 **Purge** The process of removing students from class rolls due to non-payment of tuition and fees.

38 **Quality Points** The value obtained by multiplying the numerical grade point received in a course by the number of credit hours for the course. For example, a grade of 4.0 (A) in a 3-credit course equals 12 quality points.

39 **Registration** The process of completing a schedule for classes, including advisement as well as choosing and enrolling in classes.

40 **Required Course** A course that must be completed for a specific curriculum.

41 **Schedule of Classes** A college publication or online listing of all courses offered during a term. It includes dates, times, and locations of class meetings, names of instructors, credit hours, and other important registration information.

42 **Scholarship** Financial assistance to qualified students based on need, talent, or other selection.

43 **Scholastic Suspension** Not being allowed to enroll in the college for one term as the result of not keeping the minimum required GPA for two terms.

44 **Section Number** A numerical code used to identify each class section of each course

offered. Each class has a different section number. Section numbers are listed in the schedule of classes.

45 **Semester** An academic period of time, usually 16 weeks. There are two regular semesters each year. Sometimes called a term.

46 **Sophomore** A degree-seeking student with 30 or more credit hours.

47 **Student Classification** Ways in which students may be classified: full-time, part-time, career, freshman, transfer, commuter, etc.

48 **Student ID** The identification card students receive after paying their fees. Used for college events, the library, etc.

49 **Syllabus** One or more pages that tells about course requirements. Given to students on the first day of class and may

also be available online. The syllabus may include detailed information about a course. It should include the grading system, attendance policies, and test and assignment due dates.

50 **TBA** Abbreviation for "to be announced." This tells that a course is available but the specific time, place, or instructor has not been decided.

51 **Transcript** Official record detailing the courses taken by a student and grades achieved in them.

52 **Transfer Student** A student who comes from or goes to another school when completing educational requirements.

53 **Withdraw(al)** The official process of stopping attendance in a class after the drop date. Student receives *W* for a grade.

VOCABULARY   The words in the catalog glossary refer to courses or degrees, grades, people, money or payments, academic documents (official papers), or time periods. Decide which category in the chart below best fits each word or phrase. Write the term under the correct category in the chart below. NOTE: Some terms may fit in more than one category.

Terms that refer to courses or degrees	Terms that refer to grades	Terms that refer to people	Terms that refer to money or payments	Terms that refer to academic documents	Terms that refer to time periods

VOCABULARY
BUILDER

List five words or phrases from the catalog glossary, other than the defined terms themselves, whose meanings you do not know. Look up each word in the dictionary and write its meaning based on how it is used in the sentence. Use the words in a sentence of your own.

1. _____

_____

2. _____

_____

3. _____

_____

4. _____

_____

5. _____

_____

COMPREHENSION

How much did you understand in the catalog glossary? Read the questions below and write your answers in the blank lines that follow.

1. Tom's schedule was **purged.** Why do you think that happened?

_____

2. Ling is taking 12 hours for **credit** and **auditing** 3 hours of credit. If tuition is $100 per credit hour, what is the total of Ling's tuition?

_____

_____

3. What is another name for your **curriculum**? _____

_____

4. What's the difference between an A.A. and an **A.S. degree?**_____

_____

5. Which is worse—**academic dismissal** or **scholastic suspension?** Why?

_____

6. What's the difference between **academic warning, academic probation,** and **academic suspension?** _____

_____

7. Laurita wants a copy of all the coursework and grades she has completed. What document will provide this? _____

_____

8. Jake's art class is listed as **TBA**. What does this mean? _____

_____

9. Carlos wants to know when enrollment for the summer term will be. Which document provides that information? _____

_____

10. What's the difference between a **co-requisite** and a **prerequisite**?

_____

11. List two **student classifications** that describe you. _____

_____

12. Using your college catalog, list the categories of **general education** requirements for your institution. _____

_____

13. What's the difference between a **closed class** and a **cancelled class**?

_____

EXERCISE 7.2   **While many words are common on campuses across the United States, sometimes the definitions are different.** Pick 10 words or phrases from the catalog glossary in Exercise 7.1. Look up these words in your school's college catalog. On a separate sheet of paper, write the definitions from your college catalog. How were the definitions different? If the definition in your catalog was easier to understand, put a check by that term. Put an X by the term if the definition was less clear to you.

EXERCISE 7.3   **You will find the vocabulary of your college in many places.** Answer any two of the following questions on a separate sheet of paper.

1. Look at your campus phone directory. What information do you find there? Identify three new words that you found there and their definitions.

2. Find a bulletin board on your campus. What information do you find there? Identify three new words that you found there and their definitions.

3. Review your campus website. What information do you find there? Identify three new words that you found there and their definitions.

4. Using your college catalog, describe the information it contains. What information do you find there? Identify three new words that you found there and their definitions.

5. Obtain a copy of your campus newspaper. What information do you find there? Identify three new words that you found there and their definitions.

Types of New Words

The meanings of some words change, depending on how or where they are used. There are three types of vocabulary words: **general vocabulary words, technical vocabulary words,** and **specialized vocabulary words.** General vocabulary words are common, everyday words. They can be found in every subject. Their meanings do not change. They include words like *house, water, buy, forget,* and *each.* Adding general words to your vocabulary builds your knowledge in all subjects.

Some words and phrases can only be used in one subject. These are called technical vocabulary words. They have no meaning except when you are talking or writing about that subject. Every subject has its own technical terms, but they appear most often in science and technology courses. Examples include *ion* (in science), *treble clef* (in music), and *sauté* (in cooking). When you take a class with technical vocabulary words, you need to learn these words quickly. They will help you understand the ideas or concepts for that course.

Sometimes general words have special meanings in certain subjects. These are called specialized vocabulary words. For instance, in a theater class the general word *set* refers to a stage *set*—the place where the acting happens. In math, *set* refers to a group of numbers. Specialized terms are common in all subjects, and they can sometimes be confusing. Even if you know the meaning of a general vocabulary word, you should check its definition if you see it in one of your classes.

QUICK REVIEW

Circle the correct answer. Check your answers at the bottom of the page before reading the next section.

1. Technical vocabulary words form the basic building blocks of language. **T F**

2. Specialized vocabulary words are technical words used in general ways. **T F**

3. The meaning of some words differs according to their use. **T   F**

Quick Review Answers: 1. F 2. F 3. T

Learning New Words

Awareness is the first step in learning new words. This means that you know when a word is new to you. Whenever you hear and see new words, both in and out of the classroom, you should write them down. Then, you should check your understanding of the word. One way to do this is to use a rating system like the "Vocabulary Check" in this text. If you know the word but don't understand how it is used, it may be a specialized term. If the word is new to you, it may be a technical term or a general vocabulary word. Whatever the case, you need to learn the new meaning. You need to remember the word. To do this, you can use the same kinds of strategies you use to learn information for a test (see the "Learning Tip" in Chapter 2). Word cards and word maps are two other strategies for remembering words.

Word Cards

Word cards are a good way to learn terms. There's no one right way to make a word card. One of the easiest ways is to use index cards. Write the term on the front and its meaning on the back.

It helps if you think about the word in as many ways as you can. For instance, you could add the rating system from this chapter on the card. You would write the term and your beginning rating on the front. Then define the term in your own words on the back. You might add some examples. You could include **synonyms** (words that mean the same) and even an **antonym** (a word that means the opposite). Writing a sentence using the word will help you keep the meaning in context. You could even draw a picture of what the word means to you.

Your goal is to increase your learning, so it is good to review your word cards on a regular basis. When you're ready for a test, you can rate the words again. Review each one until you rate it a 2 or 3. Figure 7.1 shows how your card might look.

Front

Back

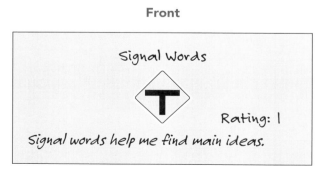

Signal Words

Rating: 1

Signal words help me find main ideas.

Words that show that how a text is organized; may help you find main ideas

Examples: *however, since, but, likewise*

Figure 7.1   Example of a Word Card

Word Maps

Learning a word's meaning is often not enough. You need to know how the word relates to other words. You can use your word cards to create a word map. Word maps help you remember and make connections between terms. To make a word map, first choose the words you want to learn. Next, pick general headings that describe the connections you want to make. For example, you could choose synonyms for your term. You could choose **homonyms** (words that sound alike but have a different meaning, such as *weak* and *week*). You could choose antonyms. The more connections you make, the better you understand the word. For specialized vocabulary words, you might want to include subheadings. You might include different subject areas, such as history or science. For example, in history, *weak* can describe leaders or governments. In science, *weak* might describe electrical charges or solutions. Then you draw a map showing these connections.

Take a look at the word map in Figure 7.2. It shows how synonyms, homonyms, and antonyms for *weak* might look. Synonyms for a weak

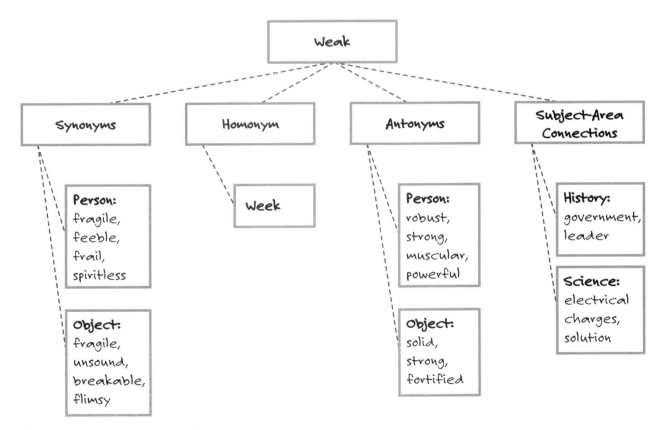

Figure 7.2 Example of a Word Map

person are *fragile, feeble, frail,* and *spiritless. Fragile* can also be a synonym for a weak object. *Unsound, breakable,* and *flimsy* also apply to weak objects. Antonyms for a weak person are *robust, muscular,* and *powerful.* The opposite (antonym) of a weak object include *solid* and *fortified.* The antonym *strong* can be used for both people and objects. The map also shows history (*government, leader*) and science (*electrical charges, solution*) connections.

QUICK REVIEW

Circle the correct answer. Check your answers at the bottom of the page before reading the next section.

1. Rating your understanding is the first step in learning new words. **T   F**

2. There's no one right way to make note cards. **T   F**

3. A word map helps you develop associations among words. **T   F**

EXERCISE 7.4   **Word cards are a good way to study vocabulary.** Choose 10 words from one of the earlier exercises or from one of your courses. Make a word card for each of the 10 words. Include your rating of the term, the definition, and a synonym. Write a sentence of your own using the word. Add a drawing to help you recall the word.

EXERCISE 7.5   **Word maps let you see connections among new words.** Make a list of 20 words or phrases that you associate with your college. On a separate sheet of paper or in your notebook, make word maps for at least 10 of them.

WRITING CONNECTION

Respond to the following on a separate sheet of paper or in your notebook.

Which is more difficult for you to learn—specialized or technical terms? Why?

Quick Review Answers: 1. F   2. T   3. T

LEARNING TIP

Computing Grade Point Average

College grades are important. Why? Grades determine a student's **academic standing** (rank). Students who don't make **satisfactory progress** (a minimum C average) are placed on probation. If their grades don't improve, they flunk out. An average of C, then, is the lowest average you can have and still stay in school. This academic standing is called "good standing."

Luckily, grades are something you know about. After all, you probably have received grades your whole life. A grade is a grade is a grade, right? Maybe not. In high school, the grades you get in most courses were alike. That is, the A you got in math was the same as the A you got in English. The C you got in French was the same as the C you got in music. When put into point value or numbers, an A = 4, B = 3, C = 2, D = 1, and F = 0 points. To get a high school GPA (grade point average), you usually add the point values of each course and divide by the number of courses. For example, if you had a C in math (2) and an A in PE (4), you would have a B average (2 plus 4 = 6; 6 divided by 2 = 3).

So, you may think the same holds true in college. But in college, the point values for grades are not the same for each course. The point value of grades depends on the credit hours for the course. To figure out your GPA, you multiply the number of credit hours for each course by each grade's point value. Then you divide this total by the total number of credit hours. The result is your GPA.

For instance, look at the following:

Math 100	*3 credit hours*
English 101	*3 credit hours*
History 103	*3 credit hours*
Music 100	*1 credit hour*
Health 101	*2 credit hours*
TOTAL	**12 credit hours**

At the end of the term, suppose Student 1 makes these grades in the following courses:

Math 100	*3 credit hours × C (2.0) = 6*
English 101	*3 credit hours × C (2.0) = 6*
History 103	*3 credit hours × C (2.0) = 6*
Music 100	*1 credit hour × C (2.0) = 2*
Health 101	*2 credit hours × C (2.0) = 4*
TOTAL	**12 credit hours**

24 points divided by 12 credit hours = 2.0 GPA

In this case, Student 1 has a C (2.0) average. Student 1 is in good academic standing. Now let's look at the grades Student 2 has made:

Math 100	*3 credit hours × C (2.0) = 6*
English 101	*3 credit hours × D (1.0) = 3*
History 103	*3 credit hours × F (0) = 0*
Music 100	*1 credit hour × A (4.0) = 4*
Health 101	*2 credit hours × B (3.0) = 6*
TOTAL	**12 credit hours**

19 points divided by 12 credit hours = 1.58

Student 2 has a 1.58 grade point average—less than a C. Since Music 100 had only 1 credit hour, the A in that course did not count enough to balance out the F in History 103, which had 3 credit hours. Student 2 would be placed on academic probation.

EXERCISE

On a separate sheet of paper or in your notebook, figure out the GPA for each of the following students. Record your answers below.

1. Student A   GPA = _____

Course	Credit Hours	Grade
Psychology 101	3	B
Phys Ed 105	1	A
Math 120	3	C
English 111	3	D
Geography 103	3	C
Orientation 101	1	A

(continued)

2. Student B   GPA = _____

Course	Credit Hours	Grade
Sociology 1020	3	D
History 1010	3	B
Math 1600	3	A
Biology 1002 with lab	4	D

3. Student C   GPA = _____

Course	Credit Hours	Grade
English 100	3	A
Speech 101	3	A
Math 102	3	D
Chemistry 107 (with lab)	4	D
Economics 100	3	F

4. List the courses you are now taking. Write down the grades you think you will have at the end of this term. Figure out your predicted GPA.

CHAPTER SUMMARY

1. Each campus has its own vocabulary.
2. Each course has a vocabulary of its own. The goal of the course is to think like a content expert using the language of the course.
3. General vocabulary words are common words that apply to any subject.

4. Technical vocabulary words are words that apply only to specific subjects.
5. Specialized vocabulary words are common words that have special meanings in specific subjects.
6. You learn new words by becoming aware of them, learning their meaning, and remembering them.
7. You add new words to your vocabulary by making word cards and/or word maps.

CHAPTER REVIEW

On a separate sheet of paper, answer briefly but completely.

1. List five words or phrases that you've learned on your campus. Provide their meanings.
2. Examine the glossary of this text or any other text. Find two words or phrases that are examples of each of the following: general vocabulary, technical vocabulary, specialized vocabulary.
3. Which type of vocabulary (general, technical, or specialized) poses most problems for you in learning? Why?
4. Which do you like using more—word cards or word maps? Why?
5. Tell how a word's meaning can change depending upon which class you are in.

ACTION SUMMARY

- Which ideas from this chapter do I already use?

  _____

  _____

- Which ideas from this chapter are new to me?

  _____

  _____

- The best idea I learned from this chapter is . . . . Why?

  _____

  _____

- Ideas from this chapter I would like to try are . . . .

  _____

  _____

- How will I put the new ideas I've learned into action?

_____

_____

LEARNING ONLINE

Go to http://developmentalenglish.wadsworth.com/atkinson-longman to find the website for *Reading Strategies for Today's College Student*. This website is designed for students using this book. Here you will find:

- fun and interesting websites related to reading
- web exercises and reading quizzes that will help you become a better reader
- a list of chapter objectives
- a glossary of terms used in the chapter
- flashcards
- crossword puzzles

CHAPTER VOCABULARY REVIEW

Go back to the "Vocabulary Check" at the beginning of the chapter. Now that you've read this chapter, rate how well you understand the vocabulary words in the "After-Reading Ratings" column. If you rate any word less than a 3, read the information about that term again.

CHAPTER 8

Reading for Main Ideas

OBJECTIVES

After you finish this chapter, you should be able to

- Identify and find topics, main ideas, and details
- Tell the steps in skimming for main ideas
- Mark key points
- Label main ideas

CHAPTER OUTLINE

CHAPTER MAP

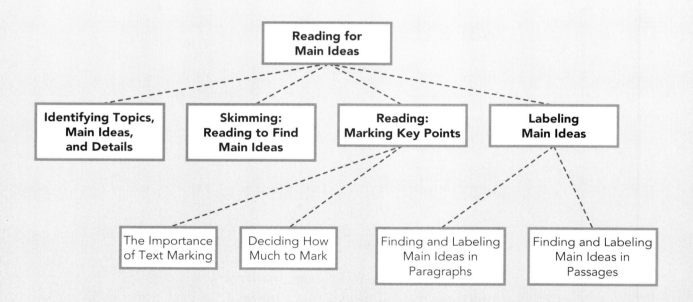

VOCABULARY CHECK

Below are the vocabulary words you will need to know in this chapter.

If you see a word that's brand-new to you, write a 0 in the "Before-Reading Ratings" column. If you have seen the word before but don't know what it means, write a 1. If you think you know what the word means, write a 2. If you know the word and can use it in a sentence, write a 3.

If you wrote a 0 or 1, look up the word in the Glossary at the back of the book. Then, after reading the chapter, look at these words again and rate them in the "After-Reading Ratings" column

If you come across new words in the chapter that are not on this list, underline them or write them in your notebook, and look them up in your dictionary. This will help you increase your vocabulary.

Before-Reading Ratings	Vocabulary Words	Pronunciation Guide (How do I say this word?)	After-Reading Ratings
	topic	'tä-pik	
	main idea	'mān ī-'dē-əz	
	details	di-'tālz	
	skimming	'skim-iŋ	
	text marking	'tekst 'märk-iŋ	
	topic sentence	'tä-pik 'sen-tən(t)s	

Perhaps I have trained myself to see what others overlook.

Sir Arthur Conan Doyle

Nineteenth-century English Author

Remember the children's story "Goldilocks and the Three Bears"? A little girl named Goldilocks goes into a house that belongs to a family of three bears. The bears are not home, but Goldilocks doesn't let that stop her. She makes herself right at home. Goldilocks sits in each chair in the house. One is too big. One is too small. One is just right. Then she tastes the porridge, the bears have cooked. One bowl is too hot. One is too cold. And, then she finds one bowl that is just right. She eats the whole bowl of porridge. Now she is ready for a nap, so she tries the bears' beds. She thinks one is too hard. She thinks one is too soft. But she finds that one bed is just right. She is sound asleep when the bears come home.

You might be wondering what this story has to do with main ideas. Sometimes students are in the same situation Goldilocks was in. They enter an unknown place—a sentence, a paragraph, a textbook chapter. They look for main ideas. But, some ideas they find are too big. These statements are too general to be useful. Sometimes students find ideas that are too small. These statements are too detailed to be useful. When you look for a main idea, you need to find a statement of information that is "just right." It cannot be too broad (big) or too exact (small). In the topic, you must find the key point. This is the main idea. Note the main idea for future use. Main ideas should be marked (highlighted or underlined) and labeled (written about). Let's look more closely at main ideas, marking, and labeling.

Identifying Topics, Main Ideas, and Details

Think about a popular TV show, such as *The West Wing*. The **topic** is what the show generally is about. The topic of *The West Wing* is about people who work in the White House. The **main idea** changes from show to show. It is affected by the **details** of that show's plot. One week the main idea of the show may be the president's office trying to get a bill passed in Congress. The next week it might be about working out a trade deal with another country. The details will change as the main idea changes. The topic concerns the broad general theme—people who work in the White House. The main ideas—different stories, details and how the characters react—change.

Paragraphs and longer reading selections, or passages, all consist of topics and main ideas. The topic is the general message in each paragraph or passage. (Some people call it the "subject.") The main idea tells the key concept about the topic. Figure 8.1 shows the relationship between topic, main ideas, and details.

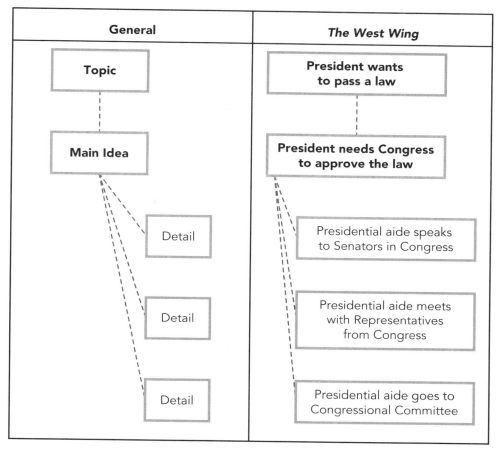

Figure 8.1   Relationships among Topic, Main Idea, and Details

QUICK REVIEW

Circle the correct answer. Check your answers at the bottom of the page before reading the next section.

1. A topic is sometimes called a subject. **T   F**

2. A main idea expresses the key concept about a topic. **T   F**

3. Details describe the main idea. **T   F**

EXERCISE 8.1

Topics, main ideas, and details go from most general to most specific.
Each box lists related items. Decide which item in each box is the general topic, which is the main idea, and which are the details. Write your answers in the blanks on the right. Look up any words you do not know in your dictionary.

Quick Review Answers: 1. T   2. T   3. T

20/20 TV shows *60 Minutes* *Good Morning, America* news shows	1. Topic _____ Main Idea _____ Detail _____ Detail _____ Detail _____
tulips plants roses flowers daisies	2. Topic _____ Main Idea _____ Detail _____ Detail _____ Detail _____
athletics tennis team sports softball hockey	3. Topic _____ Main Idea _____ Detail _____ Detail _____ Detail _____
physical fitness running shoes aspects of jogging stronger muscles better health	4. Topic _____ Main Idea _____ Detail _____ Detail _____ Detail _____
forests wild animals trees nature birds	5. Topic _____ Main Idea _____ Detail _____ Detail _____ Detail _____

post-secondary education University of Maine Coastal Community College Northwest Junior College 2- and 4-year schools	6. Topic _____ Main Idea _____ Detail _____ Detail _____ Detail _____
tuition educational expenses application fees campus expenses lab fees	7. Topic _____ Main Idea _____ Detail _____ Detail _____ Detail _____
staying up all night tests coffee final exams study groups	8. Topic _____ Main Idea _____ Detail _____ Detail _____ Detail _____
junk food potato chips candy soft drinks nutrition	9. Topic _____ Main Idea _____ Detail _____ Detail _____ Detail _____
paintings sculpture museum pottery fine arts	10. Topic _____ Main Idea _____ Detail _____ Detail _____ Detail _____

WRITING CONNECTION

Respond to the following on a separate sheet of paper or in your notebook.

How does understanding main ideas and details help you "get" a joke?

Skimming: Reading to Find Main Ideas

Imagine exploring the attic of an old house. You see many things. You find broken chairs. You see stacks of old newspapers. You look at a trunk holding worn-out clothes. After skimming the attic, you summarize what you find in a single sentence: *The attic contains junk.*

Skimming is reading quickly to find main ideas. It is like going into an attic and quickly looking around. In skimming, your focus is wide. When you skim, you can skip some words. For instance, articles (*a, an, the*), conjunctions (*and, but, or*), and prepositions (*of, with, to*) are not always important. (See Chapter 6 if you need a quick review of parts of speech.) What if these words were skipped? Then you would find that almost half of the words were left out. You could focus on the more important nouns and verbs.

Here are the steps in skimming:

1. Read the first few sentences (or paragraphs) as quickly as possible. These tell you about the passage's content.
2. Start skipping words. On the third or fourth sentence, let your eyes hit only key words and phrases. Key words are usually nouns or verbs.
3. Read the last few sentences (or paragraphs). They will often summarize main ideas.
4. Try to find the main idea and a few facts. Skimming will give you a general idea of content rather than specific details.

Textbooks usually give clues about what to skim. Chapter outlines, introductions, and graphics condense main ideas. (Look at the material at the beginning of this chapter, for example.) Skimming them provides an overview of the chapter's main ideas. Next, chapter headings and subheadings show key information. Skim these as well. Finally, skimming the chapter summary will also give you the main ideas.

EXERCISE 8.2 **Removing less important words from a paragraph or passage makes it easier to find the main idea.** Cross out the articles, prepositions, and conjunctions in the passage below. Then underline its main idea.

Community colleges are a big player in undergraduate teaching and learning. More than half of America's undergraduate students are enrolled in community colleges. The missions and goals of these two-year colleges are varied. They serve the needs of different groups of students. Community college programs include vocational training for the high-tech workplace. They also provide people with chances for learning throughout their lives. Some special programs positively affect the quality of life in the communities they serve. In the twenty-first century, community colleges are equal partners in U.S. higher education.

QUICK REVIEW

Circle the correct answer. Check your answers at the bottom of the page before reading the next section.

1. Skimming is reading slowly and carefully to find details.   **T   F**

2. You should skip over nouns and verbs when you skim.   **T   F**

3. Textbooks give clues that help you know what to skim.   **T   F**

Reading: Marking Key Points

You will take many courses in college. Some, like art and music, are courses in which you perform. You learn by creating art or music. Others, like math, ask you to solve problems. You learn by thinking through a problem to find its answer. But many courses are lecture courses. Much of what you learn will come from reading textbooks. Reading textbooks requires little or no action . . . or does it? When you read, it may look as if you are doing nothing. But reading should not be a passive activity. It should be active, especially if you are reading to study.

Your reading should be an active process as you look for information. Once you find what you think is important, you need to save the information for future use. One way to do this is to mark information you find by underlining or highlighting it.

The Importance of Text Marking

Text marking sounds simple. You get your pencil or highlighter pen and find and mark key ideas. You highlight or underline what you want to remember. But, how do you know what to mark?

First, the more you know, the less you mark. The less you know, the more you mark. This means if you already know some of the information you are reading, you don't need to mark it. Let's say you are reading your history book. The chapter you are reading has a section on Abraham Lincoln. You studied Abraham Lincoln in another class so you already know some of the information. You would not need to mark any facts about Lincoln that you already know.

Quick Review Answers: 1. F   2. F   3. T

Second, when you set learning goals, what you mark should help you meet your goals. Chapter 2 discusses asking questions to set goals. You do this by turning headings and subheadings into questions. Or, you could use chapter objectives or review questions to help you set goals. Whatever goal you set, mark the information that meets your goal. Then you might mark supporting details. These might be the steps in a sequence, other kinds of lists, reasons, conclusions, and so on.

Knowing what kinds of details your instructor thinks is important can help you choose what to mark. You can find this out by carefully looking at returned tests. The form on page 93 helps you find out how and why you missed test questions. Use this information to guide future text marking. You can also look at course handouts to figure out what your instructor thinks is important. Or, you could look at your notes and see what the instructor talked about the most. This helps you see how your instructor thinks about information.

Deciding How Much to Mark

Look at the textbook marking in Examples 8.1, 8.2, and 8.3. In Example 8.1, too much information is marked. You should mark information to separate key ideas from minor details. In example 8.1, there is no difference. Even if you know nothing about a new subject, you should only mark half or less of the text.

In Example 8.2, the reader marked too little. This could mean that the reader already knew the information. On the other hand, it could show that the reader wasn't paying attention. Maybe the reader didn't understand what was being read. Or maybe the reader just couldn't figure out what to mark.

The third example, Example 8.3, shows a well-marked text.

Example 8.1   Example of Over-Marking a Text

> ## Majors and Minors
>
> Students working toward bachelor's degrees must show evidence of depth of study. This is achieved by completing majors and minors. There are three options. First, a student can complete a major and a minor. Second, a student can complete a double major. Third, a student can complete a functional major. The double major and functional major provides preparation in two fields. A functional major is a comprehensive program that combines, with the primary field, coursework in fields that are closely related.

Example 8.2   Example of Under-Marking

Majors and Minors

Students working toward bachelor's degrees must show evidence of depth of study. This is achieved by completing majors and minors. There are three options. First, a student can complete a major and a minor. Second, a student can complete a double major. Third, a student can complete a functional major. The double major and functional major provides preparation in two fields. A functional major is a comprehensive program that combines, with the primary field, coursework in fields that are closely related.

Example 8.3   Example of Good Text Marking

Majors and Minors

Students working toward bachelor's degrees must show evidence of depth of study. This is achieved by completing majors and minors. There are three options. First, a student can complete a major and a minor. Second, a student can complete a double major. Third, a student can complete a functional major. The double major and functional major provides preparation in two fields. A functional major is a comprehensive program that combines, with the primary field, coursework in fields that are closely related.

QUICK REVIEW

Circle the correct answer. Check your answers at the bottom of the page before reading the next section.

1. Text marking makes reading a more active process.   **T   F**

2. The more you know about a topic, the more you should mark.   **T   F**

3. You should only mark main ideas when marking text.   **T   F**

Quick Review Answers: 1. T   2. F   3. F

Labeling Main Ideas

> **The palest ink is better than the best memory.**
>
> *Chinese Proverb*

So now you've marked information. But what happens a few days or weeks later when you look back at what you've marked? You might forget why you marked what you did. One way to help you remember is to use labels. Labels give you clues or reminders. They summarize main ideas. They contain your comments on main ideas. They organize details that support main ideas. They help you remember what you read.

Text labels differ according to their purpose. If you mark stated information such as lists, dates, people, places, events, main ideas, explanations, or descriptions, your label would be a brief summary of items in the list or sequence. Because your labels appear next to the text they describe, you can abbreviate them to save time. For example, a label for a section on stress management might be abbreviated (made shorter) as follows:

Three Relaxation Techniques	3 RELAX TECH
1. deep breathing	1. dp. breath
2. visualization	2. visualize
3. meditation	3. meditate

You might want to add your own opinions or comments about text that you've marked. If you disagree with the text, your label might say: I DO NOT AGREE WITH THIS! If you didn't understand the text, your label might say: Relax tech?? Ask instructor! If you think something will appear on a test, your label might say: KNOW FOR TEST!

Your labels can also show relationships between information, such as cause and effect, likenesses and differences, or conclusions. A label that shows the relationship between stress and physical symptoms might say: Emotional Stress = physical symptoms and effects.

One way to keep labeling simple and short is to use symbols such as question marks, arrows, or equals signs. A list of some simple symbols and their meanings appears in Table 8.1. Your list may change with your needs and the courses you take. You can also come up with your own symbols. Example 8.4 shows a text with labels.

Table 8.1   Examples of Shorthand Symbols and Meanings for Text Labels

Symbol	Meaning	Symbol	Meaning
??	unclear information	=	equals or results
MI	main idea	imp or ★	important
( ) or { }	encloses related information	T or Test	possible test question
C	cause	E	effect
PROB	problem	SOL	solution
→	related to	✓	check this
#	number	<	smaller, less than
>	bigger, greater than		

Example 8.4   Marked and Labeled Text

BA/BS → need evidence of degree depth?? 3 Ways ★Imp★ 1) major with a minor 2) double major 3) functional major Functional major & double major = prep in 2 fields Functional major = major with concentration of related subjects	Students working toward bachelor's degrees must show evidence of depth of study. This is achieved by completing majors and minors. There are three options. First, a student can complete one major with a minor. Second, a student can complete a double major. Third, a student can complete a functional major. The double major and functional major provides preparation in two fields. A functional major is a comprehensive program that combines, with the primary field, coursework in fields that are closely related.

EXERCISE 8.3   **You get better at finding main ideas with practice.** Read the following selection and look for the main ideas and key details. Then read the labels from the list following the reading. Choose the best label for each paragraph or section. Write the letter of the label on the line next to each passage. If you find words you don't know, look them up in your dictionary.

ALTERNATIVES TO THE USUAL WAY OF GETTING CREDIT

1 The usual way to get credit in college is by taking courses listed in the catalog. The number of credits you get for the course is often the same as the number of hours of lecture you attend each week.

2   There are many other ways to get credit. Not all colleges allow all of these methods. Thus, you need to check your college's catalog. Also, check to see how many units can be granted for each method.

1. Credit by examination

3 _____ **1a.** High school students can get college credit by taking Advanced Placement tests. If you know people who are in high school, tell them to ask their school counselors about this.

4 _____ **1b.** Some colleges give English exams to see how well you read, write, or speak. In this case, you take a test. If you pass, you get credit. You may get three to six units of credit. There is also a standardized test called the College-Level Examination Program (CLEP). Some colleges use it to test your English **competency.**

5 _____ **1c.** There are many other CLEP tests. Math and natural sciences have CLEP exams. There are CLEP tests for humanities. Social science CLEP tests are offered as well. Your college catalog tells about the tests you can take. It also says how many credits you may get by taking CLEP tests. Suppose you choose to take a CLEP test. You may want a book that gives advice on how to pass the tests. It will also contain **sample** questions.

6 _____ **1d.** Any department may allow students to show skill by passing a standardized test. You might be able to skip an introductory level class if you do well on the test. Talk to the instructor who gives the standardized test you wish to take. Ask if there are old tests that you can see. Ask what books you should read. Ask about other ways to prepare for the test.

_____ **2. Instructional television**

7 Some colleges show educational programs on television. Or, they may subscribe to services that offer televised classes. The range of courses is usually small.

_____ **3. Cooperative education**

8 Sometimes you can get college credit for work. This work may be paid or voluntary. These programs are called cooperative education. They may involve some classes. Often guest speakers teach the class. On the whole, all you do is work and then report on it. After your boss evaluates you, you get credit. Cooperative education teaches you how to act in the workplace. It increases your self-esteem. It helps you make choices about careers.

_____ **4. Directed or independent study**

9 Many schools let students gain some credits for work that they do on their own. Usually

---

Source: Modified from http://www.wadsworth.com/colsuccess_d/special_features/studyskills, © Bruce, M. Rowe

each department says what you have to do for credit. Often, you meet with an instructor. The instructor may be someone that you have had for another course. You arrange to do an **independent study.** There may be things you have to do before you can do this. For instance, you may need 6 or 9 credits in the department.

____ **5. Extension and correspondence courses**

10 Some schools allow credit through college extension (off-campus) programs. Others allow credit from correspondence courses (coursework completed through mail). You must show proof that these courses were equal to regular courses.

____ **6. Prior experience**

11 Some schools give credit for learning you gained before you came to college. Schools set their own rules for giving credit.

____ **7. Noncollege-sponsored courses of instruction**

12 Some colleges give credit for training programs. If you have been in a training program, see your counselor. He or she can tell you if you can get credit.

____ **8. Credit for military service**

13 Some colleges give credit for time in the military. They may set an amount of time

you will have needed to serve. You may also get credit for courses completed while you were in the service. These courses must meet certain standards. See your counselor to apply for this credit.

Labels

A. Credit for training programs? See couns. for info.
B. Televised classes, but # of classes small.
C. High school students can take Adv Pl.
D. Cred for mil exp possible. See counselor for info.
E. Can take test of English or College-Level Exam Prog (CLEP) for Eng skill
F. Credit from col ext or correspondence courses. Need doc. of level of work required.
G. Can get college cred for paid or voluntary work = cooperative ed. Good career tool.
H. Many kinds of CLEP tests. Math, sciences, & humanities. Catalog has info. Test books for practice.
I. Can get cred for work by self with instructor = independent study. ✓ for more info.
J. Depts give standardized tests. Ask instructor for info.
K. May get credit for learn before college. ✓ with institution.

VOCABULARY   These vocabulary words are in the article you just read. Answer each question. For words you do not know, check your glossary or a dictionary.

1. *Competency* means _____.
   A. ability
   B. kind of writing
   C. credit
   D. way of speaking

2. A *sample* is _____.
   A. a test
   B. an example
   C. a complete exam
   D. an essay question

3. *Independent study* is completed _____.
   A. in a small group
   B. in a large group
   C. alone
   D. as part of a training program

VOCABULARY BUILDER

List three words from the passage, other than the boldfaced terms, whose meanings you do not know. Look up each word and write its meaning based on how it is used in the sentence. Use the word in a sentence of your own.

1. _____

    _____

    _____

2. _____

    _____

    _____

3. _____

    _____

    _____

COMPREHENSION

How much did you understand in the reading? Read the questions below and circle the correct answer.

1. What is the main idea of the article?
   A. There are many ways to get credit.
   B. You must pay tuition in order to get credit.
   C. Military service is one way to get academic credit.
   D. CLEP tests are a way to get credit by examination.

2. Which of the following is true of CLEP exams?
    A. CLEP tests and AP tests are the same.
    B. You can take CLEP tests in science and social science, but not in the humanities.
    C. Some colleges use CLEP tests to assess English proficiency.
    D. All of the above are true.
    E. Only A and C are true.
3. Preparation books are available to help you succeed _____.
    A. in extension courses
    B. on standardized exams
    C. in televised courses
    D. with prior experience

Finding and Labeling Main Ideas in Paragraphs

Most textbooks contain hundreds or thousands of paragraphs. Shorter readings are also usually broken into paragraphs. It is important that you know how to find and label the main ideas in paragraphs. Every paragraph contains a key concept or main idea. The main idea tells the central point of the paragraph. To find the main idea, you:

1. Reread the information you marked.
2. Ask yourself what one thing the paragraph covers. This is the main idea.
3. Look for details that point to or support the main idea.
4. Look for or write a sentence that states this key concept.

Now read the following example:

> Career services help you find possible careers. You can take career workshops. You can check out books from the Career Library. You can take tests to help you identify interests. You can schedule appointments with a career counselor. The counselor also helps you study the job market before you graduate. The Career Center has current information on available jobs. It has a career hotline that is updated each day. It also offers workshops on writing resumes and interviewing. You can go to career fairs and talk to employment recruiters. The Career Center also provides employer referrals. It schedules interviews. Finally, career services can help you get a job. From start to finish, career services serves college students like you.

What is this paragraph about? It discusses what career services offers students at each step of their careers. Text labels for this paragraph might look like this:

Original Text	Label
Career services help you find possible careers. You can take career workshops. You can check out books from the Career Library. You can take tests to help you identify interests. You can schedule appointments with a career counselor. The counselor also helps you study the job market before you graduate. The Career Center has current information on available jobs. It has a career hotline that is updated each day. It also offers workshops on writing resumes and interviewing. You can go to career fairs and talk to employment recruiters. The Career Center also provides employer referrals. It schedules interviews. Finally, career services can help you get a job. From start to finish, career services serves college students like you.	CAREER SERVICES • Career workshops • Career library books • Career tests—what am I interested in CAREER COUNSELOR—study job market before graduation CAREER CENTER • Jobs I can get now • Workshops—resumes, interviewing • Career fairs with recruiters • Makes referrals • Schedules interviews

Finding the main idea of paragraphs is important to your understanding. There may be a sentence that just states the topic (subject) of the paragraph. A **topic sentence** contains the stated main idea. The first sentence is often the topic sentence. But not always! If it were always the first sentence, you might not read the rest of the sentences in each paragraph. The truth is that the topic sentence can appear anywhere in a paragraph.

Finding and Labeling Main Ideas in Passages

Finding the main idea of a passage is much like finding the main idea of a paragraph. Here are the steps:

1. After having set your learning goal, read each paragraph in the passage.
2. Find the main idea for each paragraph.
3. Identify the topic that all or most of the paragraphs have in common.
4. Locate a sentence that says what the paragraphs have in common. It might be found in the introduction or in the summary of the passage. If you can't find one, write one of your own. The sentence should answer your goal-setting question for the section.
5. Shorten your sentence. Use it for your text label.

Reading and understanding a whole passage is often harder than understanding a single paragraph. A passage's whole meaning depends on the sentences and paragraphs within it. To find the main idea of a passage, first find the meaning of each part. Then use the meaning of those parts to find the main idea.

QUICK REVIEW

Circle the correct answer. Check your answers at the bottom of the page before reading the next section.

1. Labels summarize the text's main ideas; your personal comments are not included. **T   F**

2. The main idea tells the central meaning of the paragraph or passage. **T   F**

3. Finding main ideas in paragraphs is harder than finding them in passages. **T   F**

EXERCISE 8.4   **Here's an exercise that will help you when you read social science textbooks (such as history, geography, and government).** The following section asks you to find main ideas in paragraphs and passages about history. Read each paragraph and find the main idea. If the main idea is stated, underline it in the paragraph. If the main idea is not stated, write the main idea on the lines provided. After several paragraphs, you will be asked to write the main idea of the passage. At the end of all the paragraphs, you will be asked to write the main idea of the whole reading.

Quick Review Answers: 1. F   2. T   3. F

A HISTORY OF KILROY

1   The phrase "Kilroy was here" began during World War II. It quickly became a part of American **folklore.** The words "Kilroy was here" appeared all over Europe and Japan during World War II. No one really knew where it came from. So, it makes sense that people wondered who Kilroy was. They created stories about him. At least four of these stories are **documented.** One is true.

PARAGRAPH MAIN IDEA: _____

_____

2   During World War II, metal was very **scarce.** America needed it to make guns, tanks, and ships. One story about Kilroy was about an admiral who wanted to save metal. Supposedly, he saw that bolts on ships had seven or more threads above the nuts. He ordered that all bolts be made so that only three threads stuck out. When American soldiers went on the ships, they saw the shortened bolts. They concluded that Kilroy had been there.

PARAGRAPH MAIN IDEA: _____

_____

3   A third story is a romantic one. This story tells of a soldier named Kilroy who met a woman in Boston. They met at a restaurant every day. They sat at the same table each time. They fell in love. The couple found out that they were both Irish-Americans. Kilroy drew an Irish fairy looking over a wall on his wallet. The woman liked the small drawing. The night before Kilroy was sent to war, the two planned to meet. The young woman was hurt in a car accident. She did not come. Kilroy waited for her. He drew the fairy. He carved the words "Kilroy was here" on their usual table. Soldiers from Boston saw this

message. Then they wrote it wherever they went.

PARAGRAPH MAIN IDEA: _____

_____

4   During World War II, James Kilroy was an inspector. He worked at the Bethlehem Steel Yards, which made battleships. These **yards** were near Quincy, Massachusetts. His job was to count the number of rivets on the ships so the women who built them could be paid. Kilroy marked the rivets with chalk as he counted them. The workers started erasing the chalk marks. When Kilroy counted the rivets again, the workers got paid twice. Kilroy figured this out. He changed his marker to crayon. He added the words "Kilroy was here." The workers could not **erase** his crayon marks. Painting the ship should have covered Kilroy's marks. However, there was a rush to get ships to war. Sometimes the ships never got painted. Soldiers were shipped to England. On the way, the soldiers saw the words "Kilroy was here." They didn't know who Kilroy was. They just knew that he had been there before them. As a joke, they began writing "Kilroy was here" wherever they went somewhere new.

PARAGRAPH MAIN IDEA: _____

_____

5   Who was the real Kilroy? There were 62 people in the army with the name of Kilroy. In 1946, the Transit Company of America held a contest to find the real Kilroy. They promised a real trolley car to the man who was Kilroy. Forty men said they were Kilroy. One of these was James Kilroy, the shipyard inspector. He brought **officials** and riveters from the shipyard with him. They proved his claim. James

Kilroy won the trolley car. He moved it to his front yard. His children used it as a playhouse.

PARAGRAPH MAIN IDEA: _____

_____

6   The cartoon figure that is now known as Kilroy began in Great Britain. He was first named Mr. Chad. Around the time of World War II, Mr. Chad appeared in advertisements. He had the words "Wot [What], no _____?" below him. The British had few supplies. The blank line contained whatever the British needed at the time. Sometimes it was cigarettes. Sometimes it was eggs. It could be anything the British missed.

PARAGRAPH MAIN IDEA: _____

_____

7   George Edward Chatterton was a cartoonist at this time. He may have created Mr. Chad. However, the *Oxford English Dictionary* lists Chad's **origin** as *obscure*. Sometime during the war, Chad and Kilroy merged (came together). The American phrase began appearing under the British drawing.

PARAGRAPH MAIN IDEA: _____

_____

8   In World War II, Kilroy was the **ultimate** soldier. He had been everywhere. He had done everything. When young American soldiers hit the beaches, Kilroy had already been there. When they went into towns, he was there before them. Soldiers visited caves for safety. They saw "Kilroy was here" on the walls. They believed a fellow **comrade** had been there before them. For example, soldiers spoke of

seeing Kilroy on the buildings in France. They saw him on enemy forts on Japanese-held islands. Soldiers saw him in Southern Italy. They even found Kilroy in Rome.

PARAGRAPH MAIN IDEA: _____

_____

PASSAGE (Paragraphs 1–8) MAIN IDEA:

_____

_____

9   American soldiers were helped by Kilroy's presence. How? When people have support, they **cope** better with stress. When soldiers saw the words *Kilroy was here* they knew that they were not alone. Kilroy, a fellow soldier, had already been there. He had lived to tell about it. Kilroy became part of their support group. This made them feel a little safer.

PARAGRAPH MAIN IDEA: _____

_____

10   Changing the **environment** also helps reduce stress. Soldiers could not change the war or its outcome. But they could change how it looked. They could add Kilroy's **signature.** This would remind them of their support group. It would be humorous. It would also greet the next group of soldiers who passed by.

PARAGRAPH MAIN IDEA: _____

_____

PASSAGE (Paragraphs 9–10) MAIN IDEA:

_____

_____

11   American soldiers left Kilroy in odd places. This was one way soldiers helped

(continued)

distract themselves from the war around them. Perhaps one of the strangest places Kilroy was found was at the Potsdam Summit in 1945. Josef Stalin was the leader of Russia. He went there to meet President Roosevelt and Winston Churchill. Churchill was the Prime Minister (leader) of England. Stalin was the first to use a bathroom reserved for "The Big Three." When he left the marble bathroom, he asked, "Who is Kilroy?"

PARAGRAPH MAIN IDEA: _____

_____

12   American soldiers have taken Kilroy with them into other wars. Kilroy was found in Korea. Soldiers saw him in Vietnam. He showed up in Kuwait and Iraq. When American soldiers came home, he came with them. He has a special place in American **culture.** Kilroy's picture appears on antique salt-and-pepper shakers. He can be seen on dishes. Some people eat olives off Kilroy cocktail sticks (fancy toothpicks). His face can be seen on political buttons.

PARAGRAPH MAIN IDEA: _____

_____

13   Kilroy has appeared in war movies. Old movies like *To Hell and Back* and *On Our*

Merry Way show his image. More modern movies like *Kelly's Heroes* and *Patton* have Kilroy scenes. There was even a movie called *Kilroy Was Here.*

PARAGRAPH MAIN IDEA: _____

_____

14   Kilroy has not only appeared in movies. Cartoons like *Bugs Bunny, Popeye the Sailor Man,* and *Reboot* also have Kilroy references. You can see Kilroy on reruns of some television shows. These include *M*A*S*H, Home Improvement,* and *Seinfeld.* Kilroy was the inspiration for the rock group Styx. They released a recording titled "Kilroy Was Here." Kilroy has even entered the computer age. He can be found on eBay.

PARAGRAPH MAIN IDEA: _____

_____

PASSAGE (Paragraphs 11–14) MAIN IDEA:

_____

_____

READING (Paragraphs 1–14) MAIN IDEA:

_____

_____

_____

VOCABULARY   The following words are boldfaced in the reading. First, rank these words using the "Vocabulary Check" that begins each chapter in this book as a guide. Then use a dictionary to find the pronunciations and meanings of the words you rated a 0 or 1. Second, use context to be sure you have located the correct definition. Third, when you understand the definition, write it in your own words. Finally, write a sentence using each word.

Word	Rating	Pronunciation	Definition from dictionary	Definition in your words	Your sentence
1. folklore					
2. documented					
3. scarce					
4. yards					
5. erase					
6. officials					
7. origin					
8. obscure					
9. ultimate					
10. comrade					

(*continued*)

Word	Rating	Pronunciation	Definition from dictionary	Definition in your words	Your sentence
11. cope					
12. environment					
13. signature					
14. distract					
15. culture					

VOCABULARY BUILDER

List five words from the reading, other than the boldfaced terms, whose meanings you do not know. Look up each word in the dictionary and write its meaning based on how it is used in the sentence. Use the words in a sentence of your own.

1. _____

_____

2. _____

_____

3. _____

_____

4. _____

_____

5. _____

_____

COMPREHENSION   How much did you understand in the reading? Read the questions below and circle the correct answer.

1. Who was probably the real Kilroy?
   A. an American soldier
   B. a ship inspector
   C. a man who fell in love with a woman from Boston
   D. an English advertising character

2. Which of the following countries has NOT been associated with Kilroy's origin?
   A. Ireland
   B. England
   C. Japan
   D. United States

3. What kind of support did Kilroy give American soldiers?
   A. He let them know they weren't alone.
   B. He offered humor in a time of war.
   C. He took their attention away from the situation they were in.
   D. All of these are true.

4. Which of the following statements are true?
   A. Kilroy's popularity ended with World War II.
   B. Kilroy is kept alive only in World War II movies.
   C. Kilroy is a part of American culture.
   D. Kilroy's origin will never be completely known.

LEARNING TIP
Reading Literature

Reading literature is different from reading textbook chapters. Literature is usually a narrative (tells a story). You need special skills when reading narrative text. For example, you look at the words that are used and the figurative language (images). You find the theme (basic message), main idea, and plot (what happens in the story). You study the characters (people in the story), tone (writing style), and setting (the place where the story happens).

So how do you read and mark literature? How do you use all the skills you learned in this chapter? Unlike a textbook chapter, narrative text contains no special features to guide your reading. But the techniques for marking and labeling textbooks also work for narrative text. The table below shows guidelines for previewing, reading, and judging narrative text.

As you read, you need to note plot, characters, setting, and theme. One teacher has created a way to take notes when reading literature (L. M. Tomlinson, 1997).

In the first step, you create code letters for each character and/or idea you need to follow. For example, you might use initials for each character. You could use *SET* for setting. You could use *PL* for plot. Second, you list these codes in the front of your book or in your notebook. Leave space between the codes. In the third step, you read. As you read, write the code letters next to useful information. The fourth step is to write in your list the page numbers where you wrote the code letters. In the final step, you list each character or concept on a separate sheet of paper. Then you write a brief summary or make notes about important details. You should also note important page numbers.

Questions for Previewing, Reading, and Evaluating Narrative Text

Previewing
1. What kind of literature is this (novel, drama, short story, etc.)?
2. What can you tell from the title, size of print, illustrations, and chapter titles?
Plot
3. Is this an interesting story?
4. Could this have really happened? How do events in the story build to a climax (high point)?
Setting
5. Where does the action take place? How do you know?
6. When did the story take place? How do you know?

Theme
7. Does the story have a theme (or message)?
Characterization
8. Are the characters convincing? Do they seem like people you know? People you know?
Judging Style
9. Is the style of writing easy to read?

Tomlinson, L.M. "A Coding System for Notetaking in Literature: Preparation for Journal Writing, Class Participation, and Essay Tests." *Journal of Adolescent and Adult Literacy,* 40 (1979): 486–73.

CHAPTER SUMMARY

1. Finding the main ideas is an important part of reading.
2. Skimming can help you find main ideas.
3. Marking and labeling main ideas will help you to understand and recall them more easily.
4. Some students undermark or overmark; thus, when marking, you need to decide how much is too much or how little is too little.
5. Finding and labeling main ideas in each paragraph in a passage is the first step in finding the main idea of the passage.

CHAPTER REVIEW

On a separate sheet of paper, answer briefly but completely.

1. What is the purpose of skimming?
2. What do you do more often—undermark or overmark text? Why?
3. What is the relationship between text marking and text labeling?
4. How are text labels similar to and different from topic sentences?

ACTION SUMMARY

- Which ideas from this chapter do I already use?

  _____

  _____

- Which ideas from this chapter are new to me?

  _____

  _____

- The best idea I learned from this chapter is . . . . Why?

  _____

  _____

- Ideas from this chapter I would like to try are . . . .

  _____

  _____

- How will I put the new ideas I've learned in action?

  _____

  _____

LEARNING ONLINE

Go to http://developmentalenglish.wadsworth.com/atkinson-longman to find the website for *Reading Strategies for Today's College Student*. This website is designed for students using this book. Here you will find:

- fun and interesting websites related to reading
- web exercises and reading quizes that will help you become a better reader
- a list of chapter objectives
- a glossary of terms used in the chapter
- flashcards
- crossword puzzles

CHAPTER VOCABULARY REVIEW

Go back to the "Vocabulary Check" at the beginning of the chapter. Now that you've read this chapter, rate how well you understand the vocabulary words in the "After-Reading Ratings" column. If you rate any word less than a 3, read the information about that term again.

CHAPTER 9

Reading for Details

OBJECTIVES

After you finish this chapter, you should be able to

- List the steps in scanning
- Identify organizational patterns in paragraphs and passages

CHAPTER OUTLINE

CHAPTER MAP

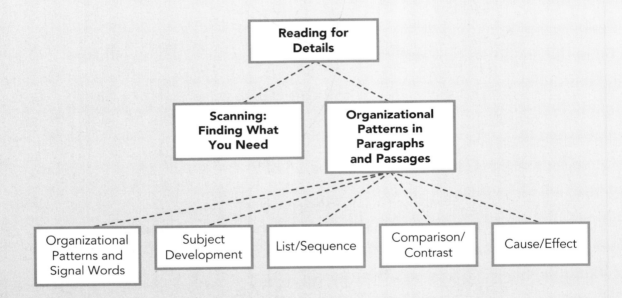

VOCABULARY CHECK

Below are the vocabulary words you will need to know in this chapter.

If you see a word that's brand-new to you, write a 0 in the "Before-Reading Ratings" column. If you have seen the word before but don't know what it means, write a 1. If you think you know what the word means, write a 2. If you know the word and can use it in a sentence, write a 3.

If you wrote a 0 or 1 next to a word, look it up the word in the Glossary at the back of the book. Then, after reading the chapter, look at these words again and rate them in the "After-Reading Ratings" column.

If you come across new words in the chapter that are not on this list, underline them or write them in your notebook, write them down, and look them up in your dictionary. This will help you increase your vocabulary.

Before-Reading Ratings	Vocabulary Words	Pronunciation Guide (How do I say this word?)	After-Reading Ratings
	scanning	'skan-iŋ	
	organizational patterns	'òr-gə-nə-'za-shnəl 'pa-tərnz	
	subject development	'səb-jikt di-'ve-ləp-mənt	
	list/sequence	'list/'sē-kwən(t)s	
	comparison/contrast	kəm-'per-ə-sən/ kən-'trast	
	cause/effect	'kòz/i-'fekt	
	signal words	'sig-nəl 'wərdz	

**In the successful
organization, no
detail is too small
to escape close
attention.**

Lou Holtz

American Football
Coach

As you learned in Chapter 8, the *main idea* of a topic is the key point. It often tells the *what* of a topic—what the topic is about. But details are important, too. They give you facts about the main idea. They tell *how, when, where, how much, who,* and *why.* Their points add to your understanding. In this chapter, you'll learn how to find details by scanning text. You'll also learn about four ways details can be organized in a reading.

Scanning: Finding What You Need

Scanning, or reading quickly, is something you already know how to do. It's what you do when you look for a name in a phone book, for example. When you look for a name in the phone book, you don't read every name in the book. You scan the pages until you find the right name. It's also what you do when you look for a street address. Your eyes quickly look at street signs while driving until you see the one you are looking for. Scanning is a fast and useful way to find information. Here are the steps in scanning for information:

1. Look at how the reading is organized. Look at major headings and subheadings to pinpoint topics. This helps you focus and narrow your search.
2. Decide what question you need to answer. For instance, are you looking for names *(who)* or numbers *(when* or *how much)*? Are you looking for verbs *(what happened)*?
3. Read quickly and search for clues to the answer. Which words or numbers point to the answer you seek?
4. Check your answer. Slow down and read the information in context. Did you find the answer to the question you asked?

When you scan, your eyes quickly pass over words and look for clues. The clues you look for depend on what you want to find—names, dates, specific terms. The clues also depend on the questions that you, your instructor, or your book are asking. Take a look at Table 9.1 on the next page. It shows clues for finding the answers to different kinds of questions. For example, perhaps you want to know when the Civil War began for your history class. You are asking a "when" question: *When* did the Civil War begin? So now you scan your chapter looking for clue words to answer "when"—words that show time, such as days, months, years, or numbers. Once you find a possible answer, you read slowly to see if it is really correct. This slow reading helps you know if what you found is right.

Table 9.1   Questioning Words and Appropriate Clues

If your question asks . . .	such as . . .	look for . . .	such as . . .
Why?	Why do college students need to know how to use the Internet?	words and phrases like *because, for that reason, consequently, as a result, in order to*	Knowing how to use the Internet is important for college students *because* faculty often use it in making assignments and communicating information. *As a result,* students who already know how to use the Internet have an advantage over those who do not.
How?	How do students register for classes?	a sequence or a list (identified by words like *first, second, after, next, last, finally*); words like *by, through, as a result of*	Students register for classes by *first* seeing an advisor. *After* talking to the advisor, students self-enroll online. *Finally,* students are billed for the classes they choose.
How much?	How much does each course cost?	numbers	Undergraduate students pay *$105* per credit hour. For example, a three-hour course costs *$315.*
Which?	Which courses satisfy general education requirements?	nouns and adjectives	Students must complete 42 hours of *general education requirements.* These include *courses in composition, speech, science, math, humanities, and social studies.*

(*continued*)

Table 9.1   Questioning Words and Appropriate Clues (*continued*)

If your question asks . . .	such as . . .	look for . . .	such as . . .
When?	When does the semester start?	capitalized words like days, months, or other time periods; time of the day (written in numbers or words); numbers that show months, days, and years (such as *6/10/05*); words like *before, during, after, soon, later, prior*	The first day of class will be *August 23rd.*
Where?	Where do students get their ID cards?	capitalized place names (cities, states, countries); addresses; words like *at, behind, across*	New students can get ID cards *at Harris Hall (across from the Student Center).*
Who?	Who is the teaching assistant for my class?	capitalized names, nouns	*Pat Carter* is the TA for Biology 110.

Read the following passage with these questions in mind: (1) *Where* was SQ3R started? (2) *Who* developed SQ3R? (3) *When* were colleges flooded by Army staff?

During the 1940s, colleges were flooded by Army staff. All needed to take courses on specialized topics. The courses were hard. Lessons had to be learned fast. Courses placed huge learning demands on students. The Ohio State University administrators went to Professor Francis Robinson. They asked him to head a new Learning and Study Skills program. This program would teach students to learn better by reading. Robinson reviewed research about effective study skills. Then he came up with an idea for study that has lasted for 60 years. He developed the SQ3R method of reading and studying.

The words *where, who,* and *when* in the questions above give clues about what to look for when you scan. *Where* points to a place. So when scanning the passage, you look for capital letters or nouns. Doing so, you find the words *The Ohio State University. Who* points to people. You scan for capital letters, nouns, or names. You find the words *Army staff.* You also see *administrators.* Next, you find the name *Francis Robinson.* Depending on your question (who wanted the program, who needed the program, or who developed the program), one of these is your answer. You need to read this section again, slowly, to find out which one is correct. *When* points to time, so you scan for numbers or dates. You find *During the 1940s.* You have found the answers: (1) SQ3R was started at The Ohio State University; (2) SQ3R was developed by Francis Robinson; (3) Colleges were flooded by Army staff during the 1940s.

EXERCISE 9.1   **When you ask someone a question (such as "Where are you going?"), you expect a certain kind of answer ("I'm going to the library"). It's the same when you read. You need to keep in mind that the question you ask determines the kinds of words you need to look for in scanning.** Read each question below, then scan the answers that follow. Circle any words that could answer the question.

1. Who is in the building?

administrators	Dean Jones	classrooms	students	counselors
residential hall	faculty	Houts Hall	Mr. Thomas	desks

2. Where are you going after class?

work	two-thirty	Friday, Jan. 9	pizza place	Kate's number
Tom's room	library research	math assignment	Writing Center	football game

3. When do you have to work?

during the summer	at the residence hall	in the morning	across from the bookstore	on the third floor
before math class	two-thirty	from math to history	in the bookstore	from one to four

4. Which classes will apply to your major?

electives	Speech 105	study group	classroom attendance	foreign languages
Writing Center	residential college	Fall semester	Geography 101	April

5. How are you going to pay for tuition?

working overtime	by completing assignments	as a result of working during the summer	after completing a GED	through student loans
through time management	by working in the residence hall	working out	over $2500	through scholarships

6. How much did you save for college?

over $4000	as the result of time management	by working after school	through a scholarship	3.2 GPA
each paycheck	in high school	$45 per week	at night	$3350

EXERCISE 9.2   **Scanning for information is harder than scanning for individual words or phrases.** Many passages or chapters have questions you need to answer at the end. You can look at the questions before reading and use them to know what kinds of information you need to find when scanning. Before reading the following passage, look at the "Comprehension" questions at the end. Use them to look for the answers you need. After quickly answering the questions, go back and reread to make sure that the answers you found were the correct ones. Complete the vocabulary exercises as usual.

ARE STUDENTS BEING EMPOWERED?

1 There has been a big change in the way leaders lead. CEOs (Chief Executive Officers) and sports coaches use it. They lead under the idea of **empowerment.** This means that leaders give feedback to subordinates. They also get and think about feedback from subordinates. It seems the Elon University administration did not stick to the idea of empowerment when it decided to raise tuition. This announcement came Wednesday.

2 Gerald Whittington is the vice president for business at the college. Whittington did hold open budget **forums.** They were attended mostly by faculty and staff. But how open were the forums? We at the campus newspaper did not know about the forums. Perhaps had the forums been better advertised, more students would have attended. They would have been students with real concerns.

3 Allowing students a chance for feedback would serve two purposes. One, student involvement would calm students' concerns. Two, it would give University President Leo Lambert an idea of what students thought. And, after all, North Carolinians expect to be treated with more respect.

4 Granted, the tuition increase for Fall 2005 is not **drastic.** But do Elon students have the right to know plans that concern their future?

5 We don't expect the administration to inform and grant dialogue on every thing it does. Yet, larger matters, like tuition, deserve input from Elon students.

Reprinted by permission from *The Pendulum* Volume XXVIII, Issue 21; Elon University; Elon, NC. Originally published March 13, 2003.

COMPREHENSION How much did you understand in the reading? Read the questions and scan the reading for the answers to each question. Write your answers on the lines below.

1. What is the name of the school? _____

2. Where is the school located? _____

3. Who is the president of the school?_____

4. Who held hearings about tuition? _____

5. What position does Whittington hold? _____

6. When will the tuition increase happen?_____

7. Why are students upset? _____

_____

VOCABULARY The words listed on page 202 are boldfaced in the reading. First, use a dictionary to find the pronunciation and meanings of these words. Second, use context to be sure you have located the correct definition. Third, when you understand the definition, write it in your own words. Finally, write a sentence using each word.

Word	Pronunciation	Definition from Dictionary	Definition in Your Words	Your Sentence
1. empowerment				
2. forums				
3. drastic				

VOCABULARY BUILDER

List five words from the reading, other than the boldfaced terms, whose meanings you do not know. Look up each word in the dictionary and write its meaning based on how it is used in the sentence. Use the words in a sentence of your own.

1. _____

   _____

2. _____

   _____

3. _____

   _____

4. _____

   _____

5. _____

   _____

EXERCISE 9.3

Here's another chance to improve your reading and scanning skills!
Your Music Appreciation instructor has given you the following information about the history of guitars. There are five paragraphs. First, read the questions below each paragraph. Next, scan each paragraph, looking for the answer to those questions. Write your answer on the lines.

A HISTORY OF GUITARS

A. There are many different kinds of guitars. They range from contrabass to treble. Guitars with different numbers of strings are played in Spain and Latin America. The twelve-string guitar has six double courses in standard tuning. The Hawaiian guitar is also known as a steel guitar. It is laid across the knees of the player. The player stops the metal strings by gliding a metal bar along the neck. The strings are usually tuned to the notes of a given chord.

1. How many double courses does the twelve-string guitar have? _____

2. From what state does the steel guitar come?

_____

B. The electric guitar was invented in the 1930s. It usually has a solid, nonresonant body. A player **amplifies** the sound of its strings. He or she also controls the sounds electronically. An American musician and inventor made the electric guitar popular. His name was Les Paul. He worked during the 1940s.

3. What type of body does an electric guitar have? _____

4. Where did the man who made the electric guitar popular come from? _____

5. When was the electric guitar made popular?_____

C. Les Paul made the electric guitar popular. Then in the early 1940s, a California inventor made some custom guitars. His name was Leo Fender. He worked in a radio shop. He also made amplifiers. He made an amplifier that had no controls. With it, he made a matching lap steel guitar. This guitar had tone and volume controls. At this time, the guitar and amplifier came together. You did not buy one without the other.

6. Who made an amplifier with no controls?

_____

7. In what kind of shop did this man work?

_____

8. Of what state was this man a resident?

_____

D. Leo Fender knew about the technology that **existed** during his time. He thought he could improve the amplified hollow-body instruments. In 1948 Fender created the Telecaster. It was first named the Broadcaster. The Telecaster became known as The Tele. It was a solid-body electric Spanish-style guitar. It was the first ever to go into commercial production.

9. Why did Fender invent the Telecaster?

_____

10. What was its original name? _____

_____

11. In what year was it created?_____

E. George Beauchamp was one of the first people to work with electric instruments. He began in work in 1925. He owned **shares** in a company called Electro String. In 1940 he became ill. He decided to pursue a different area. He started designing fishing **lures.** He patented one. He thought that he could produce it to sell. To raise the money to do so, he sold his shares in his music company to Harold Kinney. Adolph Rickenbacker was another famous person in electric instruments.

(continued)

Kinney was his bookkeeper. Not too long after Beauchamp sold his shares, he went deep sea fishing. He had a heart attack and died. His funeral **procession** was over two miles long.

12. Who was Rickenbacker's bookkeeper? _____

13. Besides electric instruments, what did Beauchamp design? _____

14. How many fishing lures did Beauchamp patent? _____

15. Name two famous people who worked with electric instruments. _____

_____

_____

VOCABULARY   The words below are boldfaced in the reading. First, use a dictionary to find the pronunciation and meanings of these words. Second, use context to be sure you have located the correct definition. Third, when you understand the definition, write it in your own words. Finally, write a sentence using each word.

Word	Pronunciation	Definition from Dictionary	Definition in Your Words	Your Sentence
1. amplifies				
2. existed				
3. shares				
4. lures				
5. procession				

QUICK REVIEW

Circle the correct answer. Check your answers at the bottom of the page before reading the next section.

1. You find main ideas through scanning. **T F**

2. Scanning is a skill most people use when looking for a name in a phone book or searching for an address. **T F**

3. The words *where, when,* and *who* provide clues about what to look for when you scan. **T F**

Organizational Patterns in Paragraphs and Passages

Finding relationships among the details within a paragraph or passage helps you organize those details into a whole. When you see how details connect to each other, you start to see what the paragraph or passage means. It helps you understand main ideas. There are four common **organizational patterns:** (1) subject development; (2) list/sequence; (3) comparison/contrast; and (4) cause/effect. We'll be looking closely at each of these later in this chapter.

Understanding organizational patterns helps you connect details to the main idea. Knowing these patterns also helps you relate what you already know to what you are reading. This is because details relate to one another in predictable ways. Instead of recalling many single details, you recall large blocks of information. For example, think about a town that you know. You probably don't recall each separate building or street in the town. Rather, you think about the town as a whole, and where the buildings and streets are in relation to each other. Buildings and streets relate in predictable ways. Streets either cross one another or are parallel to each other. Buildings are either behind, next to, or in front of each other.

So, how does this way of thinking work with a textbook? Let's look at an example. The following paragraph about psychology discusses causes of stress.

> Stress is the body's response to a demand. Demands on the body can take many forms. Academic stress is a demand that affects many college students. It includes test pressures, scholastic failures, and competition. Personal stress affects students, too. This includes daily hassles and frustrations as well as financial or relationship problems. Finally, life stressors such as change and loss affect students as well as other people.

Quick Review Answers: 1. F 2. T   3. T

You can find 10 details in the paragraph:

1. the definition of stress
2. academic stress: test pressures
3. academic stress: scholastic failures
4. academic stress: competition
5. personal stress: daily hassles
6. personal stress: daily frustrations
7. personal stress: financial problems
8. personal stress: relationship problems
9. life stress: change
10. life stress: loss

The main idea of the paragraph is "types of stress." The details tell about some types and their causes. Instead of trying to remember each cause separately, you can group the details as "different kinds of stress." Grouping the details lets you see likenesses and differences among them. You can see there are three different kinds of stress—academic, personal, and life. This is the organizational pattern, or relationship between details, in this passage.

Organizational Patterns and Signal Words

The organizational patterns used will depend on what you are reading, the topic of the reading, and what the author is trying to tell you. Seeing a pattern will help you find the main idea and supporting details. So, you need to know what patterns might be used. You also need to know how to find them.

One pattern often found in textbooks is **subject development.** In this pattern, an author tells you about a topic. A second pattern is **list/ sequence.** An author gives you a list of points. They may or may not be in a particular order. **Comparison/contrast** is the third pattern. Here, an author tells you how information is alike and/or different. The fourth pattern is **cause/effect.** With this pattern, an author tells you about an event and what led to the event happening. However, these patterns often mix or blend with each other. A textbook chapter's organization might move from subject development to cause/effect and then to comparison/ contrast.

You find organizational patterns by looking for **signal words.** Signal words help put the patterns in order. We'll look at each pattern of development more closely, but first look at Table 9.2 for an overview. It lists the four patterns, a short description of each, and corresponding signal words. An example of each pattern will follow, in the discussion of each type.

Table 9.2   Organizational Patterns and Signal Words

Pattern	Description	Signal Words
subject development	names the topic and gives numerous facts about it	no specific signal words; identified by headings and/or combination of headings and initial sentences
list/sequence	lists main points, orders a list of main points, or presents a problem and steps for its solution	*first, second, third,* etc.; *next, then, finally*
comparison/ contrast	describes ways in which people, places, things, or concepts are alike or different	comparison: *similarly, both, as well as, likewise* contrast: *however, on the other hand, on the contrary, but, instead of, although, yet*
cause/effect	describes results and the factors that cause them	*because, as a result, cause, effect, then, results in*

Subject Development

In *subject development,* an author names the topic. Then the author tells about the topic. Details describe and define the topic. The details relate to the topic but may not otherwise relate to each other. For instance, a biography is an example of subject development. A biography tells the story of a person's life. The topic is the person. The details would include the person's name, age, where the person was born, and so forth. Without the topic—the person—the details do not have anything to do with each other. They are just a name, a number, and a place.

In a textbook chapter, the headings and first sentences in a paragraph often signal the subject development pattern. The selection that follows shows an example of this pattern. Here the heading "Complex of a College Computer Lab" tells what the topic is. The paragraph defines *complex* in Sentence 2. An example is identified in Sentence 3. Details about the example are given in the rest of the paragraph.

Complex of a College Computer Lab

[1] What is a *complex*? [2] It is related items grouped together. [3] An example is the college computer lab. [4] The complex contains all the programs on the computers. [5] It includes the computer screens, computers, and printers in the lab. [6] It also includes the desks and chairs in the lab. [7] Computers all across the campus are part of it, too. [8] So are the users of these computers. [9] That means you are a part of the complex of your college computer lab.

EXERCISE 9.4   **You can use the content of a paragraph to know what kind of paragraph you are reading.** Using what you know about subject development, read the paragraph below, then answer the questions that follow

Before writing a research paper, you must choose a topic for your paper. Your instructor sometimes will assign topics. If that happens, your job is to find information on that topic. Then you write about it. If this doesn't happen, you may be asked to choose a topic from a list your instructor gives you. Or, you may have to find a topic on your own. The topic you select depends on your interests, how relevant the topic is to your class, and how much information you can find about it.

1. What is the subject of this paragraph? _____

   _____

2. What is the main idea of this paragraph?_____

   _____

3. List three details about this subject.

   A. _____

   B. _____

   C. _____

4. If you pick a research topic for yourself, what three things must you consider?

   A. _____

   B. _____

   C. _____

List/Sequence

The *list/sequence* pattern shows key points in one of two ways. In a list pattern, items appear in a somewhat random (unorganized) order. They share equal importance or rank. Grocery lists are examples of this type of list pattern. Think about items on a grocery list. They might include potato chips, eggs, bread, and milk. No one item is more important than the other. Writers or speakers sometimes use signal words like *first, second, next, finally,* or *last* when describing a list. These help the reader or listener keep track of the number of points that are being made. For example, a writing instructor might say the following:

> You will need to turn in a portfolio or collection of your work at the end of the term. You should have four kinds of materials in your portfolio. First, you need to include all the papers you've written this term. Next, you need to include all of your class notes. Third, your portfolio should contain an analysis of your papers. Finally, your portfolio should contain all your exams. You can put the items in any order as long as you include all four kinds of materials.

This example uses signal words to track the points but the points are not ranked in any order.

If items on a list are in a specific order, the list is in a sequence pattern. A sequence is a step-by-step progression of ideas. Sequence patterns are commonly found in answers to questions and solutions to problems. A good example of this is in math. When you work math problems, you follow the same sequence each time. For example, in adding large numbers, you begin adding from right to left. In dividing large numbers, you divide from left to right. Giving directions is another example of the sequence pattern. Think about giving someone directions to your campus library. If you changed the order in which you gave them, the person would get lost. You use signal words like *first, next,* and *then* to tell a person the order they need to go in to get to the library: *First,* you go past the Student Union; *next,* take the second right on Maple Avenue; *then,* make a left on Oak Street. Keep in mind that the number of steps in the sequence is not always given. This means you may not always begin your directions by saying, "There are 5 turns you need to make to get to the library."

Sequence patterns can also include:

- alphabetical order—Chelsea Anderson, Rose Billings, Max Crawford . . .

- hours in a day—7:00 wake up; 8:00 breakfast; 9:00 history; 10:15 math . . .

- rank—President Eden, Vice-President Williamson, Secretary Harding

- size—small, middle, large; least to most, most to least

- date—October 15th math midterm; October 28th Spanish exam; November 3rd biology lab report due

To find this pattern, you identify: (1) the topic, concept, process, or problem; (2) the number of points to be discussed or steps in the sequence; and (3) the signal words that show the order of the points or steps. It is a good idea to count and write numbers next to each point or step. This will tell you that the number of points or steps you find matches the number that is supposed to be there. You will know that you haven't missed anything. There's no easy way to know if information is a list or a sequence. Sometimes writers will let you know if what you are reading is a list or a sequence by the words they choose. For instance, your instructor's syllabus might include a phrase such as *"To log in to the course bulletin board, you need to do the following: First. . . and then. . . last. . . ."* Or, the text author might write, *"Several researchers contributed to this theory. First. . . and then. . . last. . . ."* Because both patterns use the same signal words, you often have to read through the items and decide for yourself if the information forms a list or a sequence.

Take a look at the reading below. This is an example of a list pattern. The heading "Choosing Classes" shows that the topic of the paragraph is finding classes. Sentence 1 tells you that the process is long. Information you need to know is ordered by numbers. By following the highlighted words, you find that there are five factors you need to consider.

Choosing Classes

¹ The process of deciding what college courses to take is a long one. ² First, you should understand what you know and what you don't know. ³ Counselors and the placement tests help you there. ⁴ Second, you should be careful of taking too many hard courses in one term. ⁵ It's better to spread these over a few semesters. ⁶ Third, you need to think about how much free time you have. ⁷ This means you need to know how many hours you plan to work. ⁸ It also means you need time to study. ⁹ Most courses require three hours of work outside class for each hour in class. ¹⁰ Fourth, you need to look at your overall goal. ¹¹ Do you just want to graduate? ¹² Or, do you want to graduate with honors? ¹³ Fifth, you should take courses that interest you. ¹⁴ All of these are factors to consider before deciding what courses you'll take.

The next reading is an example of a sequence pattern. The topic, "A Top-Down Process: Writing a Research Paper," is given in the heading. The first sentence also identifies the topic. The word *first* in the third sentence identifies the start of the sequence. The fourth sentence also states that this is the *top* of the process. Sentences 5 and 6 identify the *next* (*second*) step. At first reading, you might not know how Sentence 7 fits into the process. Sentence 8 explains that dividing the section into paragraphs is the *third* level or step. Again, you may not know how Sentence 9 fits into the sequence until you read Sentence 10. The word *finally* lets you know that the fifth stage is the last one.

A Top-Down Process: Writing a Research Paper

[1] You use top-down processing when you start at the end of a process and work your way back to the beginning. [2] Consider how you might write a research paper. [3] ① First, you decide what the entire paper is to cover. [4] This is the top. [5] Next you break the material into sections. [6] These are the ② second-level parts. [7] You divide each section into paragraphs. [8] This is the ③ third level. [9] Within those are sentences. [10] These form the ④ fourth level. [11] Finally, comes the ⑤ fifth level. [12] These are the words themselves.

EXERCISE 9.5   **Understanding a list or sequence depends on noting the number of details in it and knowing if order is important.** Read each paragraph below and answers the questions that follow it.

---

1. International students do not speak English as their first language. Thus, they often find they need special tips for adjusting to learning in the new country. Here are some tips. First, they should preview texts before class. This helps them predict what the lecture will be about. It helps keep them from misunderstanding. Second, watching successful American classmates can provide models for them. This helps with notetaking. It also aids talking with instructors and other students. Third, they should study with an American student. In this way, they could practice English. Being in a study group with an American helps them learn the American dialect, speed, and slang used at their institutions. Their language skills will improve as they hear more English. Fourth, they should get active on campus. This means they should go to as many campus meetings as possible. This helps them improve listening skills and meet new friends. Fifth, if possible, they should meet with an American family. The campus's international office or a local place of worship may keep lists of families who want international students to visit. Sixth, international students should learn more about American culture through the media. This means they need to watch TV and listen to the radio. They should see movies. They need to read newspapers, magazines, and books. They should visit museums, shops, parks, and so on. The more they understand American culture, the more comfortable they will be in the campus community.

1. What is the main idea of this paragraph?_____

_____

2. Is this a list or sequence pattern? How do you know? _____

_____

_____

3. How many items are in the list or sequence? _____

4. Identify the signal words in the paragraph._____

_____

5. List the issue identified by each signal word. Then list two details about each of these issues. _____

_____

_____

_____

_____

_____

_____

2. Over 150 campus organizations exist on this campus. If you can't find one that meets your needs, you can start one. How? First, identify a purpose and name for the group you want to form. For example, you might form the X-Box Players Group, Chocolate Fans, or Society of Math Majors. Next, get a petition to form a campus organization from the Student Services Office in 122 Gates Hall. Third, ask 11 other students to sign the petition. You sign it, too. Our campus requires a minimum of 12 signatures. Next, ask someone to be the faculty advisor. That person needs to sign the petition also. Last, submit the petition for approval.

1. What is the main idea of this paragraph? _____

_____

2. Is this a list or sequence pattern? How do you know? _____

_____

_____

3. How many items are in the list or sequence? _____

4. Identify the signal words in the paragraph.

_____

_____

Comparison/Contrast

The *comparison/contrast* pattern shows connections between people, places, objects, or concepts. Comparisons show how they are alike. Contrasts show how they are different. Thus, comparison/contrast patterns tell about likenesses and differences.

These patterns compare details in one of two ways. First, they might compare or contrast a detail of one thing with a corresponding (similar) detail of another thing. For example, a sentence might describe the location of a college: *City Community College is in the heart of an urban area.* The next sentence would describe the location of another college: *State College is located in a small town.* The rest of the paragraph would follow the same pattern. One sentence would give a detail (such as number of students or kinds of courses) about City Community College. The next sentence would give that same detail (number of students, kinds of courses) about State College.

A second type of this pattern might list all details about one thing and compare or contrast that list to corresponding details about another thing. For example, a paragraph might give all the details about one college: *City Community College is in the heart of an urban area. Over five thousand students attend classes there. It offers associate degrees in 21 areas.* Then, the paragraph would give details about a different college: *State College is located in a small town. Over eighteen thousand students attend classes there. It offers 31 undergraduate degrees. It also has 9 graduate programs.*

This pattern can also show how two things are alike. Signal words such as *similarly* or *both* show likenesses. For example, a paragraph could describe how the two colleges are alike: *Both City Community College and State College offer small class sizes and affordable tuition. They are also both conveniently located so students can either walk to school or take public transportation.*

The pattern can also tell ways in which two things differ. Signal words such as *however, but,* and *whereas* show differences. For example, a paragraph could describe differences between two colleges: *State College offers scholarships in tennis, football, and baseball, but City Community College has no sports programs. State College also offers students on-campus housing, whereas City Community College has no residence halls.*

To use this pattern, you need to find: (1) the items that are related, and (2) the signal words that show comparisons and/or contrasts. Take a look at the example that follows. In this reading, the items to be compared or contrasted are identified in Sentence 1 as *different kinds of jobs on a college campus.* Sentence 2 gives a similarity among the groups. Sentence 3 tells that workers differ. Sentence 4 identifies one of the groups. Sentence 5 gives examples of people in that group. Sentence 6 identifies another group and gives examples. Sentence 7 identifies the biggest differences between the groups. Sentence 8 tells the outcome of the difference. Although only one group is described in Sentence 9 *(Administrators and faculty are more highly educated and make more money),* you can draw conclusions about the other group ("thus, clerical and janitorial staff must be less educated and make less money"). Sentence 10 cites another difference. Sentence 11 gives additional details about the difference. Sentence 12 states that *interests differ as well.* The rest of the paragraph describes how interests vary by worker type.

Work on a College Campus

¹ Here is a more complete picture of different kinds of jobs on a college campus. ² Everyone works on the same campus. ³ But what each does and how each thinks may differ. ⁴ At the high end, you find the people who run the institution or teach there. ⁵ These are administrators and faculty. ⁶ At the lower end, you find clerical and janitorial staff. ⁷ The biggest differences between the two groups involve money and education. ⁸ Administrators and faculty are more highly educated and make more money. ⁹ What work is called differs between the groups. ¹⁰ The administration and faculty hold positions, not jobs. ¹¹ Interests differ as well. ¹² Administrators and faculty focus on education. ¹³ Administrators focus on education from a business side. ¹⁴ Faculty are usually more concerned with classes and students. ¹⁵ In contrast, lower-level staff are concerned about maintaining offices and buildings.

EXERCISE 9.6   **Much of what you read adds to your understanding by giving you details which compare or contrast one thing with another.** Read the paragraphs below and then answer the questions that follow each of them.

1. Other than cheating on tests, the most common type of cheating in college is plagiarism. Plagiarism means stealing another person's work and presenting it as your own. There are two types of plagiarism: unintentional and intentional. Unintentional plagiarism is plagiarism that occurs by accident. This might occur through inaccurate note taking, by incorrectly citing references, or from poor writing skills. Intentional plagiarism, on the other hand, is deliberate. It is planned theft of another person's work or printed information. It includes getting a paper from a friend, a term paper service, or the Internet. Even though the motives for unintentional and intentional plagiarism differ, the consequences remain the same.

1. What is the main idea of this paragraph?_____

_____

2. Is this a comparison passage, a contrast passage, or both? How do you

   know?_____

_____

3. How many items are being compared or contrasted? _____

4. Identify the signal words in the paragraph._____

_____

2. Daily to-do lists vary. Some people create time lists and schedule activities for specific times during the day. Other people create task lists and accomplish one job at a time. Either method or a combination of both works as long as you rank your list in order of importance before doing anything. This lets you complete those activities that are truly priorities, rather than what is most fun or what can be done quickly.

1. What is the main idea of this paragraph?_____

_____

2. Is this a comparison passage, a contrast passage, or both? How do you know?_____

_____

3. How many items are being compared or contrasted? _____

4. Identify the signal words in the paragraph. _____

_____

3. Instructors often assign themes or essays, reports, and research papers or term papers. Themes require little or no research. Somewhat short in length, they usually contain your personal opinions about a single topic. Other kinds of papers vary in length and purpose. Reports narrate or describe something that you have experienced firsthand. They sometimes include information that you derive from the accounts of others. Research papers are required assignments, written as a culmination or synthesis of a course's content. They often require supporting research. Called term papers by some instructors, research papers involve much library work. They focus on either part or all of a course's content or a related topic.

1. What is the main idea of this paragraph?_____

_____

2. Is this a comparison passage, a contrast passage, or both? How do you know?_____

3. How many items are being compared or contrasted? _____

4. Identify the signal words in the paragraph. _____

_____

Cause/Effect

The *cause/effect* pattern shows that an action or response happened because of an earlier event or reason (cause). It tells what happened (effect). It may also explain why the action or response happened (cause). For example, in a zoology class you might write: *The decline of the bald eagle population was due, in large part, to the use of the pesticide DDT.* In a health class you might write: *Government research shows that teens (ages 12–17) smoke the cigarettes that are advertised the most.*

To find this pattern, you identify: (1) the effect and (2) the cause or causes of the effect. The following reading shows an example of the cause/effect pattern. The heading of this passage is "How Low Grades Affect You." Paragraph 1 introduces the main idea. In Paragraph 2, the causes of poor grades are discussed. All of the sentences of Paragraph 3 discuss the effects of lower grades.

How Low Grades Affect You

1 Are grades important once you are out of school? Some employers will care about your grades. Others won't. If this is true, why worry about bad grades?

2 ① First, low grades are unnecessary. If you take courses you have the skills to complete, you shouldn't have a problem. If you run into problems, you should drop the course or get help before it affects your grade point average.

3 ② The main reason you should worry about grades is because they affect your life in school. Minimum (the lowest allowable) grade-point averages are needed to take certain courses. Grades affect transferring from a community college to a four-year school. They affect admission into graduate school such as law or medical school. Low grades can keep you from playing your sport or joining some groups. They affect financial aid. Low grades can force you out of school. ③ Finally, low grades can hurt your self-image.

EXERCISE 9.7   **In reading, it is often important to know what and why something happened.** Read the paragraphs below looking for details about causes and effects. Answer the questions that follow.

What happens when students get caught cheating? Some charges of academic dishonesty may stay between the student and instructor. But the student will get an *F* for that paper or test. However, if the instructor suspects cheating on previous papers, assignments, or tests, or if the amount of plagiarism is extreme, he or she could bring the case to a formal committee of other students, professors, or campus administrators.

If the committee finds the student guilty of academic dishonesty, disciplinary actions include probation, suspension, or expulsion. This committee's decision is not final, however. Students have the right to appeal academic disciplinary actions. But the student will need strong evidence to overturn the committee's recommendation.

1. What is the main idea of this paragraph?_____

_____

2. What is the cause(s)? _____

_____

3. What is the effect(s)? _____

_____

4. Identify the signal words in the paragraph._____

_____

EXERCISE 9.8   **An author seldom tells you which pattern of details you are to find. Rather, you need to be able to read and recognize patterns of details for yourself.** Read the paragraphs below. Circle the signal words in each paragraph. Then decide which organizational pattern (subject development, list/sequence, comparison/contrast, cause/effect) each paragraph uses. Write the name of the pattern below each paragraph.

1. Exercise plays a role in reducing stress. It helps you work off excess energy. Surprisingly, exercise also increases your energy level. When this happens, you cope better with stress because you no longer feel exhausted or overwhelmed. As a result, exercise decreases fatigue. This is particularly true when you use it as an alternative to challenging mental processes. For example, brisk walking for thirty minutes breaks the intensity of a long study session. Another benefit of exercise is that it tends to have a positive effect on your lifestyle. That is, if you exercise regularly, you'll probably find yourself drinking, smoking, and/or overeating less often. This, in turn, causes you to feel and look better. If you worry about your appearance, as do many people, exercise eliminates this potential stressor as well. Exercise affects your long-term health. It increases strength and flexibility while it decreases your chances of cardiovascular or skeletal-muscular problems. Exercise even tends to slow the natural aging process

Organizational pattern: _____

2. A weekly plan is your personal game plan for your life. It helps you transform long-term commitments into more manageable

(continued)

short-term objectives. A weekly plan consists of a written weekly schedule of events and a daily to-do list. Together, they allow you to manage your time so you can accomplish your long-term objectives and lifetime goals.

Organizational pattern: _____

3. During an exam, you can manage stress by pausing for about 15 seconds and taking a few deep breaths. You need to breathe smoothly and slowly. This calms your nerves and steadies your mind. A second way to manage stress while taking a test is to use smart test strategies. For example, answering questions you know first and making notes of information you're afraid you might forget eases stress. A third way to reduce stress during an exam is to ask your instructor for help if the way a test is constructed or the wording of a question causes you stress. Fourth, positive self-talk can help you control stress.

Organizational pattern: _____

WRITING CONNECTION

Respond to the following on a separate sheet of paper or in your notebook.

History books are often organized according to list/sequence or cause/ effect patterns. Describe these patterns and explain why this is so.

QUICK REVIEW

Circle the correct answer. Check your answers at the bottom of the page before reading the next section.

1. Organizational patterns provide the structure for relating details to the main idea. **T   F**

2. Organizational patterns do not change according to content, topic, and author's purpose. **T   F**

3. Signal words help you identify organizational patterns. **T   F**

4. Subject development pattern provides a topic and facts about the topic. **T   F**

5. List/sequence paragraphs always have numbered steps. **T   F**

Quick Review Answers: 1. T   2. F   3. T   4. T   5. F

LEARNING TIP

Thinking in New Ways

At first, college seems a lot like high school. Math, English, social studies, and science are all courses you've had before. However, most students say college courses are somehow "different." Why? The difference is in how you are asked to think about the content of the course. High school teachers may tell their classes exactly what to learn. They may tell them which questions to expect. Often students only need to memorize to do well on high school tests. College instructors assume you already know how to do that. They ask you to do more. They ask you to find relationships among ideas, such as ways that main ideas and their details relate. College instructors expect you to use what you learn in new ways. They expect you to break information apart and think about each part. They expect you to create new ideas. They expect you to assess ideas for their value.

Levels of Thinking: Bloom's Taxonomy

You know how to do the kinds of thinking required by college courses. You already know that the thinking you do when you daydream differs from the thinking you do when solving a problem. The thinking you use when looking for a phone number differs from the thinking you use when making a decision. What you need to know now is how to identify different kinds of thinking. You need to also know when to use each kind. You need a way to organize your thought processes.

On the next page are the levels of thinking according to a system called "Bloom's Taxonomy of Educational Objectives" (Bloom 1956). A *taxonomy* is a way to classify information. This taxonomy classifies the ways people think. It progresses from basic to advanced kinds of thinking. Table 9.3 shows levels of thinking. The most basic level (recall) is at the top. The highest level of thinking (evaluation) is at the bottom. You may think these levels sound unfamiliar, but you already know how to think at different levels. The examples in the following table show how you might use Bloom's levels of thinking in terms of a pizza.

Notice that you make sense of the world based on what you already know. For example, if you had never seen pizza, you would not recognize it at a buffet. You would not be able to move to any of the next levels in thinking about pizza. Why is this important? Because you learn by linking new ideas with what you already know. You connect thoughts at different levels.

Table 9.3   Bloom's Taxonomy of Educational Objectives

Level	Description of Thinking	Example
recall	You recognize and remember information.	You go to a buffet and recognize pizza as one of the choices.
translation	You put information in your own words.	You describe a pizza as "baked dough with sauce, cheese, and other toppings."
interpretation	You understand information in relation to other ideas (comparison, contrast, cause and effect, etc.).	You know that pizza crusts can be thick or thin. Pizzas can be different sizes. They can have different toppings. These differences affect taste and texture.
application	You use information to solve new problems.	You follow a recipe and make your own pizza.
analysis	You break difficult ideas apart and look at them piece by piece.	You go to a party where a combination pizza is served. After eating a piece, you identify each of the toppings. Based on its taste and look, you can also determine which pizza restaurant made the pizza.
synthesis	You use information to summarize, conclude, predict, or create.	You invent a new pizza flavor—a cornbread crust with turkey and cranberry sauce on top.
evaluation	You judge worth, correctness, truth, relevance, or other factors.	You decide if the new flavor of pizza tastes good or not.

Bloom, Benjamin S. and David R. Krathwohl. "Taxonomy of Educational Objectives: The Classification of Educational Goals," *Handbook I: Cognitive Domain*. New York, Longmans, Green, 1956.

The next table shows kinds of learning tasks found at different levels. Thinking at each level depends on and involves thinking at the levels below it. For example, in a foreign language, you have to know vocabulary (recall) in order to put information in your own words (translation). In trying to solve a math problem (application), you compare it to other problems you do know how to solve (interpretation). You also often use higher levels of thinking. For instance, you use synthesis to write a paper. In debating a topic, you use analysis to identify errors in thinking. You use evaluation in deciding which instructor to take for a class.

Table 9.4 Examples of Learning Tasks by Level of Thinking

Level	Learning Task
recall	foreign language vocabulary lines of poetry musical phrases or melodies mathematical facts (such as multiplication tables) rules of grammar
translation	paraphrasing information (putting in your own words) note taking reducing equations to lowest terms making a chart, diagram, or other visual from written information describing art, music, process, or other event
interpretation	generalizing drawing conclusions comparing and contrasting determining causes and effects identifying relationships
application	solving problems different from those you've already seen using a formula to solve problems following directions to complete a task or project grouping or classifying (putting similar items together) information based on a rule solving word problems in math

(continued)

Table 9.4   Examples of Learning Tasks by Level of Thinking (*continued*)

Level	Learning Task
analysis	identifying stated or inferred details that support a main idea or conclusion looking at the form or style of music, literature, or art identifying a math or science problem by type identifying information needed to solve a problem identifying statements of fact, opinion, or expert opinion identifying figures of speech identifying errors in logic (thinking) determining how text format (headings, subheadings, and so on) affects information organization
synthesis	writing a research paper writing music creating a work of art making a new solution for a problem solving a mystery designing an experiment drawing conclusions to form a main idea predicting outcomes
evaluation	checking internal consistency (details agree with each other) within a document determining consistency across several texts making decisions judging worth

CHAPTER SUMMARY

1. You can find important details by scanning a text.
2. The questions *how, when, where, how much, who,* and *why* are answered through scanning.
3. Organizational patterns help you understand main ideas more fully.
4. The subject development pattern names a topic and gives numerous facts.
5. The list/sequence pattern lists main points, orders a list of main points, or presents a problem and steps for its solution.
6. The comparison/contrast pattern describes ways in which people, places, things, or ideas are alike or different.
7. The cause/effect pattern shows that an action or response had an earlier basis or reason (cause).

CHAPTER REVIEW

On a separate sheet of paper, answer briefly but completely.

1. How is scanning different from skimming?
2. What are the steps in scanning?
3. What question words help you in scanning?
4. What is the purpose of organizational patterns?
5. What are signal words?
6. List and define each of the organizational patterns discussed in this chapter.

ACTION SUMMARY

- Which ideas from this chapter do I already use?

  _____

  _____

- Which ideas from this chapter are new to me?

  _____

  _____

- The best idea I learned from this chapter is. . . . Why?

  _____

  _____

• The ideas from this chapter I would like to try are. . . .

_____

_____

• How will I put the new ideas I've learned in action?

_____

_____

LEARNING ONLINE

Go to http://developmentalenglish.wadsworth.com/atkinson-longman to find the website for *Reading Strategies for Today's College Student*. This website is designed for students using this book. Here you will find:

• fun and interesting websites related to reading
• web exercises and reading quizzes that will help you become a better reader
• a list of chapter objectives
• a glossary of terms used in the chapter
• flashcards
• crossword puzzles

CHAPTER VOCABULARY REVIEW

Go back to the "Vocabulary Check" at the beginning of the chapter. Now that you've read this chapter, rate how well you understand the vocabulary words in the "After-Reading Ratings" column. If you rate any word less than a 3, read the information about that term again.

CHAPTER 10

Drawing Conclusions

OBJECTIVES

After you finish this chapter, you should be able to

- Draw logical conclusions
- Find the author's point of view
- Recognize propaganda

CHAPTER OUTLINE

(handwritten note: I'm know what this are)

CHAPTER MAP

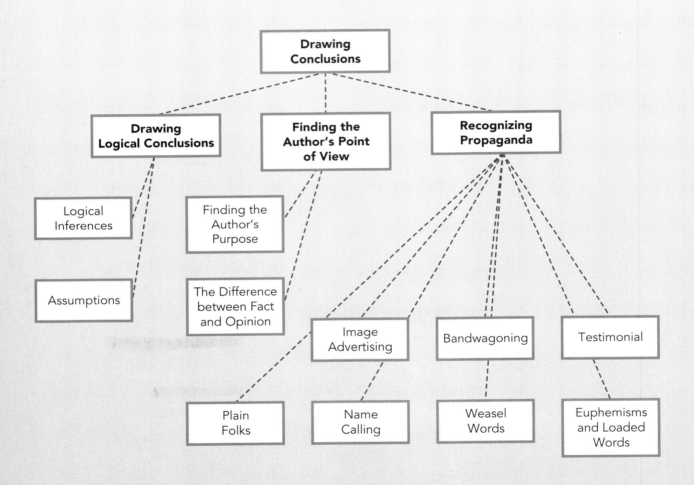

VOCABULARY CHECK

Below are the vocabulary words you will need to know in this chapter.

If you see a word that's brand-new to you, write a 0 in the "Before-Reading Ratings" column. If you have seen the word before but don't know what it means, write a 1. If you think you know what the word means, write a 2. If you know the word and can use it in a sentence, write a 3.

If you wrote a 0 or 1, look up the word in the Glossary at the back of the book. Then, after reading the chapter, look at these words again and rate them in the "After-Reading Ratings" column.

If you come across new words in the chapter that are not on this list, underline them or write them in your notebook, and look them up in your dictionary. This will help you increase your vocabulary.

Before-Reading Ratings	Vocabulary Words	Pronunciation Guide (How do I say this word?)	After-Reading Ratings
	inferred *knowledge were what*	in-ˈfərd	
	drawing conclusions	ˈdrȯ(-)iŋ kən-ˈklü-zhənz	
	logical inference	ˈlä-ji-kəl ˈin-f(ə-)rən(t)s	
	assumption	ə-ˈsəm(p)-shən	
	stereotype	ˈster-ē-ə-ˌtīp	
	fact	ˈfakt	
	opinion	ə-ˈpin-yən	
	bias	ˈbī-əs	
	expert opinion	ˈek-ˌspərt ə-ˈpin-yən	
	propaganda	ˌprä-pə-ˈgan-də	

Before-Reading Ratings	Vocabulary Words	Pronunciation Guide (How do I say this word?)	After-Reading Ratings
	image advertising	'i-mij 'ad-vər-ˌtīz-iŋ	
	bandwagoning	'band-ˌwa-gən-iŋ	
	testimonial	ˌtes-tə-'mō-nē-əl	
	plain folks	'plān 'fōks	
	name calling	'nām 'kȯ-liŋ	
	weasel words	'wē-zəl 'wərdz	
	euphemism	'yü-fə-ˌmi-zəm	
	loaded word	'lō-dəd 'wərd	

The art of reading between the lines [drawing conclusions] is as old as manipulated information.

Serge Schmemann

Professor and Journalist

There are a lot of reasons for reading. You need to read and understand the instructions for connecting a new computer. You may read for fun, choosing books on topics that you enjoy. And, of course, you must read to learn in your college classes. Sometimes what you need to learn comes from your textbooks or lecture notes. Sometimes, however, your instructor wants you to think about this information. Sometimes you are asked to draw conclusions about what you have read or heard.

Most reading involves *literal* (factual or true) information. When you read your biology textbook or your history textbook, you are reading literal information. When you are asked to answer questions from these textbooks, the answers to literal questions are found in the text. Look at this example:

AIDS affects young and old, rich and poor, men and women. As of this writing, an estimated 50 million people worldwide have already been infected with the virus that causes AIDS. This virus is called HIV. Almost all of them are expected to develop the disease, and most will die from it. Prevention and treatment are important concerns of medical workers around the world. HIV uses the T-cells of the immune system to copy itself. When it does this, it kills T-cells. The job of T-cells is to tell your body that you need protection from a disease. When the T-cells get below a certain number, you have AIDS.

Suppose your professor asks you: *How many people are estimated to have the virus that causes AIDS?* You can point to the word or phrase that answers these questions. Answers to literal questions are the stated details of a text.

Inferred information is not found directly in the text. Suppose your professor asked you this question: *Are AIDS and HIV the same?* Unlike the question asking for literal information, for this you cannot point to the word, phrase, or sentence that answers the question. You can use information in the text. However, you also must use your background knowledge. For instance, look again at the paragraph about AIDS. You may have already known that it affects the immune system. If you did, this knowledge helped you better understand what was being said. This is called **drawing conclusions.** This answer might be a detail. It might be a main idea. Unlike a literal reading, however, inferred information is not plainly stated. Instead of reading what the lines of text say, you have to read "between the lines" to know what they mean.

Drawing Logical Conclusions

Suppose you come home from school one day and find your house is a mess. Your lamp is broken into pieces. Your plant is upside down on the floor. Books are scattered on the floor. Your rug is crooked. Based on the facts—a broken lamp, an upended plant, displaced books, and a crooked rug—you conclude that you have been robbed. However, once you start looking more closely, you find your cat playing with a big bug. He chases the bug all over the room, bounding from one place to another. You realize you jumped to the wrong conclusion. A burglar did not break into your house. It was just your cat chasing a bug.

You can draw different conclusions from almost any situation. Sometimes the right conclusion will be easy to make. Sometimes it will be hard. Sometimes you will look at all the facts, both stated and inferred, and still come up with the wrong conclusion. You can get better at drawing conclusions as you get more practice. That is what this chapter is all about. There are two main types of conclusions: *logical inferences* and *assumptions*.

Logical Inferences

A **logical inference** is a conclusion that cannot be avoided. There is no other reasonable conclusion to be drawn from the information. For instance, what would happen if you skip class and fail every exam and assignment in a course? The logical inference is that you would fail the course. Or, suppose you make an *A* on every test and project. You fulfill all other course requirements. You can logically conclude that you will pass the course.

Assumptions

An **assumption** is a conclusion based on your background knowledge. You may have no other facts or proof. For instance, you assume that your instructors have skill and knowledge in the subject they are teaching. Or, you assume that a textbook author knows about the topic of the textbook. You make these assumptions because your background knowledge tells you that instructors should know about the subjects they teach. Your background knowledge also tells you that authors should know about the subjects they write about. Such assumptions are often true. But they may be false.

Some assumptions become generalizations (conclusions applied to a larger group). This happens when you think all examples of something are alike. For instance, if you think your college is great, you might assume that all colleges are great. Or, you might think that because a course is easy for you, it is easy for everyone. That may or may not be true.

A generalization about a group of people is called a **stereotype.** Stereotypes can be based on gender (male or female), ethnic background (such as American, French, or Chinese), religion (such as Christian or Muslim), age, job, location, or other factors. For instance, some people think that everyone who goes to a private college is rich. Some people think student athletes are spoiled. Some people think all college presidents are men. None of these statements is true. Not everyone who goes to a private college is rich. Not every student athlete is spoiled. Not all college presidents are men.

WRITING CONNECTION

Respond to the following on a separate sheet of paper or in your notebook.

Do you stereotype people? Give an example of when you did so. Describe how you have changed or could change this way of thinking.

QUICK REVIEW

Circle the correct answer. Check your answers at the bottom of the page before reading the next section.

1. Literal information is stated in the text. **T   F**

2. The two main types of conclusions are logical inferences and stereotypes. **T   F**

3. Assumptions are never true. **T   F**

EXERCISE 10.1   **Cartoons often provide some of the best opportunities for drawing conclusions.** Look at the cartoons. Then answer the questions that follow.

Used by permission of Richard M. Longman. All rights reserved.

"I hate giving finals in the Chemistry building."

1. What is happening in this cartoon?_____

2. How do you know?_____

3. Who are the people in the cartoon? _____

4. How do you know?_____

Quick Review Answers: 1. T   2. F   3. F

Used by permission of Richard M. Longman. All rights reserved.

Rural Parking. . . Urban Campus

1. What is happening in this cartoon?_____

2. How do you know?_____

3. Who is the person in the cartoon?_____

4. Why do you think that? _____

Finding the Author's Point of View

Authors write because they have something to say. They write to inform you or to try to get you to believe something. They do this through the words they use. They also do this by each **fact** and **opinion** they include. Facts are true details about a topic. Opinions are what the author believes about a topic. Sometimes, it is hard to tell the difference between the facts and opinions in a book. An author's **bias** (feelings or beliefs) may affect what and how information is presented. This can happen by accident or on purpose.

Finding the Author's Purpose

Authors want a response from their readers. For instance, authors who write to inform—such as textbook authors—want students to learn. Authors who write to persuade may want you to think differently about a topic. You can find this kind of writing on the editorial page of your campus newspaper. Authors who write to entertain may want you to feel amused. A short story or novel is an example of this type of writing. These form the three purposes authors have when writing. They write to inform, persuade, or entertain.

An author sometimes mixes the three purposes. For instance, an author might add humor when trying to inform or persuade. Sometimes textbooks use humor to get you interested. But, for the most part, what you read in college will either inform or persuade. Thus, only these two types will be discussed in this chapter.

Informative Writing

In textbooks, authors write in order to teach. Their writing is informative. To write informatively, an author tries to give information in clear and understandable ways. Informative writing can include examples, dates, and expert opinions. (You'll learn more about expert opinion later in the chapter.)

Such writing might:

1. explain—*How do hydrogen particles combine with oxygen to make water?*
2. analyze—*What caused the Depression in America in the early 1900s?*
3. describe—*How did propaganda affect the public's beliefs about World War II?*
4. demonstrate—*Show how the body's nervous system works.*
5. define—*What are trade tariffs?*

Persuasive Writing

In another kind of writing, the author's goal is to persuade you. Authors write persuasively to try to change your beliefs. Then, they ask for a promise of action. Like informative writing, persuasive writing includes examples, data, comparisons, contrasts, and expert opinions. For instance, a student might write a letter to the editor of the campus newspaper. In it, she might try to persuade students that a college rule is unfair. She could compare the rule with ones at other colleges. She could give opinions from faculty or professional staff. After reading the student's letter, you might agree that the rule is unfair. This would be a change in belief. The letter's author might ask readers to sign a petition (a collection of signatures that support an appeal) in order to change the rule. This would require an action on your part.

EXERCISE 10.2   **What you read and hear on campus provides many opportunities for drawing conclusions.** Read each of the following paragraphs. Think about the source of the information as well as the content. Decide whether the purpose of each paragraph is to inform or to persuade. Circle your response.

1. Source: Campus Handbook

   What is a bursar? A bursar is the person on campus that handles student financial accounts. The Office of the Bursar tracks charges to and payments from students at the college. This includes tuition and fees. It also includes charges such as library fines or parking tickets. The Bursar's office issues bills to student email accounts on the first working day of each month. Students may pay with check, credit card, or cash.

inform   persuade

2. Source: Discussion by Student Orientation Leader with New Students

OK. The question is: Should a new student join a campus organization the first semester or just concentrate on studies? New students should definitely join something. It doesn't really matter what you join as long as you become part of the campus community. Our campus has everything. You can join a fraternity or sorority. You can be in a musical or sports group. You can be in a religious group or a political group. You can even think of a campus job or a study group as something you've joined. Becoming part of the campus is good for your social life. But, it's even better for your academic success. Students that get involved tend to be more successful.

inform   persuade

3. Source: Sign on Campus Bulletin Board

WORRIED ABOUT YOUR GRADES?

READY FOR MIDTERM EXAMS?

WE'VE MADE THE DIFFERENCE FOR OTHERS!

WE CAN MAKE THE DIFFERENCE FOR YOU, TOO!

Academic Center College Success Workshops

presents

ACING YOUR NEXT TEST!

Tuesday, September 24

1 PM, 108 Jackson Hall

inform   persuade

4. Source: Heard on Campus Radio Station

The events calendar at the Union for November 8th:

Nontraditional Students Breakfast Club	7 am	Union Dining
Career Workshop	10 am–noon	Ballroom
Spanish Club Honors Lunch	noon–1 pm	Union Dining
Art Show	noon–5 pm	Gallery
College Republicans Meeting	7 pm	Union 233
College Democrats Meeting	8 pm	Union 145
International Student Association	8 pm	Union 301

inform   persuade

The Difference between Fact and Opinion

Is everything you read true? Can you always trust experts—people who have special skill or knowledge about a topic? Do you accept as fact everything you see? Should you believe everything you hear? Hopefully, you answered no to each of these questions. Everything you read is not true. Not all experts can be trusted. And you should not believe everything you see and hear.

In a free country like the United States, almost anything can be printed or spoken. Good examples are the newspapers and magazines you see at grocery store checkouts. Their "reports" range from untrue stories about famous people to space aliens living among us to sightings of Bigfoot. In order to make good decisions, you need to be able to tell the difference between fact and opinion in information.

Facts

Facts are statements of truth. For example, there are seven days in a week. That's a fact. Canada is north of the United States. That's a fact. Facts also exist in the form of events we know have happened. For instance, George Washington was the first president of the United States. The bombing of Pearl Harbor occurred on December 7, 1941. These are facts.

You must decide if what you read is factual. Facts come from observation or experience. The observations and experiences can be personal or they can be from reliable sources. For example, you don't have to have personally seen George Washington to know that he was the first U.S. president. You don't have to personally experience space travel to know that it exists. Facts also come from established standards. For example, water freezes at a Celsius temperature of 0 degrees. Twelve inches equals one foot. The chemical symbol for water is H_2O. These standards are considered to be facts.

Established standards, however, sometimes change. For instance, a fact for science used to be that the earth was the center of the universe. It is now an established fact that the earth revolves around the sun. Your ability to separate fact from fiction (information that is not true) comes from learning. The more you learn about a subject, the more you will be able to know if it is factual.

When reading, you may see descriptive words that tell about facts, such as *long* (the *long* class), *hard* (a *hard* test), *nearby* (the bookstore *nearby*), *early* (the *early* meeting), and *delicious* (a *delicious* meal). Some words limit facts. They show that other options are possible. Compare these statements: "I make good grades." "At times, I make good grades." Look at the difference in these two. The words *at times* limit the facts. Some of the words that limit facts are *often, sometimes,* and *seldom.*

Opinions

Opinions are a kind of truth. An opinion is what someone thinks. It is a viewpoint, belief, or judgment. Opinions reflect personal attitudes or feelings. It is an opinion if you say: *The sunsets in Maryland are more beautiful than the sunsets in Texas.* However, facts are true for everyone. For example, it is true for everyone that the sun rises in the morning and sets at night.

Words that describe opinion often vary according to who uses them. Consider the word *smart.* One person may think that a friend is smart because he makes good grades. You might think he is not smart because he spends all his money for college on music CDs. It depends on how each of you defines *smart.* Words that describe opinions are called qualitative words. Examples of qualitative words include *cute, ugly, funny, hot, cold, bad,* and *sour.*

Bias

When you express opinions as facts, you show *bias.* For instance, look at this statement: *Blue is the prettiest color in the world.* It is stated as a fact. However, it is a fact to only one person. It is one person's opinion that blue is the prettiest color in the world. Bias can come from personal opinions, feelings, or beliefs. Bias weakens the truth and value of what you read. Some phrases show that an opinion follows. These help you know that the information you are hearing or reading is an opinion. Such phrases include *in my opinion, I believe,* and *I think.*

Expert Opinions

People's backgrounds affect the value of an opinion. In other words, people who know about a topic usually can provide more helpful opinions than those who do not. Anyone can give an opinion, but an **expert opinion** is one given by a professional. Your high school friend might look at a college course description and say, "This is a good class." A faculty advisor might look at the same course and say, "This is a good class." Which person would you trust to know more about the class?

An expert opinion depends on many factors. In reading, you should look at an author's education and professional experience. You should find out where the author works. You can ask your instructors if that place has a good record. Often an author's background affects his or her point of view. It affects what is said about a topic. It can even change how facts are reported. For instance, suppose an American author and a British author both write about the American Revolution. They might discuss the same battles. They might talk about the same generals. But their versions would be different because of their backgrounds. You can find background information about an author in the introductory or ending statements of an article or a book. You can also find this out by asking others in the same field.

QUICK REVIEW

Circle the correct answer. Check your answers at the bottom of the page before reading the next section.

1. Authors have three purposes when writing—to inform, to persuade, and to entertain. **T   F**

2. Facts only result from what you have personally seen or experienced. **T   F**

3. Opinions reflect judgments, attitudes, or feelings. **T   F**

4. Words describing opinions are interpretive. **T   F**

5. Expert opinions come from someone who is experienced in a field. **T   F**

EXERCISE 10.3   **You often need to differentiate between facts and opinions in what you hear and read on campus.** Read the phrases on the next page. Tell which is a fact or an opinion by writing an *F* before each phrase that is a fact and an *O* before each phrase that is an opinion.

Quick Review Answers: 1. T   2. F   3. T   4. T   5. T

_____ 1. a difficult exam

_____ 2. 126 credits in the curriculum

_____ 3. a degree in elementary education

_____ 4. the highest grade in the class

_____ 5. section 23 in English 100

_____ 6. the best course for history majors

_____ 7. a boring class

_____ 8. a grade of 88 on the third exam

_____ 9. the tallest building on campus

_____ 10. the most attractive campus in the United States

EXERCISE 10.4

Sometimes what seems like a fact or an expert opinion is really just someone's opinion. Can you tell the difference? Read the following sentences. Do they give facts, opinions, or expert opinions? Write _F_ for _fact_, _O_ for _opinion_, or _X_ for _expert opinion_ before each one.

_____ 1. According to my science textbook, carbon has an atomic weight greater than that of hydrogen.

_____ 2. According to a student in my English class, our teacher is the best poet on campus.

_____ 3. According to my advisor, four courses in physical education are required for graduation.

_____ 4. According to our state senator, athletics have no place in higher education.

_____ 5. According to an editorial in our campus newspaper, most students fail to study enough to get good grades.

_____ 6. According to registration figures, more students have enrolled part-time than ever before.

_____ 7. According to my math instructor, Greek organizations are a waste of time.

_____ 8. According to my roommate, I'm the neatest roommate he has ever had.

_____ 9. According to the head of campus security, this is a very safe campus.

_____ 10. According to my grades, I will be on the Dean's List this semester.

WRITING CONNECTION

Respond to the following on a separate sheet of paper or in your notebook.

In your American history class, a graduate student in history gives a speech. She states that Abraham Lincoln was the best president. Do you consider hers an expert opinion? Explain your answer.

Recognizing Propaganda

Propaganda is a form of persuasion. It is used to change opinion. Propaganda is one-sided. It tells only one side of an issue to make you believe that side is the right one. It does not try to present a balanced viewpoint. It usually has more to do with opinion than with facts.

When you know what propaganda is and how it works, then you can make your own decisions. Common types of propaganda include **image advertising, bandwagoning, testimonial, plain folks, name calling, weasel words, euphemisms,** and **loaded words.** (Look at Table 10.1, page 240.) Because propaganda is often used in advertising, we'll look at examples in advertising. However, once you know what to look for, you also can find propaganda in other, written text.

Image Advertising

Have you seen TV commercials with beautiful celebrities trying to sell makeup? Celebrities often sell products. Advertisers want you to connect the product with the person. They want you to think that you will be more like the celebrity if you use their product. Or think about political ads. Have you seen one with a candidate standing next to an American flag? The advertisers want you to think of the candidate as patriotic. In *image advertising,* a person, product, or idea is connected to certain people, places, sounds, activities, or symbols to make you feel a certain way. The images may not have any real connection to what is being advertised. Advertisers want to create a good feeling about their product by tying it to a well-known person or symbol.

Bandwagoning

In *bandwagoning,* the theme is "join the crowd." If you, as a child, said, "Everyone has a skateboard. I want one, too," you used bandwagoning to get your parents to let you have a skateboard. You implied that you would be left out by not being like everyone else. Bandwagoning is a form of peer pressure (friends trying to get you to do what they do). For example, ads for alcoholic beverages show people drinking and laughing together.

Table 10.1 Types and Examples of Propaganda

Types of Propaganda	Examples
image advertising	ads showing rich people drinking fine wines; trucks and SUVs in rugged outdoor settings; politicians standing next to the American flag
bandwagoning	soda advertisements showing friends having fun; "Spirit Day" on campus when everyone is supposed to wear school colors
testimonial	formerly overweight celebrities recommending weight-loss products; hair products recommended by celebrities
plain folks	politicians shaking hands and kissing babies; a young woman (not a celebrity) advertising wart remover; an average man telling you to call the lawyer who got him thousands of dollars
name calling	one soft drink challenging another soft drink in a taste test; aspirin commercials that say, "It takes eight of these, four of those, but just one of ours"; competition between fast-food chains
weasel words	"Leaves your dishes *virtually* spotless"; "Cleans your teeth as white *as they can be*"; politicians promise not to ask for *unneeded* taxes; "*almost* no poisons were found in our water supply"
euphemisms	grades that *could be better* (failing grades); *five-finger discount* (theft); *collateral damage* (death or injury to civilians in a war); *passed away* (died)
loaded words	*junkie* (substance abuser); *deadbeat dad* (father who does not pay child support); *crazy* (mentally ill)

The message is that drinking alcohol is how everyone has a good time, so you should drink alcohol, too.

Testimonial

Have you seen the underwear commercials with former basketball star Michael Jordan? Or any ads with golfer Tiger Woods? In these commercials, the celebrities give a *testimonial*. In a testimonial, a famous person or authority on the subject says that a product, person, or idea is good. The advertiser hopes that if a famous person likes it, you will, too. But a testimonial is not the same as expert testimony. Famous actors and athletes often give testimonials for products they never use. They get paid to do this. It is the association or connection with the famous person that advertisers hope will hook you on their products.

Plain Folks

When the *plain folks* technique is used in advertising, people in ads seem to be average and ordinary. Many fast-food chains use plain folks advertising. The idea is to make you feel as though your friend or neighbor recommends a product. This is almost the opposite of a testimonial. This ad wants you to trust the advice of an average person.

Name Calling

In *name calling*, a product or cause is made to appear better than another by using unfair comparisons. Unpopular or unflattering language is used to describe the competition. For example, one salsa (a common condiment in the Southwest) claimed that a competitor's product was made in New York City—a city not known for its salsa. The ad suggests that salsa made in New York City must not be the "real thing." Or, a hamburger chain claims that its burgers are "grilled" not "fried." Fried burgers sound worse than grilled ones.

Weasel Words

Weasels are animals with keen sight and smell that are known for their quickness and slyness. This quickness and slyness helps them slip out of trouble. Because of these characteristics, words that lack exact meanings are called *weasel words*. Their meanings cannot be pinned down. Promises are not guarantees. Weasel words leave the speaker with a quick and sneaky way out. For instance, consider a commercial that says "Will leave your dishes virtually spotless!" The word *virtually* means "almost." How is that different from your usual dish detergent? It is a weasel word.

Euphemisms and Loaded Words

Euphemisms and *loaded words* are also forms of propaganda. These are used less often in advertising than are other forms of propaganda. Nonetheless, they work to change your view.

Euphemisms replace "bad" or unpleasant phrases with "good" or pleasant phrases. Saying that someone *passed away* instead of saying they *died* is a common euphemism to soften a negative statement. Euphemisms can also hide the truth. For example, perhaps a friend sets you up with a blind date. You ask what the date looks like. You are told that the date has a *great personality*. This may mean that the person is not very attractive.

Loaded words, on the other hand, make people, issues, and things seem as bad as possible. Think about the difference between calling someone a *bum* and someone else *homeless*. The *connotations* for these two words differ, but they describe the same situation. When you hear loaded words, think about why the author is using them. Would you react the same way if different words were used?

QUICK REVIEW

Circle the correct answer. Check your answers at the bottom of the page before reading the next section.

1. In image advertising, a person, product, or concept is linked with certain people, places, sounds, activities, or symbols. **T   F**

2. In bandwagoning, the theme is "join the crowd." **T   F**

3. Testimonial ads are based on an average person. **T   F**

4. Name calling is a form of propaganda that compares products or issues unfairly. **T   F**

5. Unlike other forms of propaganda, euphemisms and loaded words do not try to change your beliefs. **T   F**

EXERCISE 10.5   **Propaganda techniques are often used in newspaper ads because advertisers want you to buy their products. They are also found in editorials because writers want to influence your beliefs and actions. Can you identify the use of propaganda techniques in the newspapers you read?** Get a copy of your campus or local newspaper. Use its advertisements and editorial page to find examples of each of the terms on the following page. On a separate sheet of paper, list each term and the example, and tell why you think it is a good example.

Bring your examples to class for discussion. Ask other students to match your examples to these terms. Then tell them what you thought. Discuss any differences of opinion.

Quick Review Answers: 1. T   2. T   3. F   4. T   5. F

- image advertising

- bandwagoning

- testimonial

- plain folks

- name calling

- weasel words

- loaded words

- euphemisms

EXERCISE 10.6   **There are examples of bias all around us—even in the classroom.** Read the article below on bias in the classroom. After you read it, answer the questions that follow.

EDUCATION EXPERT: CLASSROOM GENDER BIAS PERSISTS
by Jill Goetz

1 American educators—no matter their **gender** or the grade level they teach—pay more attention to male students than to female students. This was the statement of education expert David Sadker in a lecture at Cornell University. Sadker's lecture was sponsored by the Public Service Center. It was titled "Gender Bias in the College Classroom and Strategies for Change." Sadker and his wife have spent more than two decades of research on this topic.

2 This research shows that gender bias in the classroom hurts females. It lessens girls' self-esteem. It reduces prospects for females. It limits opportunities for women later in life. Sadker showed the subtle and obvious ways that teachers support male students and **hinder** females. He said this happens from kindergarten through college

3 Sadker spent the first half of his lecture offering clear instances of sexism. He discussed a book published in 1970. The book's title was *I'm Glad I'm a Boy! I'm Glad I'm a Girl!* In this book, boys become doctors and girls, nurses. Boys fix things, and girls need things fixed. Boys will one day build houses. Girls will clean them.

4 Sadker asked two male and two female students to come on stage. He asked them to pretend they were sitting in a classroom. He played the role of the teacher. During the "class," he stood next to the men. He called on them to answer questions. He asked them follow-up questions. He nodded rarely at the women. Otherwise, Sadker ignored them.

5 Next, Sadker showed less obvious examples of classroom gender bias. He showed a clip of a 1992 **segment** of *Dateline NBC.* He and his wife observed a teacher in classroom for two days. They watched from behind a one-way mirror.

From the *Cornell Chronicle*, Vol. 27, No. 31, Apr. 25, 1996. Reprinted with permission from Cornell University.

(*continued*)

6   The show's producers failed at first to see any bias on the part of the teacher they watched. Some members of the Cornell audience agreed. However, the Sadkers pointed to several examples. They showed that the teacher faced the boys more often. Also, the teacher spent more time with them as she moved around the classroom. And this teacher knew the Sadkers were watching her.

7   "What we have here is a pattern that **pervades** our classrooms," Sadker told the Cornell audience.

8   Sadker noted two points. First, because of such unequal attention, girls become less active learners. Second, girls ask and answer questions less often than boys. Such differences in the classroom are most marked at the college level.

9   The *Dateline* segment also addressed the recent debate over the value of single-sex schools and colleges. This has been spurred by studies that have shown such schools can increase girls' self-esteem. Increases in leadership skills and interest in science and math is also shown.

10   "I think single-sex schools are a wonderful option," Sadker said. "But the lesson from our research is not to abandon the **coed** classroom. Instead, we need to make it a better place for all students."

11   In his lecture Sadker showed ways that teachers can do just that. For example, he suggested that teachers ask more girls to take part in class demonstrations. He asked that they give girls more time to answer questions before calling on more vocal male students. He said they should seek books that show women in non-traditional roles.

VOCABULARY   The words below are boldfaced in the reading. First, use a dictionary to find the pronunciations and meanings of these words. Second, use context to be sure you have located the correct definition. Third, when you understand the definition, write it in your own words. Finally, write a sentence using each word.

Word	Pronunciation	Definition from Dictionary	Definition in Your Words	Your Sentence
1. gender				
2. hinder				

Word	Pronunciation	Definition from Dictionary	Definition in Your Words	Your Sentence
3. segment				
4. pervades				
5. coed				

VOCABULARY BUILDER

List five words (other than those boldfaced) from the passage whose meanings you do not know. Look up each word and write its meaning based on how it is used in the sentence. Use the word in a sentence of your own.

1. _____

2. _____

3. _____

4. _____

5. _____

COMPREHENSION How much did you understand in the reading? Read the questions below and circle the correct answer.

1. According to Sadker, which of the following is an example of *gender bias*?
    A. same-sex schools
    B. giving female students more time to answer before calling on a male student
    C. a teacher who faces male students more often than female students
    D. all of the above

2. Who was Sadker's partner in the research?
    A. his son
    B. his daughter
    C. his wife
    D. his grandchild

3. Where was Sadker speaking?
    A. Yale University
    B. Cornell University
    C. Stanford University
    D. City University of New York

4. How long have Sadker and his research partner focused on the topic of gender bias?
    A. less than twenty years
    B. exactly twenty years
    C. over twenty years
    D. The article does not say.

5. Which of the following statements does NOT make Sadker's an expert opinion?
    A. He had conducted research in the field for over two decades.
    B. He has written articles and given lectures in the field.
    C. His wife was his partner in research.
    D. He has consulted with nationally known television shows.

6. Which of the following is true of Sadker's observation of a teacher as described in a 1992 *Dateline* clip?
    A. The teacher was aware that she was being observed.
    B. The teacher was observed daily for two weeks.
    C. The teacher did not show characteristics of gender bias.
    D. Sadker observed the teacher by sitting in the back of the classroom.

7. When was *I'm Glad I'm a Boy! I'm Glad I'm a Girl!* published?
   A. 1970
   B. 1980
   C. 1992
   D. The article does not say.

8. What news program was mentioned in the article?
   A. *60 Minutes*
   B. *CBS Evening News*
   C. *20/20*
   D. *Dateline NBC*

9. Who sponsored Sadker's lecture?
   A. a news program
   B. the Public Service Center
   C. the College of Education
   D. the U.S. Department of Education

10. According to Sadker, gender bias is most evident in _____.
   A. kindergarten
   B. elementary school
   C. high school
   D. college

LEARNING TIP
Directed Test Preparation Activity

To prepare for a test, you need to answer three questions: (1) What do I know? (2) What do I need to learn? (3) What will my instructor expect me to know? Determining what you know and don't know is an important first step. Your next step is to predict test questions. This requires you to draw conclusions. A *directed test preparation activity* (DTPA) helps you make these inferences.

In the DTPA, you divide review information into one of three types: (1) Is it *completely known?* (2) Is it *partly known?* (3) Is it *unknown?* Your goal is to change *unknown* and *partly known* information to *completely known* information.

The DTPA uses a chart to organize the types. (See the chart on page 248.) It helps you predict test questions, too.

(continued)

To use the DTPA, first look at your reading and lecture notes. Decide what information is familiar to you and what is less familiar. Write what you know and what you don't know in the correct columns in the chart. Now, look at what you have in columns 2 and 3. Think about what you need to do to make that information "completely known." For instance, you might choose an acronym to help you recall steps in a sequence. (See Chapter 2 if you need to review acronyms.) You actively think about the information when you write the mnemonic in your notes.

The DTPA also helps you prepare for tests. For instance, pretend you're on a quiz show. Look at information in column 2. What question does this information answer? Write that question in column 4. This is a way of predicting the questions your instructor might ask.

Now write your questions and answers on note cards. You have created an active test study tool.

Example of DTPA Chart

What do you really know? KNOWN INFORMATION	What do you somewhat know? PARTLY KNOWN	What don't you know? UNKNOWN	What do you need to learn this information?	What question might get this information as the answer?

CHAPTER SUMMARY

1. When you draw conclusions, you think about both stated and unstated information.
2. Logical inferences and assumptions are types of conclusions.
3. You can draw conclusions about the author's purpose for writing.
4. You can draw conclusions when you identify bias and propaganda techniques.

CHAPTER REVIEW

On a separate sheet of paper, answer briefly but completely.

1. Make a chart that defines and gives an example of each type of conclusion (logical inferences and assumptions) for the topic of *test preparation*.
2. Create and label three statements of opinion and three statements of fact concerning the last exam you took in this course.
3. Compare and contrast *euphemisms* and *loaded words*. How might these affect an author's purpose for writing?
4. How do euphemisms and loaded words relate to bias?
5. Define each of the types of propaganda and locate a current example of each.

ACTION SUMMARY

- Which ideas from this chapter do I already use?

  _____

  _____

- Which ideas from this chapter are new to me?

  _____

  _____

- The best idea I learned from this chapter is. . . . Why?

  _____

  _____

- The ideas from this chapter I would like to try are. . . .

  _____

  _____

- How will I put the new ideas I've learned in action?

_____

_____

LEARNING ONLINE

Go to http://developmentalenglish.wadsworth.com/atkinson-longman to find the website for *Reading Strategies for Today's College Student*. This website is designed for students using this book. Here you will find:

- fun and interesting websites related to reading
- web exercises and reading quizzes that will help you become a better reader
- a list of chapter objectives
- a glossary of terms used in the chapter
- flashcards
- crossword puzzles

CHAPTER VOCABULARY REVIEW

Go back to the "Vocabulary Check" at the beginning of the chapter. Now that you've read this chapter, rate how well you understand the vocabulary words in the "After-Reading Ratings" column. If you rate any word less than a 3, read the information about that term again.

CHAPTER 11

Reading Graphics

OBJECTIVES

After you finish this chapter, you should be able to

- Find main ideas in graphics
- Use charts to understand information
- Use graphs to understand data

CHAPTER OUTLINE

I. Finding Main Ideas in Graphics

  A. Charts: Analyzing Concepts

  B. Graphs: Drawing on Data

  C. Maps: Physical Locations

CHAPTER MAP

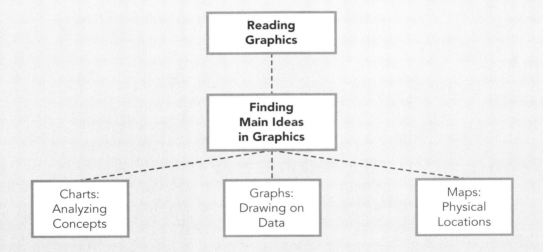

Reading
Graphics

Finding
Main Ideas
in Graphics

Charts:
Analyzing
Concepts

Graphs:
Drawing on
Data

Maps:
Physical
Locations

VOCABULARY CHECK

Below are the vocabulary words you will need to know in this chapter.

If you see a word that's brand-new to you, write a 0 in the "Before-Reading Ratings" column. If you have seen the word before but don't know what it means, write a 1. If you think you know what the word means, write a 2. If you know the word and can use it in a sentence, write a 3.

If you wrote a 0 or 1, look up the word in the Glossary at the back of the book. Then, after reading the chapter, look at these words again and rate them in the "After-Reading Ratings" column.

If you come across new words in the chapter that are not on this list, underline them or write them in your notebook, and look them up in your dictionary. This will help you increase your vocabulary.

Before-Reading Ratings	Vocabulary Words	Pronunciation Guide (How do I say this word?)	After-Reading Ratings
	graphics	ˈgra-fikz	
	caption	ˈkap-shən	
	keys	ˈkēz	
	legends	ˈle-jəndz	
	trends	ˈtrendz	
	data	ˈdā-tə	
	table	ˈtā-bəl	
	headings	ˈhe-diŋz	
	flowchart	ˈflō-ˌchärt	
	timeline	ˈtīm-līn	
	bar graph	ˈbär ˈgraf	

Before-Reading Ratings	Vocabulary Words	Pronunciation Guide (How do I say this word?)	After-Reading Ratings
	units	'yü-nətz	
	line graphs	'līn 'grafs	
	map	'map	
	special-purpose map	'spe-shəl 'pər-pəs 'map	
	thematic map	thi-'ma-tik 'map	
	political map	pə-'li-ti-kəl 'map	
	physical map	'fi-zi-kəl 'map	
	scale	'skāl	

A good map is both a useful tool and a magic carpet to faraway places.

Anonymous

Before people could write, they used pictures to express ideas. The pictures were tools used to show others how new things or places looked. Today, we use both words and pictures to communicate ideas. **Graphics** organize information visually. As you remember from the "Learning Tip" in Chapter 1, some people are visual learners. They learn more easily if they can see information in graphic form. Graphics include different kinds of charts, graphs, and maps. You may think that graphics are hard to read. In this chapter, you'll see that reading graphics is fast and easy once you learn how. This is because graphics help you read and remember visual details.

Finding Main Ideas in Graphics

As you already know, it is important to find main ideas when you are reading. It is also important to find main ideas in graphics. Graphics show information visually. This visual information forms the *context* for graphics. (Look back at Chapter 5 if you need to review context.) Thus, reading graphics is similar to reading written words.

A good place to start with any graphic is the title or **caption**. A graphic's title tells the subject. A caption is a sentence which tells something about the graphic. Graphics have labels and headings that name information. They also have **keys** or **legends** that tell what symbols mean. These highlight key details about the graphic. It's important that you think about why the author is using a graphic. For instance, an author might use a graphic to help you see relationships clearly. Table 11.1 gives steps in reading all types of graphics.

Table 11.1 Steps in Reading Graphics

1. Decide why you think the author included the graphic.
2. Read the title. Look at the labels, headings, key, or legend. Use these to find the graphic's main idea. Note the main idea in the margin of your book or in your text notes.
3. Check your understanding with your text or instructor.

Charts: Analyzing Concepts

Charts reduce and simplify information. They can show a lot of information in an easy-to-understand format. Common types of charts are tables, flowcharts, and timelines. Charts help you compare features. They organize information by topic, order, or time. They stress key points. They show **trends.** Trends show movement of **data** (factual information). For instance, data amounts could increase, decrease, or stay the same.

A **table** is one form of chart. Tables show relationships among details. They put information into rows and columns. A row runs from left to right across the page. A column runs from top to bottom on the page. **Headings** tell what the rows or columns contain. Tables show specific details of what is being compared. For instance, look at Figure 11.1. It is an instructor's gradebook. By looking at the items in the table, you can compare one student with another. Or, you can compare how one student did on several tests. Table 11.2 shows steps in reading tables.

Another example of a chart is a **flowchart.** Flowcharts show the order of steps in a complex or hard-to-understand process. Arrows show the route through the steps. Text within circles, boxes, or other shapes tell what happens at each step. Flowcharts also show relationships. They show how pieces of information are above, at the same level, or below each other. A **timeline** is a flowchart that shows the order of events. You will often see timelines in history textbooks. For instance, a history timeline might show all the major events in American history from 1960 to 2004. Figure 11.2 shows a flowchart of steps in college registration, and Figure 11.3 shows a timeline for registration. Table 11.3 tells how to follow a flowchart.

Instructor's Gradebook, Fall Semester

Name	Date				
	10/07 Test 1	10/14 Test 2	10/21 Test 3	10/28 Test 4	11/14 Test 5
Galvez, L.	—	61	71	75	81
Grant, R.	98	80	80	72	65
Long, V.	90	81	93	60	—
Monroe, R.	70	71	81	86	93
Moore, S.	48	0	59	73	68
Smith, B.	88	74	81	79	0
Wells, S.	65	53	81	79	70

Figure 11.1   Example of a Table

Table 11.2   Steps in Reading Tables

1. When you read about a table in your textbook, find its purpose before turning to it. What does the author want you to know from the table? In this chapter, the authors want you to see an example of a table.

2. Read the title. This tells the table's subject. In Figure 11.1, the title is "Instructor's Gradebook, Fall Semester."

3. Identify what the table shows. Look at the table's headings. These tell what and how items are compared. In Figure 11.1, the headings are *Name, Date, Test 1, Test 2, Test 3, Test 4,* and *Test 5.* A table shows the quantity (how much) or quality (what kind) of a feature. You can see what grades are recorded and which ones aren't. In this example, the numbers mean that the test was taken. A dash shows that the test was not taken.

(continued)

Table 11.2   Steps in Reading Tables (*continued*)

4. Note any general trends (how data changes over time). For example, look at how the grades for Galvez and Grant change over time. Grant's grades show a downward trend, whereas Galvez's grades show a positive trend.

5. Reread the section of the text that refers to the table. Make sure you understand what you need to know about it.

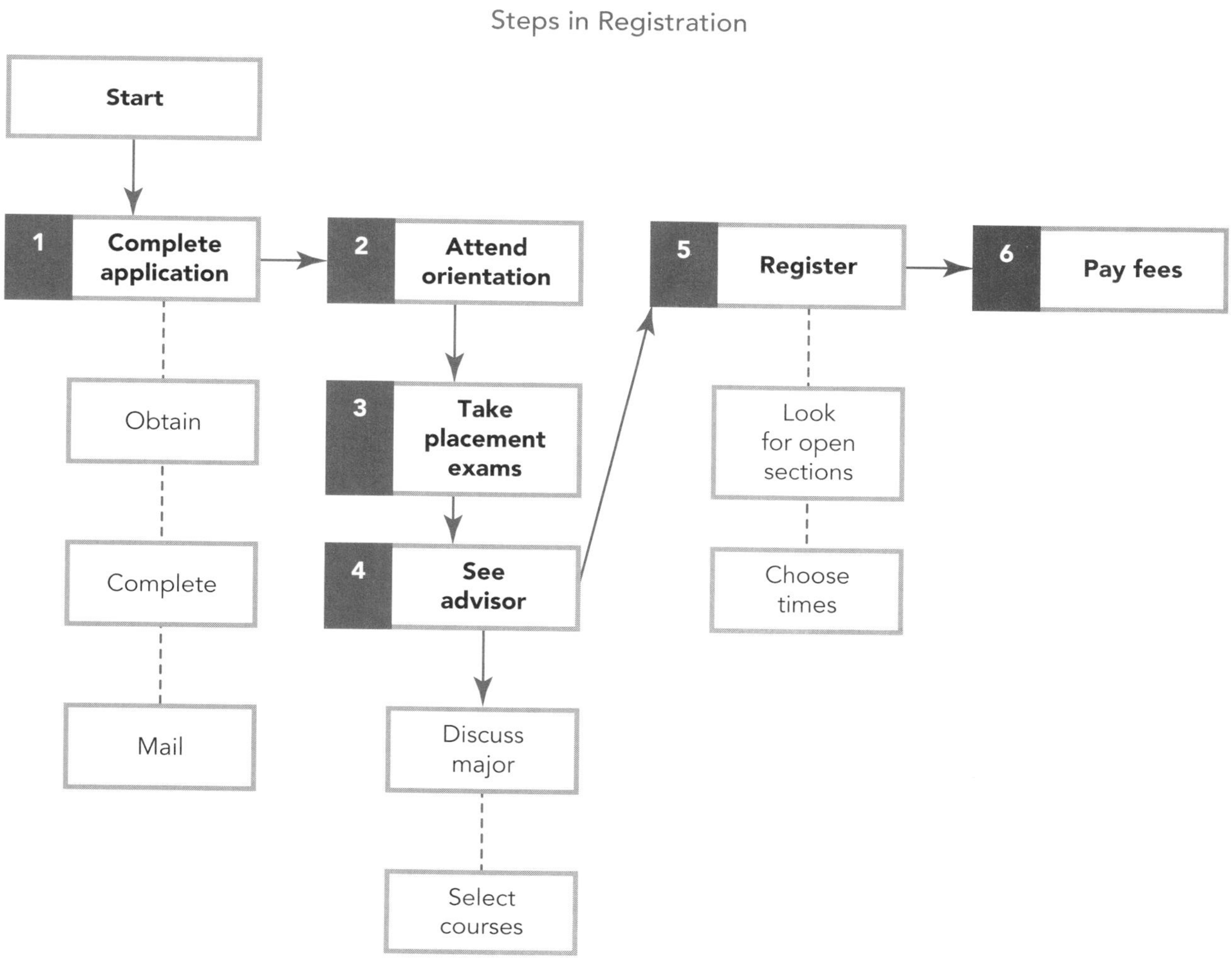

Steps in Registration

Figure 11.2   Example of a Flowchart

Table 11.3 Steps in Reading a Flowchart

1. Find the author's purpose before turning to the flowchart. Does the author point out key facts or trends? You might find a flowchart like Figure 11.2 in your student handbook. The author's purpose is for you to understand how to register for class.
2. Turn to the flowchart. Use the author's purpose to look at it.
3. Look at the title. This tells the subject. Note the starting and ending points. In Figure 11.2, the title is "Steps in Registration." It begins with "1: Complete application" and ends with "6: Pay fees."
4. Look at the steps within the flowchart. These help you know how complex the process is. Look at the total number of steps. In general, the more steps in the process, the more complex it is. Then, look at what the steps involve. For instance, in this example, steps 1, 4, and 5 involve completing several tasks. Processes with multiple tasks at each step are more complex.
5. Reread the section of the text that talked about the flowchart. Make sure you understand what the author wanted you to see.

Timeline for Admission and Orientation	
May 1	Applications for admission due
June 1	Notice of admission to college and orientation information mailed
July 15	Orientation Session I begins
July 16	Testing for Math and English placement
July 22	Orientation Session II begins
July 23	Testing for Math and English placement
July 30	Freshman Convocation
September 1	School begins

Figure 11.3 Example of a Timeline

Table 11.4 Steps in Following Timelines

1. Identify the author's purpose before turning to the timeline. For instance, does the author want you to note specific events or time periods? Use the purpose to focus on specific areas of the graphic.
2. Look at the title or caption. This tells you what time period is being covered. The title for Figure 11.3 tells you this is a timeline for the admission and orientation period.
3. Note the starting and ending dates on the timeline. In this example, the timeline goes from May 1 to September 1.
4. Note any trends or breaks in trends. For instance, in the example, only one task occurs in May, June, and September. The trend for July, however, is different. Tasks occur every few days.
5. Draw conclusions about the timeline. For instance, in the example, you could conclude that the month of July will require the most time and effort.
6. Reread the section of the text that referred to the timeline. Make sure you understand the points and relationship noted by the author.
7. If you are looking at the timeline as part of a chapter overview, now continue previewing the chapter.

Graphs: Drawing on Data

Graphs both show and inform. They organize large amounts of data. Graphs compare data for two or more sets of information. Look at Table 11.5 and read the steps for reading graphs.

A common type of graph is a **bar graph**, shown in Figure 11.4 on page 261. Bar graphs compare amounts for an item. The **units** used to measure items must be the same. They could be dollars, miles, pounds, years, and so forth. For large units, a bar graph might show estimated (approximate) rather than exact amounts. A bar graph might compare how much college textbooks cost in 2005 compared to 1975. Or, a bar graph might show the growth in the U.S. population between 1900 and 2000.

Take a look at Figure 11.4, which shows how often a college website is accessed each day. Two labels appear on this chart. The bottom of the chart is labeled "Day of Week." Each bar is labeled for a certain day. The

Table 11.5   Steps for Reading Graphs

1. Identify the graph's purpose before turning to it. Does the author want you to note facts, generalizations, or trends?
2. Turn to the graph. Use what the text has to say about the graph to look at it.
3. Read the title, heading, or caption. This tells the group of objects being compared.
4. Note labels or headings. This tells the specific objects being compared.
5. Look at the size of the units used to measure items.
6. Note general trends. What does the information tell you?
7. Reread the part of the text that referred to the graph. Make sure you understand the points and relationships noted by the author.

left-hand side of the chart is labeled "Number of Hits per Day." In this graph, the units start at 500. Each unit equals 500 hits. So, if you wanted to know how many times the website was accessed on Wednesday, you would find the label for Wednesday on the bottom of the graph. Then, where the bar for that day stops, you would read across to the left to find the number. What trends can you see about this information? You can tell that most access occurs on Mondays and Tuesdays. The least amount of access occurs on the weekends.

Line graphs are another common type of graph. Line graphs, like bar graphs, compare data. Take a look at Figure 11.5. The title, "Comparison of Website Hits for Different Weeks of a Term," tells the main idea of the graph. Instead of separate bars for each amount, amounts are shown as points on the line. The lines connect them so you can see the patterns. The units in this graph start at 500. Each unit represents 500 hits. Like the bars in a bar graph, lines may show an increase, decrease, or no change in value. But, unlike bar graphs, some line graphs show more than one line. For example, Figure 11.5 compares the number of times a college website is accessed each day for three different weeks in a term. What trends can you see about these weeks? The website is accessed more often during the middle of the semester. It is accessed least during finals week. The website is accessed least on Saturdays. This might be useful information for a

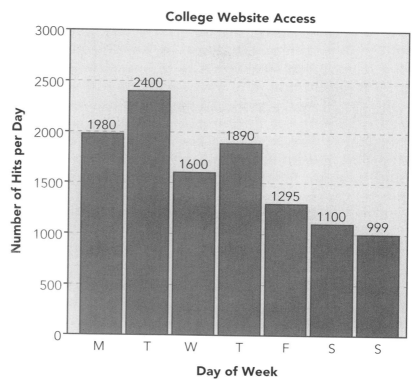

Figure 11.4   Example of a Bar Graph

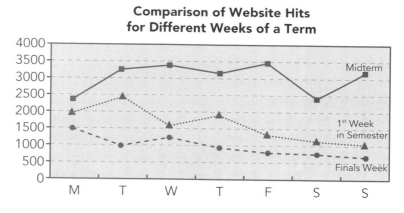

Figure 11.5   Example of a Line Graph

computer center that is hiring people to work on a help desk. Fewer people could be hired for weekend hours than for weekday hours. If the computer center needed to disrupt service for maintenance, Saturday would be the best day to do so.

EXERCISE 11.1 **You will find graphics in a variety of sources, including articles.** Read the following essay about how colleges use tuition money and answer the questions that follow it.

WHERE *DOES* THE MONEY GO?

1 Do you ever wonder what colleges do with your fees? The National Association of College and University Business Officers (NACUBO) is trying to figure out how much it costs to teach students. They plan to look at everything from instructor pay to the cost of heating and cooling buildings.

2 NACUBO surveyed over 150 schools of all sizes. You may be surprised at what they found. **Survey** results show that most schools spend more on students than the amount of tuition that students pay. How can this be?

3 Education is funded by more than what you and other students pay. **Federal,** state, and local governments also provide money for your education. **Donations** play a role, too. This is important because the price of education is increasing.

4 According to the National Center for Education Statistics (NCES), this means you have to borrow more money to go to school (see Figure 1). This is true whether you attend a public or a private school (see Figure 2).

5 How much, then, does your education cost? Table 1 shows you an answer. You are getting a bargain in terms of how much you learn and how much you pay!

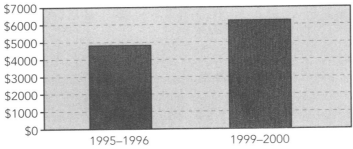

Figure 1 Comparison of Average Undergraduate Federal Loans and Grants, 1995–1996 and 1999–2000

© MMI CBS Worldwide Inc. and the Associated Press. All rights reserved.

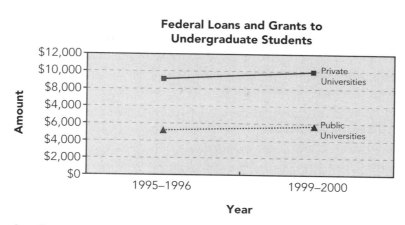

Figure 2 Comparisons of Federal Student Loan Increases at Public and Private Colleges, 1995–1996 and 1999–2000

Table 1 Comparison of Actual Costs of Education and Tuition and Differences between Tuition and Costs

Institution	Costs	Tuition	Difference
Community Colleges	$5000–9000	$2000	$3000–7000
Public Universities	$7000–15,000	$3000–5000	$4000–10,000
Private Four-Year Colleges	$10,000–40,000	$10,000–20,000	$0–20,000

VOCABULARY

These vocabulary words are boldfaced in the section you just read. Answer each question that follows. For words you do not know, check your dictionary.

1. A *survey* is _____.
   A. a way to collect information
   B. a source of funding
   C. a special fee
   D. paid for by tuition

2. *Federal* loans and grants come from _____.
   A. student fees
   B. private funds
   C. the U.S. government
   D. state funds

3. *Donations* come from _____.
   A. federal funds
   B. the U.S. government
   C. local government
   D. private sources

VOCABULARY
BUILDER
List three words from the article, other than the boldfaced terms, whose meanings you are unsure of. Look up each word and write its meaning based on how it is used in the sentence. Use the word in a sentence of your own.

1. _____

   _____

2. _____

   _____

3. _____

   _____

COMPREHENSION How much did you understand in the reading? Read the questions below and either circle the correct answer or write your answers on the lines below.

1. What is true of the price of education?
   A. Costs are going down.
   B. Costs have not changed in ten years.
   C. Costs are going up.
   D. You can't tell from the article.

2. Who pays for the cost of a college education?
   A. government
   B. student tuition and fees
   C. private donations
   D. all of the above
   E. A and B only

3. Look at Figure 1.
   a. What kind of graphic is this ? _____
   b. What is the topic of this graph? _____

      _____
   c. What two sets of years are compared? _____
   d. Do you see a trend(s)? If so, what is it? _____

      _____
   e. In what years did undergraduates need more federal loans and grants? _____
   f. What is the difference in dollars from the first set of dates to the second set? _____

4. Look at Figure 2.

    a. What kind of graphic is this? _____

    b. What is the topic of this graph? _____

    c. What two sets of years are compared? _____

    d. Do you see a trend(s)? If so, what is it? _____

    _____

5. Look at Table 1.

    a. What kind of graphic is this? _____

    b. What is the topic of this graph? _____

    c. Do you see a trend(s)? If so, what trend(s)? _____

    _____

WRITING CONNECTION

Respond to the following on a separate sheet of paper or in your notebook.

Which type of graphic is easiest for you to read? Which one is most difficult? What accounts for these differences?

Maps: Physical Locations

A **map** shows places. Maps are found in almost every subject. The **special-purpose map** is found most often in textbooks. This map is also known as a **thematic map**. Special-purpose maps highlight an aspect of a specific place. For example, the maps in both Figure 11.6 and Figure 11.7 show regions in Australia.

Maps can show two types of information. They can show physical features. These are natural features such as mountains or rivers. They can also show political features. These are features related to human populations. Political features include cities, borders between states, regions, countries, and parks. The map in Figure 11.6 is a **political map.** Figure 11.7 shows a **physical map** for Australia.

Notice that the map of Australia in Figure 11.7 is a little larger. Which size is correct? Actually, both are correct. A key or legend shows the **scale** of measurements. For instance, in the key for Figure 11.6, one inch on the map equals 1050 nautical miles. In Figure 11.7, one inch on the map equals 970 nautical miles. The scale helps you estimate size and distance. For instance, you can see that the distance across the Northern Territory in Figure 11.6 equals 0.5 inches. To estimate the distance across the Northern Territory, you would multiply the distance one inch represents (1050 miles) by 0.5. A map key or legend may also include symbols for information on the map. For example, the key for Figure 11.7 shows you that ✪ is the symbol for a capital city.

Regions within Australia

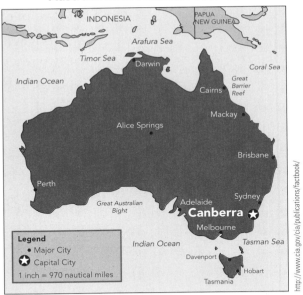

Western Australia

Northern Territory

Queensland

South Australia

New South Wales

Victoria

Tasmania

Legend
1 inch=1050 nautical miles

http://www.cia.gov/cia/publications/factbook/

Figure 11.6   Example of a Special or Thematic Map with Political Features

Australia with Political Features

http://www.cia.gov/cia/publications/factbook/

Figure 11.7   Map of Australia with Physical Features

Table 11.6   Steps for Reading Maps

1. Find the text's purpose before turning to the map.
2. Turn to the map. Use the text's purpose to look at features of the map.
3. Read the title, heading, or caption. This tells the physical location shown on the map.
4. Find the key or legend. This gives you more information about reading the map.
5. Reread the section of the text that referred to the map. Draw conclusions about information provided by the map and the text.

WRITING CONNECTION

Respond to the following on a separate sheet of paper or in your notebook.

Do you think maps are hard to read? Why or why not?

EXERCISE 11.2   **Navigating a new environment—from a college campus to a new city—is an important life skill as well as a critical learning skill.** Look at the map of a college campus below and answer the questions that follow.

LEGEND—
Building Codes

1 Administration
   Building
2 Anne Mooney
   Library
3 Fieldhouse and
   Gymnasium
4 Art Building and
   Federalsburg
   College Art Gallery
5 Campus Bookstore
6 Danielson Child
   Care Center
7 Humanities Building
8 Social Sciences
   Building
9 Science Building
10 Performing Arts
   Building

⟨E⟩ Entrance

Ⓟ   Parking

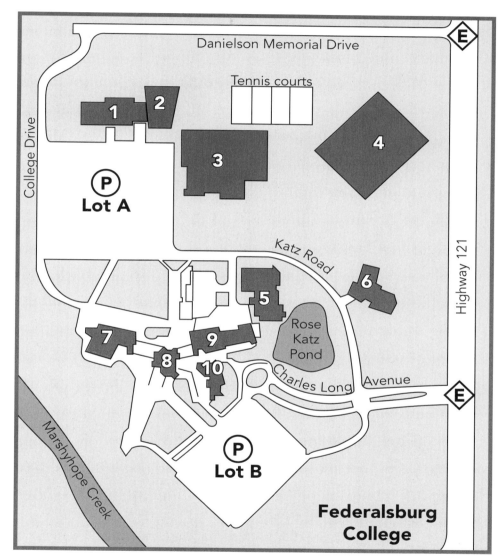

1. What is the main highway leading to the college? _____

_____

2. List the buildings that surround the Social Sciences Building. _____

_____

_____

3. Why are the tennis courts located near building 3? _____

_____

4. Where would you suggest a friend park if she has a class in the
Science Building? _____

5. Where could you see an art exhibit on this campus? _____

_____

6. If you had young children, where might they go for daycare?

_____

7. Two bodies of water are named on this map. Identify them.

_____

8. Where would you buy books at Federalsburg College? On what street
is the bookstore? _____

9. You are giving a friend directions to Lot B. He can enter the college
campus in two places. Give him directions to Lot B from each
entrance. _____

_____

_____

10. What two items are identified on the map by letters? _____

_____

QUICK REVIEW

Circle the correct answer. Check your answers at the bottom of the page
before reading the next section.

1. Bar graphs are more exact than line graphs. **T**   **F**

2. Special-purpose maps are also called thematic maps. **T**   **F**

3. A timeline is a special type of line graph. **T**   **F**

4. Graphics organize information visually. **T**   **F**

Quick Review Answers: 1. F   2. T   3. F   4. T

LEARNING TIP

Using Graphics to Organize Information

You, too, can use graphics to organize what you need to learn. Making your own graphics makes learning more active. It lets you use different *learning styles*. (See the "Learning Tip" in Chapter 1 if you need to review learning styles.) As you connect ideas on paper, you make connections in your mind. This helps you understand more clearly. This also helps you remember information more easily.

For example, perhaps you are studying for a history test. You could make your own timeline of important dates. You would list the dates. Then, you would place them in order on a line from left to right:

1492	1624	1776	1803	1860
▲	▲	▲	▲	▲
Columbus	Pilgrims	Declaration of Independence	Louisiana Purchase	Civil War

Or, if you were writing a comparison/contrast paper about apples and oranges, you could use a diagram to help you join and separate your facts. The information in the left circle is about oranges. The information in the right circle is about apples. The overlapping part contains information that applies to both apples and oranges.

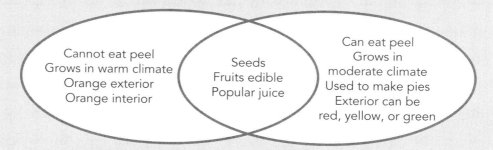

You could use a table to help you organize information for a psychology course. The following table compares two theories of personality.

	Psychodynamic Theory	Trait Theory
associated with . . .	Freud	Allport; Cattell
key terms	id, ego, superego, defense mechanisms	surface traits; source traits
definition	forces move through the personality and determine behavior	aspects of personality that are inferred from behavior
weaknesses of theory	overemphasis on sexuality and underemphasis on social relationships; possible biases in collecting evidence	descriptive theory but not explanatory; situational variability

You can even create your own maps of ideas. These are called *idea maps* or *concept maps*. To create this kind of map, you first choose a topic. Next, you locate and list details about the topic. Then, you look at what you have. You think of ways to organize the details into groups. You add labels that identify the groups. Some students find writing details on small "sticky notes" to be helpful in arranging ideas. For example, you might list information about your college, then arrange it in a concept map like the one opposite.

football team	*professors*	*Memorial Stadium*	*Baker Hall*
Student Union	*fraternities/sororities*	*students*	*majors*
Boyd Hall	*classes*	*grades*	*graduation*
Graham Hall	*studying*	*bookstore*	

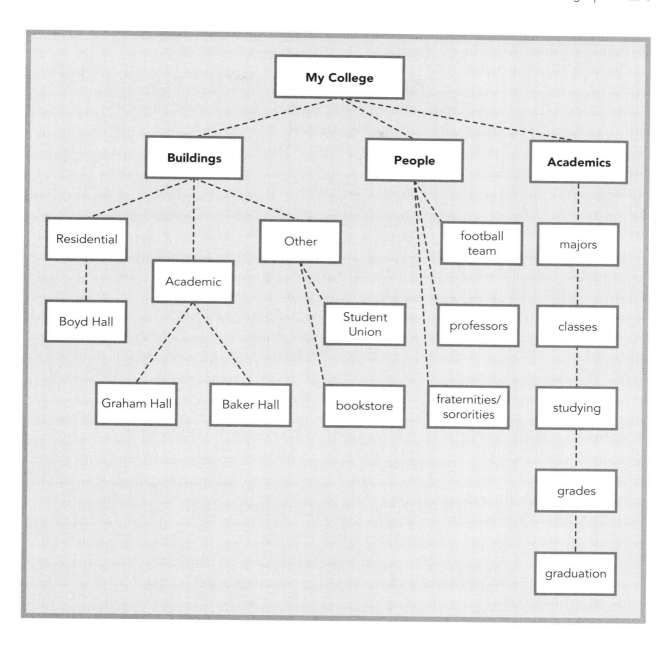

CHAPTER SUMMARY

1. Graphics show key concepts visually.
2. Charts (tables and flowcharts) organize and simplify data.
3. Graphs (bar and line) compare information.
4. Maps provide information about physical locations.

CHAPTER REVIEW

On a separate sheet of paper, answer briefly but completely.

1. List three reasons why graphics are important to understanding.
2. Why would having graphics as well as text information be more helpful than having just one or the other?
3. How do bar graphs differ from line graphs?
4. What do special-purpose maps show?
5. What does scale show on a map?
6. What is the purpose of keys or legends in reading graphs or maps?

ACTION SUMMARY

- Which ideas from this chapter do I already use?

  _____

  _____

- Which ideas from this chapter are new to me?

  _____

  _____

- The best idea I learned from this chapter is . . . . Why?

  _____

  _____

- The ideas from this chapter I would like to try are . . . .

  _____

  _____

- How will I put the new ideas I've learned in action?

  _____

  _____

LEARNING ONLINE

Go to http://developmentalenglish.wadsworth.com/atkinson-longman to find the website for *Reading Strategies for Today's College Student*. This website is designed for students using this book. Here you will find:

- fun and interesting websites related to reading
- web exercises and reading quizzes that will help you become a better reader
- a list of chapter objectives
- a glossary of terms used in the chapter
- flashcards
- crossword puzzles

CHAPTER VOCABULARY REVIEW

Go back to the "Vocabulary Check" at the beginning of the chapter. Now that you've read this chapter, rate how well you understand the vocabulary words in the "After-Reading Ratings" column. If you rate any word less than a 3, read the information about that term again.

CHAPTER 12

Using Online Information

OBJECTIVES

After you finish this chapter, you should be able to

- List features of the Internet and the World Wide Web
- Identify how online reading differs from print reading
- Tell how to use search strategies and tools
- Explain how to judge the relevance and content of online information
- Summarize and synthesize information
- Use electronic features of your campus

CHAPTER OUTLINE

CHAPTER MAP

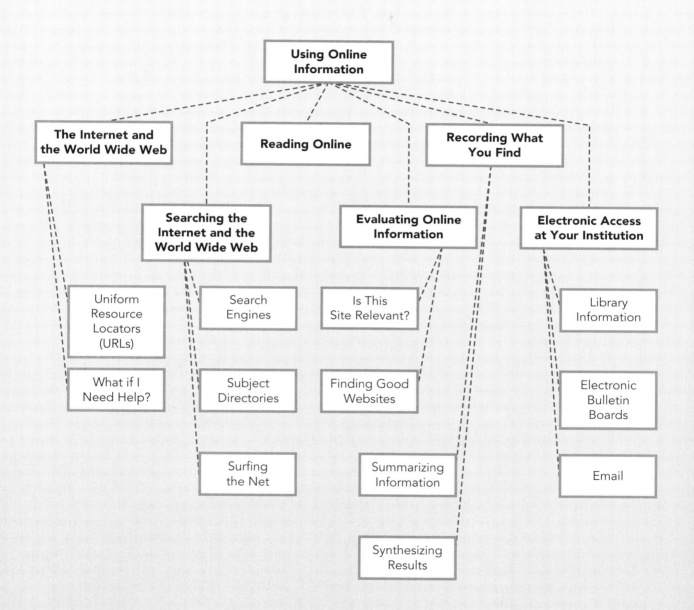

Using Online Information

The Internet and the World Wide Web

Reading Online

Recording What You Find

Searching the Internet and the World Wide Web

Evaluating Online Information

Electronic Access at Your Institution

Uniform Resource Locators (URLs)

What if I Need Help?

Search Engines

Subject Directories

Surfing the Net

Is This Site Relevant?

Finding Good Websites

Summarizing Information

Synthesizing Results

Library Information

Electronic Bulletin Boards

Email

VOCABULARY CHECK

Below are the vocabulary words you will need to know in this chapter.

If you see a word that's brand-new to you, write a 0 in the "Before-Reading Ratings" column. If you have seen the word before but don't know what it means, write a 1. If you think you know what the word means, write a 2. If you know the word and can use it in a sentence, write a 3.

If you wrote a 0 or 1, look up the word in the Glossary at the back of the book. Then, after reading the chapter, look at these words again and rate them in the "After-Reading Ratings" column.

If you come across new words in the chapter that are not on this list, underline them or write them in your notebook, and look them up in your dictionary. This will help you increase your vocabulary.

Before-Reading Ratings	Vocabulary Words	Pronunciation Guide (How do I say this word?)	After-Reading Ratings
	Internet	'in-tər-ˌnet	
	World Wide Web	'wər(-ə)ld 'wīd 'web	
	websites	'web-sīts	
	web pages	'web 'pāj-ez	
	hyperlinks	'hī-pər-liŋks	
	URL	ˌyü-(ˌ)är-'el	
	surf	'sərf	
	search engines	'sərch 'en-jənz	
	subject directories	'səb-jikt də-'rek-t(ə-)rēz	
	navigate	'na-və-ˌgāt	
	scroll	'skrōl	

Before-Reading Ratings	Vocabulary Words	Pronunciation Guide (How do I say this word?)	After-Reading Ratings
	relevant	're-lə-vənt	
	jargon	'jär-gən	
	summarize	'sə-mə-ˌrīz	
	synthesize	'sin(t)-thə-ˌsīz	
	netiquette	'ne-ti-kət	

> **When I took office, only high-energy physicists had ever heard of what is called the World Wide Web. . . . Now even my cat has its own page.**
>
> *Bill Clinton*
>
> Forty-second President of the United States

Not long ago, textbooks, some paper, and a pen or pencil were all you needed for class. Today you need much more. Computers have become a part of our daily lives. College students need to be familiar with them. Students also need to know how to use the Internet and the World Wide Web. You need to know the language of computers and the Internet. You need the right skills so you can search online for what you want. Once you find it, you need the skills to decide if that information is useful. You must be able to summarize what you find. You need to keep a record of where the information came from. Lastly, you must be able to find electronic resources on your campus. Your academic success may depend on your skills in using them. In this chapter, you will learn about each of these skills.

The Internet and the World Wide Web

The **Internet** (or the Net, as it is sometimes called) is a worldwide network (or group) of computers that are all linked together. Some are educational. These include computers from colleges and universities. Some are owned by governments. Some are used in business. Some are personal computers. Part of the Internet is called the **World Wide Web,** the Web, or WWW. It contains **websites.** These are made up of pages called **web pages.** Web pages use special links called **hyperlinks.** Hyperlinks let you jump to other information. The information could be in the same website or in a new one. Web pages provide information in many forms, such as text, pictures, audio clips, and video.

The Web has information that was once only found in libraries or museums. It can be a great way to learn about the world without leaving home. You can learn more about topics that interest you. You can learn about topics that you didn't even know existed. On the Web you can:

- read the newspaper from almost any city, state, or country
- look up your ancestors' history
- find online quizzes for your textbooks
- check the weather in Paris, Texas, or Paris, France
- explore the Rock and Roll Hall of Fame or the Whitney Museum of American Art
- learn about the history of popcorn
- learn how to build a house out of straw
- play online checkers with someone at two o'clock in the morning
- take a college course in the biology of insects
- buy tickets for a movie theater in your neighborhood
- research the requirements for the job of your dreams

Uniform Resource Locators (URLS)

How does your computer know where to find what it's looking for? Each website gets a unique, or one-of-a-kind, address called a Uniform Resource Locator, or **URL** for short. When you enter the URL in your Web browser (the software used to find Web pages), it's sort of like dialing a phone number. When you dial a phone number, you are connected to the person you are calling. When you type in a URL and hit "Go," your computer connects you to that Web address. Internet addresses are often said aloud. To do so, you say the letters, words, or names in the address. A period is said as *dot*. A slash (/) is called *backslash*. For instance, you say *http://www.the name of your college.com* as: *H, T, T, P, colon, backslash, backslash, W, W, W, dot, the name of your college, dot, com*. Sometimes people leave out the "http://" when speaking an address aloud, assuming that you will understand.

As a student, you'll use the Internet in many ways. You will find information on it. You'll use it to complete homework. You may use it most often to contact faculty and other students. Many instructors have a web page where they post information like office hours, their classes, and their syllabus.

What if I Need Help?

But what if you lack computer skills? What if you don't know what to do? Luckily, college campuses have lots of places to help you. You can sign up for a computer course in the Computer Services office or in Academic Services. You can take a Continuing Education class (short courses without degree credit) on how to use the Internet. You may find computer and Internet workshops offered at your campus library. The computer lab is another great place to find help. The people at the help desk there know how to work with computer users at all skill levels. Your instructors or advisor can also help you find the help you might need.

QUICK REVIEW

Circle the correct answer. Check your answers at the bottom of the page before reading the next section.

1. The Internet is part of the World Wide Web. **T   F**

2. Every website has a URL. **T   F**

3. College campuses have computer courses, help desks, workshops, and computer labs to help users at all skill levels. **T   F**

EXERCISE 12.1   **Many words related to computers and the Internet have become a part of our everyday language.** The chart starting on on page 280 has a list of words used about computers and the Internet. Look up each term in a specialized online dictionary like Webopedia (http://www.webopedia.com/) or glossary like Learn the Net (at http://www.learnthenet.com/), a general online dictionary like Merriam-Webster OnLine (http://www.m-w.com/), or search for the term using a search engine like Yahoo! or Google. Match each term with a meaning given in the right-hand column. In the Answer column on the left, write the letter of the correct meaning.

Quick Review Answers: 1. F   2. T   3. T

Answer	Term	Meaning
	1. archives	a. program used to search for, view, and download WWW information
	2. browse	b. the last part of a URL that tells the location of a web page; common U.S. domains are .edu (education), .gov (government agency), .net (network related), .com (commercial business), .mil (U.S. military), and .org (nonprofit and research organizations); outside the United States, domains indicate country: .ca (Canada), .uk (United Kingdom), .au (Australia), .jp (Japan), .fr (France), etc.
	3. browser	c. a company that sells Internet access; may also provide Web page hosting services for individuals, companies, organizations, or other groups
	4. chat room	d. a topic of conversation on a listserv or bulletin board
	5. cyberspace	e. also called a *host;* a computer that provides or "serves" documents on the World Wide Web
	6. domain	f. as a verb, to write a message and place on an electronic bulletin board system; as a noun, the messages on an electronic bulletin board system
	7. download	g. to follow links on a page or to explore without specific direction; also called *surfing*
	8. FAQ	h. web page created by an individual rather than a school, business, organization, or other group
	9. home page	i. abbreviation for *Frequently Asked Questions;* a file on some web pages that answers commonly asked questions about the site or information in it
	10. ISP (Internet service provider)	j. describes being linked to the Internet

Answer	Term	Meaning
	11. listserv	k. computer hardware that lets one computer connect to others over telephone lines
	12. modem	l. an artificial environment produced by a computer; the opposite of physical reality in which objects/people can be seen and touched
	13. newsgroup	m. first screen of a website; usually contains a site map or table of contents to other pages within the site
	14. online	n. general term that describes the virtual existence of everything on the Internet
	15. personal page	o. a special-interest email list that lets large numbers of people exchange information among themselves
	16. post	p. a destructive computer program that sometimes comes with email; it tries to stop normal computer operation or erase information from computer memory, and can sometimes damage the computer
	17. server, Web server	q. virtual place where several people can communicate at one time
	18. thread	r. to take information from the Internet and save to a hard drive or diskette; to transfer information from one computer to another
	19. virtual reality	s. a file of past communications, history, or information
	20. virus	t. a bulletin board system on a particular topic that people view

EXERCISE 12.2 **How confident do you feel about using computers and the Internet?**
Read each statement below. Using the scale below, rate how confident (or not) you feel about computers and the Internet. Write a number next to each statement. At the end of each part, add up your ratings. For example, if your ratings for one part were 2, 0, 1, 3, and 1, your total for that part would be 7. Then follow the directions below each section to figure out your score.

> *0* I cannot do this.
>
> *1* I've done this a little, but I'm not confident about my ability to do so again.
>
> *2* I think my ability to do this is OK.
>
> *3* I do this very well.

Computer Usage

_____ 1. I know how to use a computer.

_____ 2. I can fix problems with my computer.

_____ 3. I recognize most of the terms people use when discussing computers.

_____ 4. I have used a computer on campus.

_____ 5. I use a word-processing program to write essays or reports.

_____ 6. I use basic editing functions (cut, paste, etc.) in a word-processing program.

Computer Usage Total _____ *divided by 6 =* _____

Internet and World Wide Web Usage

_____ 1. I use the WWW almost every day.

_____ 2. I use URLs to find websites.

_____ 3. I can follow hyperlinks from one web page to another.

_____ 4. I know how to move backward and forward within a website.

_____ 5. I can download documents and graphics.

_____ 6. I know how to make a list of favorites sites I visited.

Internet and WWW Total _____ *divided by 6 =* _____

Finding and Evaluating Information

_____ 1. I know what kinds of information are found on the Internet.

_____ 2. I can use a search engine to find information.

_____ 3. I can use a subject directory to find information.

_____ 4. I know how to evaluate (judge) a website to see if its information is accurate.

Finding and Evaluating Information Total _____

divided by 4 = _____

Communication and Email

_____ 1. I can use my college's website.

_____ 2. I can use the campus library's electronic card catalog.

_____ 3. I can use a course bulletin board to get information.

_____ 4. I have an email account.

_____ 5. I know how to send and receive email.

_____ 6. I know the basics of "netiquette."

_____ 7. I know how to attach a document to send to someone via email.

Communication and Email Total _____

divided by 7 = _____

If your score for any section is less than 2, you need to look for ways to increase your skills and confidence.

If your score for any section is 2, you have average or satisfactory skills in that area.

If your score for any section is more than 2, your skills are strong.

Searching the Internet and the World Wide Web

Almost any information you want or need is on the Internet. You just have to find it. You may already know the URLs of companies and organizations that you see in advertisements, magazines, or on TV. For those, all you need to do is type in the URL and hit "Go." But what if you don't know the URL? What if you don't even know what sites you need? You need search tools. They help you look for information in organized ways. Or, you can find a starting point and **surf** for information. Surfing means exploring links as they appeal to you.

How you find information depends on what information you want. So, the first step is to define what you want to know. This forms the topic. Next, you list key terms connected to that topic. You may need to think of synonyms. You may need to know related words for these terms. You use this list of words as *keywords,* words to use in your search.

Defining your topic helps you choose the right search tool. There are two broad types of search tools: **search engines** and **subject directories.** *Search engines* are programs that search for keywords and return a list of the documents where the keywords were found. Some of the most common search engines are Lycos, AltaVista, and Google. *Subject directories* organize information into categories. You search in them by topic. Common subject directories include Yahoo! and About.com. Here are a few things to remember about search engines and subject directories.

Search Engines

If you have a clear topic, a search engine is a good choice. In a search engine, electronic programs create databases (collections of information). They search the Internet for information. Then they collect and sort what they find. So, when you use a search engine, you only see what that one search engine found. That's why different search engines may come up with different results. Your results come in a list of hits. A *hit* is a website that matches your search term. You could get thousands of hits if your search term is very general. Even so, you may not find the exact information you want. That doesn't mean that what you are looking for is not there. It may still be out there—it's just not in that search engine's database. Thus, you should use different search engines. Each gives a different set of results.

You should narrow your topic as much as possible. If not, you could get too many hits, and they may not be what you need. For example, suppose you want information on time management. If you searched on Google using the keywords *time* and *management,* you'd get millions of hits, or 15,500,000, to be exact! You would get some websites for time management, such as time management articles or names of companies who help people manage time, but you also might get websites for time sheets or for getting a job in management. So how do you narrow down your search? Here are a few steps you can try:

1. Some search engines (like Google) let you use symbols to focus your search. For instance, if two or more words must go together, put quotation marks around them, like this: "time management." Then the search engine only looks for those words linked together. If you add additional words, i.e. "college time management," the number of hits declines.

2. Suppose you know you don't want any books on time management. You could use a minus sign (–) to cut this word out of the search. Your keywords would look like this: "time management"–books

3. If you decided you want websites about time management for college students, you could put a plus (+) sign before "college students." You would type: "time management"–books +"college students"

4. If you want to open up your search, you can use a tilde (~) symbol. Putting this in front of a word will ask the search engine to look for synonyms. So if you did a search using ~time ~management, you might get sites with tips on organizing or time scheduling.

5. If those strategies don't work, try using different search engines. Remember, each search engine is a little different. Click on the Advanced Search features to learn exactly what to do for that search engine.

Subject Directories

When searching for broad topics, a subject directory is better than a search engine. To use a subject directory, you browse using topics or keywords. The results have been gathered and sorted by people, not computer programs. These people are often experts in their fields. They look for the best sites for each term. The resulting collection is smaller than that of a search engine and may be more current. Each hit has a sentence or two explaining it, so you can quickly see which ones might be useful.

If you use a subject directory such as Yahoo! or LookSmart, be sure to first think of the broad category in which your information might be. For example, you might be looking for information about your favorite college football team on LookSmart. Your first step is to choose a category. You find categories such as *hobbies & interests, regional, sports,* and *entertainment.* The hard part of using a subject directory is choosing the correct category. Following your favorite team might be your hobby. Your team could be a regional team. Football is a sport. You find football entertaining. But, given your choices and your background knowledge about college football, *sports* is probably your best choice. That choice leads you to another set of choices. It includes *news and scores, all sports, football,* and *outdoor recreation.* You choose *football.* That choice results in another set of choices. Now your choices include *statistics, college football,* and *players.* You choose *college football.* That choice gives you more options. You keep making choices until you reach the information about your favorite team. Some subject directories also can also be searched exactly like search engines. This also gives you a list of hits for your topic.

Surfing the Net

When surfing the Net, you move from one link or page to another without a clear purpose in mind. One of the downsides to surfing the Net is that you may waste time. Without knowing exactly what you are looking for, you spend time reading whatever you happen to find. On the other hand, you may find something unexpected and maybe more interesting than your original topic.

QUICK REVIEW

Circle the correct answer. Check your answers at the bottom of the page before reading the next section.

1. Search engines and subject directories are tools for finding information on the Internet. **T   F**

2. Using search tools let you search in less organized ways than surfing for information. **T   F**

3. Information in search directories is gathered by electronic programs. **T   F**

WRITING CONNECTION

Respond to the following on a separate sheet of paper or in your notebook.

Which do you use more often: a search engine or subject directory? Why?

Reading Online

In some ways, reading online is like reading print materials such as books or magazines. You find main ideas, you look for details, and you draw conclusions.

But reading online materials is different from reading print materials. Print materials have guides such as headings, subheadings, boldfaced terms, and so forth. They help you find what you need in the reading. But anyone can put up a website. What you find may or may not be written well. The page may or may not have an outline of topics. Documents found there may or may not have headings or subheadings. Rarely is there a list of key

Quick Review Answers: 1. T   2. F   3. F

terms. You probably won't find a glossary. There won't be objectives or review questions to help you be sure you have gotten what you need.

Online reading takes more work. Why? First, you have to figure out how to **navigate** (move through) the pages. Print materials are sequenced. You read page 1, page 2, and so on. Web pages have no sequence. You choose the order by clicking on the *hyperlinks*. Because there is no sequence, you might miss information. Second, you can't always see all of the information at once. You must **scroll** (move down) through the text. Third, websites focus your attention in different ways. Bullets (dots or graphics that call attention to information), graphics, and color may show important ideas. But not all web pages use them. You have to skim and scan to find what you want. Fourth, websites often include ads. Some ads pop up while you are looking at a web page. These can distract you. Finally, you've been reading paper documents for years. Reading online may be harder simply because it is new to you.

QUICK REVIEW

Circle the correct answer. Check your answers at the bottom of the page before reading the next section.

1. Reading online materials is the same as reading print materials. **T F**

2. Online text has predictable text guides to help users. **T F**

3. The order of pages in a website help readers make sense of them. **T F**

Evaluating Online Information

Search engines and directories are just tools. What you find may not meet your needs. You are the best judge of what you need. You must also decide if you can trust the information you find on a website. Even good sites can have wrong information.

Once you find a site that seems **relevant** (related to your topic), explore the links in it. As you read, avoid getting distracted. Unrelated information will delay your progress.

Is This Site Relevant?

When you search the Internet, you usually get many hits. Which are important? Which are not? How do you choose the right ones? You can judge importance and relevance in one of two ways. First, when possible, start your search by checking general sources like online encyclopedias or print reference books. They help you find key concepts. As you look at

Quick Review Answers: 1. F   2. F   3. F

other sites, you can compare them with these basic resources. For example, you might be writing a paper on presidential elections. Looking up *presidential elections* in an online encyclopedia will give you basic and accurate information. As you look at other web pages, use this as your standard. Check the accuracy of what you find by seeing if it agrees with your basic information.

The strength of hits is a second way to judge relevance. Search engines rank hits by strength. The first hits are supposed to be the best ones. Sometimes, though, the first few hits don't meet your needs. For instance, suppose you want to know about local beaches. If you use the search term *beaches,* the first few hits may be about resorts with beaches. You'll need to look at the first ten or so hits before you'll know if you've found what you want. If not, you may need to narrow your search by being more specific, like *Delaware beaches,* and search again. Remember, the more specific your search term, the better chance you have of finding relevant hits.

Finding Good Websites

How do you know if the information on a website is correct? First, you should look for the source. The source tells who put the website together. People with real information put their names on their work. The names of the group who sponsors their work may also be there. The site should also tell how to reach the author or sponsors. It should provide a physical address, phone number, or email address. Trustworthy sites often support their information. This could be a list of references. Or, it could be the author's educational or professional background. The credentials (qualifications) of the site's sponsor also let you know its value. For instance, perhaps you find information written by J. Smith as part of the National Aeronautics and Space Administration (NASA) website. Although you might not know who J. Smith is, you know that NASA is a good source of information. You might also see ".edu" in a URL. That means the site is related to a college or university. It will probably have accurate information.

Finding a site's purpose is the next step. Sites give you information. Some sell products and services. Others might be just for fun. Looking at how the author writes often helps you find the purpose. The author of the site could use general, technical, or specialized vocabulary. (See Chapter 7 if you need to review these terms.) If **jargon** (technical language) is a part of the site, that site may be meant for professionals. The way the web page is written also helps you find out its purpose. Is it serious? Does it include specific facts and data? Or is it humorous? Does it provide funny details and ideas? Does it appeal to your emotions? Does the site cause feelings of anger, joy, or sorrow? If so, it may be relying more on emotions than on facts.

Third, you need to know how current the site is. The importance of this depends on your purpose. Suppose you need well-known information. This might include names of all 50 states or a list of the U.S. presidents. Sites of almost any age could provide these. But suppose you need the latest news or research on your topic. Then you need sites with up-to-date information. Sites often show a "last date page updated" note. Checking this date lets you know how new the site's information is. Links within the site also give clues. You can check to see if pages within the site or links to other sites work. If they don't, then the site may be older or less dependable.

Finally, you need to try to check the information's accuracy. One way to do this is to compare what you find on one site with what you find on other sites. Comparing information from the site with books could also help. Another way is to look for facts and data. These are more objective than opinions and generalizations.

Finally, you should look for bias. (Go back to Chapter 10 if you need to review this topic.) Can you tell what the site is trying to lead you to do or believe? Is there a way the author or sponsor could make money from you? If so, you need to be careful. Remember that some people or groups have sites just for these purposes. You need to find additional sites about the same topic. You need to find sites that talk about the issue from different points of view. When you find these sites, judge them for accuracy. You can email questions or concerns to the site's author/sponsor. A reference librarian or your instructor also can help you.

QUICK REVIEW

Circle the correct answer. Check your answers at the bottom of the page before reading the next section.

1. Even good websites can have wrong information. **T   F**

2. A site's purpose helps you determine the usefulness of content. **T   F**

3. Bias can affect the value of information in a website. **T   F**

Recording What You Find

Once you find the information you want, what do you do with it? You have a couple of choices. You can print out the information that you find and keep a paper copy of it. You can also copy what you find on a website and paste it into a document for reference. It is important that you carefully identify any information you use from the Internet. You should always write down:

- the date you downloaded or printed the Web content

- the website's URL

- the author of the website

Quick Review Answers: 1. T   2. T   3. T

- the name of the website
- the name of the web page
- the website's sponsor or publisher
- the date when the site was posted or last updated

If you need to go back to the website later or if you use this information in a paper you write, you will have the information you need.

When you use the Internet, you should never "cut and paste" a research paper you find or purchase a paper from an online source. This is plagiarism. It is a form of cheating, or academic dishonesty. Academic dishonesty is a serious offense. (We'll discuss more about plagiarism in the "Learning Tip" later in this chapter.) Although you can "cut and paste" information for reference, you must then rewrite and revise the information for your own paper. Remember to identify the source in your paper to avoid plagiarism.

Now that you've gathered all this information, what do you do next? You need to **summarize** and **synthesize** your information.

Summarizing Information

Summarizing is much like taking notes in a lecture. When taking notes, you don't write each word. Rather, you write main points. You leave out small details. You might note an example but not its details. In summarizing, you also record main points. But there is a key difference. In summarizing, you record only what's important to your topic. What you record depends on its relevance. You decide what to include. For example, if you looked at nine different websites about the same topic, you could summarize them by writing down the most useful information you learned from each one.

Synthesizing Results

You *synthesize* when you combine your summaries. You begin by rereading your summaries. You look for likenesses and differences. Charts can help you organize them.

To create a synthesis chart, you first list your sources across the top of a page. Take a look at Table 12.1. The sources here are notes from Smith, Jones, Lee, and Thomas. Then, you list vertically (from top to bottom) the features you plan to compare. Table 12.1 looks at types of colleges, their focus (the types of classes/students), how long it takes to get a degree, and the type of degree they give. Now you read the information from each summary. When you find information about a feature, you write it in the chart. Your completed chart helps you see patterns and connections in information. You have synthesized the information from all your sources. Now you can use the chart to write your paper. Be sure to document your sources as you write. Example 12.1 shows how the information in Table 12.1 could be transformed into a paragraph.

Table 12.1   Synthesis Chart: Topic—Comparison of Higher Education Institutions

	SOURCE 1 (Smith 2001)	SOURCE 2 (Jones 2002)	SOURCE 3 (Lee 2003)	SOURCE 4 (Thomas 2003)
Type	community colleges	technical colleges	liberal arts colleges	universities
Focus	entry-level or general education coursework	technical career fields such as nursing, automotive technology, computer technology	mostly undergraduate education with emphasis on the humanities	wide range of programs for undergraduate and graduate students
Time	2 years	mostly 2 years; some 4 years	4 years	4 years for undergraduates
Degrees	associate's degree	mostly associate's degrees	bachelor's degree	bachelor's, master's, some doctoral degrees

Example 12.1   Synthesis Paragraph

What's the difference between schools of higher education? It depends on the level of degree you want, what you want your degree to be in, and how long you want to spend getting it. For instance, community colleges and technical schools often only offer two-year (associate) degrees (Smith 2001; Jones 2002). If you plan to continue your education at a university, a community college is a better choice for an associate's degree. That's because you can complete entry-level coursework there (Smith 2001). If you want a career focus, a technical school might be a better option (Jones 2002). To get a four-year bachelor's degree in humanities, you could attend either a liberal arts college or a university (Lee 2003; Thomas 2003). Bachelor's or advanced degrees are only available at universities (Thomas 2003).

QUICK REVIEW

Circle the correct answer. Check your answers at the bottom of the page before reading the next section.

1. A summary is the same as a synthesis. **T   F**

2. Cutting and pasting electronic information is all you need to do to complete a research paper. **T   F**

3. Charts can help you note likenesses and differences in information from different sources. **T   F**

EXERCISE 12.3 **Plagiarism has always been a problem on college campuses. However, it has become an even bigger problem since the Internet.** Students may plagiarize by accident or on purpose. This academic dishonesty is a problem for both students and faculty. Read the article and answer the questions that follow.

INTERNET HELPS PROFESSORS CATCH PLAGIARIZED TERM PAPERS

1 SEATTLE (AP)—Some years ago, college students began using the Internet to buy, sell, and copy term papers. Now instructors are using the Internet to catch plagiarism (presenting the work of others as your own).

2 "**When the world becomes your oyster,** there are many more chances to get information. There are more chances to cheat," said Gus Kravas, Vice Provost for Student Affairs at Washington State University. "We've had to become more **vigilant.**"

3 A paper on Bill Gates caught the attention of George Dyson. He teaches history of technology at Western Washington University. The words and style seemed too advanced for college students. Gates's age was also **off** by two years. Dyson checked one phrase with an search engine. **Bingo.** Up came a two-year-old paper. It was from a University of Michigan computer science class. "The wording hadn't even been changed," Dyson said. "It really was no mystery to solve."

4 The **extent** of cheating is hard to know.

5 The University of Washington found eight cases of plagiarism this year. It had ten in 1997. It had seven in 1996. "But most plagiarism is handled by instructors or deans. They do not take formal action. These cases, then, are not reflected in the numbers," said Ernest Morris. Morris is the university's Vice President for Student Affairs.

6 Fred DeKay is Associate Dean of the Albers School of Business and Economics at Seattle University. He said plagiarism is rare there. But when it happens it comes from the use of the Internet. Last year, he said, a business **ethics** student was caught taking articles from the Internet.

Reprinted with the permission of the Associated Press.

Quick Review Answers: 1. F   2. F   3. T

7   Faculty have become resourceful. They use seminars, email, and other means to catch cheaters. Some post lists of websites that offer free papers. There are also computer programs to help instructors catch cheaters.

8   Software is offered by Glatt Plagiarism Services of Chicago. It removes key words from essays. Writers must fill in the blanks. Plagiarists get low scores, owner Barbara Glatt said. Another aid to professors is the electronic coding in documents and pictures on some Internet sites. "You may change spacing between words (in a document) just by small amounts. You can put in a one or a zero," said Hector Garcia-Molina, a computer science professor at Stanford University. "A human cannot see it." Many instructors say fakes can be found through attention and common sense.

9   Kevin Laverty is a University of Washington Assistant Professor of Business in Bothell. He gets suspicious (mistrusting) when he sees writing that is more journalistic than academic. "I can often find the stolen article in 15 minutes. That's how much effort students are putting into it," Laverty said.

10   Robert Harris is an English professor at Southern California College in Costa Mesa. He suggests asking students to read from their papers. They should be able to do so without making many mistakes.

11   Web addresses or other unusual text at the top or bottom of the page are another clue. So are gray letters in the copy. These may mean material was printed directly from the Internet. This information comes from Lisa Hinchliffe. She is a University of Illinois librarian.

12   If cheaters steal from multiple sources, they can still be found out. A cut-and-paste document is not consistent. It just doesn't read smoothly. Students may get away with cheating, but they won't get a good grade.

VOCABULARY   These vocabulary words are boldfaced in the section you just read. Answer each question that follows. For words you do not know, check your dictionary.

1. The phrase *When the world becomes your oyster* means _____.
   A. when you are trapped in a shell
   B. when you have anything you want
   C. when you are a cheater
   D. when you have plagiarized a document from the Internet

2. The word *vigilant* means _____.
   A. watchful
   B. illegal
   C. secretive
   D. lenient

3. The word *off* means _____.
    A. opposite of *on*
    B. happens frequently
    C. not right
    D. added

4. The word *Bingo* means _____.
    A. there it is
    B. a game to play
    C. nothing
    D. cheater

5. The word *extent* means _____.
    A. crime
    B. source
    C. cause
    D. amount

6. The word *ethics* means _____.
    A. practices
    B. finances
    C. morals
    D. organizations

VOCABULARY BUILDER

List five words from the article, other than the boldfaced terms, whose meanings you are unsure of. Look up each word and write its meaning based on how it is used in the sentence. Use the word in a sentence of your own.

1. _____
   _____

2. _____
   _____

3. _____
   _____

4. _____
   _____

5. _____
   _____

COMPREHENSION How much did you understand in the reading? Read the questions below and circle the correct answer.

1. Ernest Morris is employed by _____.
   A. the University of Washington
   B. Stanford University
   C. Southern California College
   D. Seattle University

2. What is Barbara Glatt's occupation?
   A. vice provost
   B. librarian
   C. professor
   D. business owner

3. According to the article, which of the following is NOT a way in which faculty compare notes on cheaters?
   A. seminars
   B. email
   C. newspaper articles
   D. discussion lists

4. Which of the following does NOT indicate a plagiarized paper, according to this article?
   A. varied writing styles in the same paper
   B. technical language
   C. unusual text on the page
   D. academic writing

5. Which person is a librarian?
   A. Lisa Hinchliffe
   B. Fred DeKay
   C. Ernest Morris
   D. Hector Garcia-Molena

Electronic Access at Your Institution

Most colleges have public websites that anyone can log on to. Colleges also have other online services. Often these are only for faculty, staff, or enrolled students. Some are general references such as library services or academic calendars. Others let you look at your grades, class schedules, or information for specific courses.

Library Information

Much of the information in a library is in the form of books and journals. But you often use electronic searches to find them. Thus, you need to know how to use the electronic card catalog for your campus.

Electronic card catalogs make searching by author or title easy. You can use many of the same strategies for searching by subject that you use for a search engine or subject database search. Libraries also buy electronic materials like CD-ROMs that contain information about hundreds of topics. Libraries may subscribe to online database services that collect and index information. These resources make it easier for you to find the information you need. Libraries choose these materials for their academic content. Thus, you can depend on their accuracy. The library staff wants students to use the library easily, so ask for a library tour. And don't be afraid to ask questions. They can help you find what you need.

Electronic Bulletin Boards

Some faculty use electronic bulletin boards (special websites). These bulletin boards are somewhat like the ones you find in the hallways at school, except they are online. They contain all sorts of notes and information. Instructors post course information like homework and readings. Some give review questions or lecture notes. You can read these at any time. Students can often post comments in the bulletin board. They can also ask questions. The instructor and other students in the class answer them. Some instructors give tests through the bulletin board. Some instructors lecture online. Others ask students to meet online to discuss topics in a special chat area. There may even be ways for you to check your grades. You need to know how to use the bulletin board of a course before an assignment or a test is due. If you have problems, ask your instructor for help.

Email

Email lets you communicate quickly and easily with faculty, staff, and other students. You can attach assignments, pictures, or other information. Correspondence—the emails you get from others—can be printed or saved. If you don't have an email account, ask your instructor or advisor how to get one. When you get it, you'll also get an email address. The first part will be your user name. The user name is followed by the *at* symbol (@). The second part shows your account's source. This will most likely be your school name. So, your email address might be something like *yourname@communitycollege.edu*. All email messages include the sender's and recipient's (the person who is getting the email) email addresses. A subject line shows the topic. Table 12.2 provides basic **netiquette** (Internet etiquette, or proper behavior) tips.

Table 12.2   Basic Netiquette Tips

1. Don't write anything that you wouldn't say in person. If you write in anger or frustration, reread your message *before* sending. It's better to wait several hours and then reread it when you're calmer.
2. Include your name in the body (the main part of your message) or subject line of your emails to your instructor or classmates. They may not know you by your user name.
3. Write, think, and revise before you send an email. Check your emails for correct spelling and punctuation (periods, commas, etc.) like you would for a paper you are turning in for a grade.
4. Don't write in all capital letters. If you do that, IT MEANS YOU ARE SHOUTING OR SCREAMING!
5. Use the subject line to label the contents of your emails. In other words, give the person receiving your email a hint as to what your email is about.
6. Don't think that email is private. Most electronic communications are stored somewhere on your computer. It is possible that someone could get into your account and read your emails.

QUICK REVIEW

Circle the correct answer. Check your answers at the bottom of the page before reading the next section.

1. Some information at a university website is only accessible by students, faculty, or staff. **T   F**

2. Emails are private and not accessible by anyone but the sender and receiver. **T   F**

3. Netiquette is Internet etiquette. **T   F**

Quick Review Answers: 1. T   2. F   3. T

EXERCISE 12.4   **Every college has a website. What do you know about yours?** Log on to your campus website and answer the following questions.

1. Does the website have a campus map? If so, print a copy or write the URL for the map. _____

2. List five kinds of information provided on the website. _____

    _____

3. Can you access your campus newspaper from the web? If so, list the name of the campus newspaper and the date of the last issue

    available online. _____

    _____

4. Search for campus organizations on your website. List an organization for each of the following: (1) honors; (2) music, art, or athletics; (3) subject specific (such as an association for future teachers); and (4) special interest (such as the Chess Club or the College Republicans).

    _____

    _____

5. Does the website provide an alphabetical listing of faculty and staff? If so, where is it located on the website? _____

    _____

6. Does the website provide information for new or freshman students? If so, what kind of information is given? _____

    _____

7. Does the website list campus offices? If so, write the name of the office that provides information about financial assistance.

    _____

8. Does the website list campus administrators? If so, write the name of the person who is the head of your campus. (Look for words like *president, chancellor,* or *provost.*) _____

    _____

9. Search for one of your instructor's names. How many hits did you find? What kind of hits were they? _____

    _____

10. Does the website have an online catalog? If so, list the name and number of a course that you plan to take next term. _____

    _____

EXERCISE 12.5   **Sometimes you can learn about your campus by comparing it to others.** Log on to your campus website and answer the questions that follow.

1. Locate your campus library home page. Record the URL for the library's home page. _____

2. Choose two other colleges or universities. Go to their websites. Locate the library home pages at each one. Record the URL for each.

   _____

   _____

3. Review the information on the home page for each library. Choose a feature to compare (such as services, staff, links, general information, research tools). On a separate piece of paper, summarize what you find about each feature. Include a reference for each one.

4. On a separate piece of paper, create a synthesis chart for your sources.

5. On a separate piece of paper, write a paragraph that shows your synthesis of the topic. List your references at the bottom of the page in alphabetical order by author.

LEARNING TIP
Avoiding Plagiarism

All Internet information is copyrighted when it is created. This is true whether it contains a copyright symbol (©) or not. The content on a web page belongs to the person wrote it or who put it together. This includes everything from websites to emails.

Information on the Internet can seem so free and easy. Free, that is, for you to use and reuse as if you wrote it yourself. It is easy to cut and paste information from a web page and call it your own. It is also easy to forget to write down the URLs of sites where you find information. But if you use this information as if it were your own, it is plagiarism. It is also plagiarism if you don't tell your readers where the information came from. You need to avoid plagiarism.

Plagiarism is taking another person's words or ideas and presenting them as your own. To prevent it, you cite (identify the source of) electronic materials just as you do print materials. Each source should be cited with the summary.

There are many ways to cite print and online materials. Ask your instructors which method you should use for each class. Internet

(continued)

websites also tell how to cite electronic resources. Such sites include APA Style (www.apa.org), MLA Style (www.mla.org), and Columbia Guide to Online Style (www.columbia.edu/cu/cup/cgos/idx_basic.html). No matter which format you use, you need to include the author (if known) and the web page's title and URL. You also need to note any publication information. This includes the site's sponsor, publisher, the date the document was posted, and the date you found the material. Including these helps you avoid plagiarism.

What happens if you're accused of cheating or plagiarism? In some cases, charges of plagiarism stay between you and your instructor. You get an *F* for the paper or test. However, if your instructor thinks you cheated on previous papers, assignments, or tests, or if the amount of plagiarism is extreme, he or she could refer your case to a formal committee of other students, professors, and/or campus administrators. This committee has the right to suspend you for a semester or more, expel you from the institution, place an academic dishonesty statement on your transcript, and/or refuse you a degree from the department. If you are not sure of the guidelines for plagiarism, you might consider taking your references and a draft of your assignment to your instructor and asking for advice.

CHAPTER SUMMARY

1. Students use the Internet to find information, complete homework, and contact faculty and fellow students
2. Search strategies make finding information on the Internet easier to do.
3. Search engines and subject directories are tools for finding information on the Internet.
4. The usefulness of information in a website depends on its relevance and content.
5. Each source must be accurately summarized.
6. Sources are blended together to form a synthesis.
7. Most institutions provide electronic access to library information, course bulletin boards, and communication.

CHAPTER REVIEW

On a separate sheet of paper, answer briefly but completely.

1. What's the difference between the Internet and the World Wide Web?
2. Summarize the steps in a search strategy.
3. What's the difference between search engines and subject directories?
4. How do you judge relevance of content on websites?
5. How do you judge the validity of the content on a website?
6. Why do you need to judge information on the Internet more carefully than print information?
7. What's the difference between summarizing and synthesis?
8. When are the materials on a website protected by copyright?
9. What is plagiarism? How can you avoid plagiarism in using online sources?
10. Does your community college have electronic bulletin boards for some of its courses? How could you find out?

ACTION SUMMARY

- Which ideas from this chapter do I already use?

  _____

  _____

- Which ideas from this chapter are new to me?

  _____

  _____

- The best idea I learned from this chapter is. . . . Why?

  _____

  _____

- The ideas from this chapter I would like to try are. . . .

  _____

  _____

- How will I put the new ideas I've learned in action?

  _____

  _____

LEARNING ONLINE

Go to http://developmentalenglish.wadsworth.com/atkinson-longman to find the website for *Reading Strategies for Today's College Student*. This website is designed for students using this book. Here you will find:

- fun and interesting websites related to reading
- web exercises and reading quizzes that will help you become a better reader
- a list of chapter objectives
- a glossary of terms used in the chapter
- flashcards
- crossword puzzles

CHAPTER VOCABULARY REVIEW

Go back to the "Vocabulary Check" at the beginning of the chapter. Now that you've read this chapter, rate how well you understand the vocabulary words in the "After-Reading Ratings" column. If you rate any word less than a 3, read the information about that term again.

Appendix of Readings from the College Environment

Reading 1
Campus Voices: Student Poetry

I AM A COLLEGE STUDENT
by Anthony "Art" Arton

I am a *college* student. The college newspaper is the only thing I read.

I am a college student. I only call my family when I need money.

I am a college student. My campus telephone number only has 4 **digits.**

I am a college student. Breakfast is usually after *noon.*

I am a college student. Pizza is a **staple** of my **diet.**

I am a college student. I'm on my own for the first time.

I am a college student. Going "out to eat" no longer involves getting in a *vehicle.*

I am a college student. My college ID looks nothing like me.

I am a college student. I no longer care what I look like when I go to class.

I am a college student. I've been *known* to get *dirty clothes* off the floor and wear them again.

I am a college student. I ask, "Do you have a student *discount?*" wherever I go.

I am a college student. The library is a great place to find a **date.**

I am a college student. **Flip flops** are my favorite *shoes.*

I am a college student. I never make the bed in my dorm room.

I am a college student. Playing *video* games is my only source of exercise.

I am a college student. I sometimes get emails from my roommate.

I am a college student. My first class isn't until after lunch.

I am a college student. I stay up all night to study.

I am a college student . . . and love every *minute* of it!

Reprinted with permission of Anthony "Art" Arton. All rights reserved.

WRITING CONNECTION

Respond to the following on a separate sheet of paper or in your notebook.

Using Arton's format, write your own version of "I Am a College Student."

EXERCISE 1.1

Pronunciation. The words below are italicized in the reading. Draw a line from each word on the left to its correct pronunciation on the right.

1. college		a. klōthz
2. clothes		b. 'mi-nət
3. video		c. nün
4. shoes		d. 'vē-ə-kəl
5. minute		e. 'dis-kaůnt
6. known		f. 'kä-lij
7. noon		g. shüz
8. vehicle		h. 'vi-dē-ō
9. discount		i. 'dər-tē
10. dirty		j. nōn

EXERCISE 1.2

Blends and Digraphs. Sort the following words by their consonant sounds. If the word contains a blend, write the word in the left column of the chart below. If it contains a digraph, write it in the right column. Blends and digraphs can be anywhere in the word. Some words have no blends or digraphs. Some words may have both blends and digraphs. If so, write the word in both columns.

shoes	place	sometimes	nothing	great	playing
student	video	flip flops	class	games	breakfast
ask	get				

Consonant Blends	Digraphs

EXERCISE 1.3   **Vowel Sounds.** Sort the following words by their vowel sounds. If the word contains a long vowel sound, write the word in the first column in the chart below. If it contains a short vowel sound, write it in the second column. If it contains a vowel combination that makes a different sound, write it in the last column.

bed	place	get	looks	date	noon
ask	source	shoes	read	games	

Long Vowel Sound	Short Vowel Sound	Vowel Combination

EXERCISE 1.4   **Identifying Syllables.** A syllable is formed each time your mouth opens and makes a vowel sound in a word. For example, *mouth* has one syllable, *open* has two syllables, and *example* has three. Sort the words below by the number of syllables in each word.

video	library	source	love	every	roommate
discount	favorite	money	family	digits	staple
pizza	care				

One Syllable	Two Syllables	Three or More Syllables

EXERCISE 1.5   **Dictionary Usage.** The boldfaced words below are in the poem you just read. Look them up in your dictionary. For "a.", write the meaning of the word that matches how it is used in the reading. Look at its context for this. For "b.", write another meaning that you find in your dictionary.

1. Pizza is a **staple** . . .

    a. _____

    b. _____

2. . . . number only has 4 **digits.**

    a. _____

    b. _____

3. . . . to find a **date.**

    a. _____

    b. _____

4. . . . of my **diet.**

    a. _____

    b. _____

5. **Flip flops** are . . .

    a. _____

    b. _____

EXERCISE 1.6   **Word Study.** Look up the following words in your dictionary. For "a.", write the etymology (history) of the word. For "b.", write the definition of the word. For "c.", explain how the etymology helps you understand and recall the word's definition.

1. vehicle

    a. _____

    b. _____

    c. _____

2. digits

    a. _____

    b. _____

    c. _____

3. library

    a. _____

    b. _____

    c. _____

EXERCISE 1.7   **Reading for Meaning.** Circle the correct answer for each question below.

1. What is the author's purpose in writing this poem?
   A. to inform
   B. to entertain
   C. to persuade
2. Which of the following describes this college student?
   A. He is majoring in history.
   B. He doesn't worry about his looks.
   C. His room is very neat.
   D. He is physically fit.
3. What is the main idea of this poem?
   A. College students are unique human beings.
   B. College students wear dirty clothes.
   C. College students have no money.
   D. College students change in appearance after ID pictures are made.
4. The author likes being in college. True or false?
5. The author lives on campus. True or false?
6. The author is probably single. True or false?
7. The author likes to get up early in the morning. True or false?
8. The author is not concerned about money. True or false?

EXERCISE 1.8   **Organizing Ideas.** The following statements come from the reading. Decide if they are related to time, communication, appearance, relationships, or money. Put them by number in the correct categories in the chart on page 308. Some may fit in more than one category. Some may not fit in any category.

1. The college newspaper is the only thing I read.
2. I only call my family when I need money.
3. My telephone number only has 4 digits.
4. Breakfast is usually after noon.
5. Pizza is a staple of my diet.
6. I'm on my own for the first time.
7. Going "out to eat" no longer involves getting in a vehicle.
8. My college ID looks nothing like me.
9. I no longer care what I look like when I go to class.
10. I've been known to get dirty clothes off the floor and wear them again.
11. I ask, "Do you have a student discount?" wherever I go.
12. The library is a great place to find a date.
13. Flip flops are my favorite shoes.

14. I never make my bed.
15. Paying video games is my only source of exercise.
16. I sometimes get emails from my roommate.

Time	Communication	Appearance	Relationships	Money

Reading 2
Campus Voices: Campus Newspaper Article

WHAT'S IN A NAME? HOW TO ADDRESS A PROFESSOR IN CLASS

from *The Central Florida Future*, University of Central Florida
by Natalie Rodriguez

1   Mortimer is a graduate teaching assistant. He prefers students to *address* him by his first name. He thinks that it makes him a little more approachable to students. He says that it is more comfortable for him. He has not yet received his Ph.D.

2   His students seem to *agree*. "Using his first name dispels some of the fear students may have. After all, he has a large **body** of knowledge," freshman Patrick Sullivan, 18, said.

3   College instructors differ on how they wish to be addressed. Some do so because they have last names that are hard to say. Others want the respect that comes with earning a Ph.D.

4   Each teacher may choose his/her title in class. But one does not truly become a professor until he or she *earns* a Ph.D. When a faculty member has a doctorate, he or she enters as an assistant professor. Then they become associate professors. The highest **title** is professor. This **rank** is sometimes termed full professor.

5   Using titles sets a line between student and teacher. "There is a difference between a professor and a student," said Ronnie Hawkins, an associate professor. "We are not all on the same level. I have earned my Ph.D. I should be addressed as 'doctor'."

6   Junior Andreina Ramones agrees. "People with Ph.D.s should be recognized as 'doctor' because they deserve that recognition. After all, they went to school for a long time."

7   Associate professor Barbara Fritzsche said that she refers to her colleagues as "doctor." It shows respect.

8   Some instructors do not say to their students or colleagues how they wish to be addressed.

9   Some do not mind how students **address** them. They just want to be treated with respect. Students can show that through *tone* without using any *title*.

10   Freshman Kristen Fricke has not had a teacher say how he or she would like to be addressed. She says that she would *call* a professor by his or her last name even if they didn't say so. "Still, I think it's *cool* when professors don't care how they are addressed."

"What's in a Name? How to Address a Professor in Class" by Natalie Rodriguez; used by permission of *The Central Florida Future*; University of Central Florida, Orlando, FL.

(*continued*)

11   Some students enjoy knowing that some professors do not mind using *their* first name in classes. They do not believe this makes their teachers less professional. They think it makes a more *casual* classroom.

12   Mortimer said it is most important that his students learn. He'll use any trick that could help his students. That includes creating an informal setting. He does this by asking students to use his first name.

13   "Everyone has different styles of teaching," he said.

14   Not all teachers earn the same respect from their students.

15   Hawkins said there is a difference in how students address male and female faculty. She has observed that most male faculty will immediately be addressed "doctor." Female instructors are not.

16   "Women," she says, "have to work harder to earn students' respect." Male faculty are given that respect from the first day. She added that women do not start out on a level playing field.

17   An instructor's title may be a delicate matter. So students should *err* on the side of caution. They should address their instructors as "professor" or "doctor," unless told otherwise.

WRITING CONNECTION

Respond to the following on a separate sheet of paper or in your notebook.

Do you think it matters how you address instructors and professors in the classroom? Why or why not? Cite people from the article that you agree or disagree with.

EXERCISE 2.1   **Pronunciation.** The words below are italicized in the reading. Draw a line from each word on the left to its correct pronunciation on the right.

1. address	a. ə-'grē
2. agree	b. 'er
3. earns	c. 'kazh-wəl
4. err	d. kȯl
5. casual	e. ə-'dres
6. tone	f. tōn
7. title	g. kül
8. call	h. 'ther
9. cool	i. ərn
10. their	j. 'tī-təl

EXERCISE 2.2   **Blends and Digraphs.** Sort the following words by their consonant sounds. If the word contains a blend, write the word in the left column of the chart below. If it contains a digraph, write it in the right column. Blends and digraphs can be anywhere in the word. Some words have no blends or digraphs. Some words may have both blends and digraphs. If so, write the word in both columns.

graduate   delicate   respect   should   everyone

styles   rank   teaching   assistant   address

Consonant Blends	Digraphs

EXERCISE 2.3   **Vowel Sounds.** Sort the following words by their vowel sounds. If the word contains a long vowel sound, write the word in the first column in the chart below. If it contains a short vowel sound, write it in the second column. If it contains a vowel combination that makes a different sound, write it in the last column.

names   freshman   choose   yet   trick

cool   last   how   school

Long Vowel Sound	Short Vowel Sound	Vowel Combination

EXERCISE 2.4   **Identifying Syllables.** A syllable is formed each time your mouth opens and makes a vowel sound in a word. For example, *mouth* has one syllable, *open* has two syllables, and *example* has three. Sort the words below by the number of syllables in each word.

delicate   hard   informal   professor   female   addressed

doctor   truly   same   faculty   colleagues

One Syllable	Two Syllables	Three or More Syllables

EXERCISE 2.5   **Dictionary Usage.** The boldfaced words below are in the article you just read. Look them up in your dictionary. For "a.", write the meaning of the word that matches how it is used in the reading. Look at its context for this. For For "b.", write another meaning that you find in your dictionary.

1. . . . a large **body** of knowledge . . .

   a. _____

   b. _____

2. This **rank** is sometimes. . . . .

   a. _____

   b. _____

3. . . . how students **address** them.

   a. _____

   b. _____

4. The highest **title** is professor.

   a. _____

   b. _____

EXERCISE 2.6   **Word Study.** Look up the following words in your dictionary. For "a.", write the etymology (history) of the word. For "b.", write the definition of the word. For "c.", explain how the etymology helps you understand and recall the word's definition.

1. colleagues

    a. _____

    b. _____

    c. _____

2. doctor

    a. _____

    b. _____

    c. _____

3. faculty

    a. _____

    b. _____

    c. _____

4. graduate

    a. _____

    b. _____

    c. _____

5. instructors (Hint: see *instruct*)

    a. _____

    b. _____

    c. _____

EXERCISE 2.7   **Reading for Meaning.** Circle the correct answer for each question below.

1. Who decides how students will address instructors?
    A. the university or college
    B. administrators
    C. students
    D. the instructors themselves

2. Which of the following is highest in rank?
   A. graduate assistants
   B. full professors
   C. instructors
   D. assistant professors

3. Which of the following is NOT true of instructors?
   A. Female professors generally get more respect than male professors.
   B. Some instructors are better than others.
   C. Instructors vary in their teaching styles.
   D. Instructors depend on their students for feedback.

4. What is the purpose of author of this article?
   A. to entertain
   B. to inform
   C. to persuade
   D. both A and C

5. What is the highest degree a faculty member can achieve?
   A. BA
   B. MA
   C. Ph.D.
   D. BS

6. Which of the following is lowest in rank?
   A. graduate assistants
   B. full professors
   C. instructors
   D. assistant professors

EXERCISE 2.8   **Organizing Ideas.** The following names come from the reading. Complete the outline by placing them under the correct heading. Remember to use capital letters (A, B, C, and so on) before each name you add.

Andreina Ramones   Barbara Fritzsche
Ronnie Hawkins   Mortimer

I. Believes professors should be called by first name

II. Believes professors should be addressed as "Dr." or by last name

Reading 3
Reading from a Government Website

MYTHS AND REALITIES ABOUT GOING TO COLLEGE AS AN ADULT
from the
College Is Possible website, American Council on Education

1   **Myth:** Going to college doesn't pay. *Education* doesn't *translate* into increased *earnings*.

2   **Reality:** Nothing could be farther from the *truth!* The *average* earnings for **bachelor's** degree holders is 50 percent higher than those with a high school diploma. For many adults, the road toward success begins with college.

3   **Myth:** College is for young people. Adults don't fit in.

4   **Reality:** Today, college is for everyone. Forty percent of American college students are 25 years of age or older. This is almost 6 million people. Further, the Department of Education believes that 90 million people take part in some form of adult education each year. This includes *training* and basic education that are outside *traditional* higher education. To serve this market, colleges have structured programs and services just for adult learners.

5   **Myth:** There's no financial aid for adult students.

6   **Reality:** Most student aid programs have no age guidelines. Anyone who shows financial need qualifies. In fact, many of the neediest students are adult single parents.

7   **Myth:** There's no way to juggle parenthood, work, and going to school.

8   **Reality:** The demands of family, work, and school are great in number. Still, many adult students manage. Increasingly, colleges find ways to help students manage their many duties. Classes are offered in the evening. Student services are available at night or over the Internet. Low-cost childcare is provided on many campuses. When choosing a program, adult learners should look into whether the campus has the needs of adults in mind.

9   **Myth:** Unless you live near a college, there's no way to attend.

10   **Reality:** For years, colleges have offered courses in places other than on campus. This includes *extension* campuses. They also offered correspondence and televised classes. Many colleges and organizations now offer courses via the *Internet*. Satellite, video teleconferencing, and other media bring higher education into students' homes and workplaces.

11   **Myth:** Going to school part-time, you'll never complete a **degree.**

(continued)

> 12   **Reality:** One of the ways that colleges have helped adult learners is by devising alternate schedules. These let students complete more classes in the same amount of time. For example, a class may meet four times on Saturday for the entire day. This lets working students take four classes over the **course** of a sixteen-week semester. Adult students also can earn **credit** for workplace training and learning.
>
> 13   **Myth:** Colleges expect you take the SAT or ACT, years after **high school.**
>
> 14   **Reality:** Many colleges have changed *admission* guidelines for adults. They may not require an admissions test.

WRITING CONNECTION

Respond to the following on a separate sheet of paper or in your notebook.

Your 30-year-old friend Ahad is planning to return to college. Write a letter to him explaining the myths and realities of college.

EXERCISE 3.1   **Pronunciation.** The words below are italicized in the reading. Draw a line from each word on the left to its correct pronunciation on the right.

1. translate   a. əd-'mi-shən
2. truth   b. 'trān-iŋ
3. extension   c. tranz-'lāt
4. admission   d. ‚e-jə-'kā-shən
5. traditional   e. trüth
6. training   f. 'a-v(ə-)rij
7. earnings   g. ik-'sten(t)-shən
8. education   h. trə-'di-shə-nəl
9. average   i. 'in-tər-‚net
10. Internet   j. 'ər-niŋz

EXERCISE 3.2   **Blends and Digraphs.** Sort the following words by their consonant sounds. If the word contains a blend, write the word in the left column of the chart below. If it contains a digraph, write it in the right column. Blends and digraphs can be anywhere in the word. Some words have no blends or digraphs. Some words may have both blends and digraphs. If so, write the word in both columns.

farther	truth	offered	degree	education
training	programs	guidelines	translate	correspondence

Consonant Blends	Digraphs

EXERCISE 3.3

Vowel Sounds. Sort the following words by their vowel sounds. If the word contains a long vowel sound, write the word in the first column in the chart below. If it contains a short vowel sound, write it in the second column. If it contains a vowel combination that makes a different sound, write it in the last column.

juggle	take	courses	same	age
aid	week	helped	school	places

Long Vowel Sound	Short Vowel Sound	Vowel Combination

EXERCISE 3.4

Identifying Syllables. A syllable is formed each time your mouth opens and makes a vowel sound in a word. For example, *mouth* has one syllable, *open* has two syllables, and *example* has three. Sort the words below by the number of syllables in each word.

Internet	correspondence	media	complete
adult	serve	young	colleges

One Syllable	Two Syllables	Three or More Syllables

EXERCISE 3.5   **Dictionary Usage.** The boldfaced words below are in the article you just read. Look them up in your dictionary. For Part "a.", write the meaning of the word that matches how it is used in the reading. Look at its context for this. For "b.", write another meaning that you find in your dictionary.

1. The average earnings for **bachelor's** degree holders. . . .

    a. _____

    b. _____

2. . . . you'll never complete a **degree.**

    a. _____

    b. _____

3. Adult students also can earn **credit** . . .

    a. _____

    b. _____

4. . . . after **high school.**

    a. _____

    b. _____

5. . . . take four classes over the **course** of a sixteen-week semester.

    a. _____

    b. _____

EXERCISE 3.6   **Word Study.** Look up the following words in your dictionary. For "a.", write the etymology (history) of the word. For "b.", write the definition of the word. For "c.", explain how the etymology helps you understand and recall the word's definition.

1. diploma

    a. _____

    b. _____

    c. _____

2. televised

    a. _____

    b. _____

    c. _____

3. million

    a. _____

    b. _____

    c. _____

4. adult

    a. _____

    b. _____

    c. _____

5. media

    a. _____

    b. _____

    c. _____

EXERCISE 3.7   **Reading for Meaning.** Circle the correct answer for each question below.

1. What is the purpose of this article?
    A. to entertain
    B. to persuade
    C. to inform
    D. both B and C
2. What is a myth?
    A. fiction
    B. true statement
    C. fact
    D. reality

3. What is the main idea of this article?
   A. Education doesn't translate into increased earnings.
   B. Adults fit in college as well as the young.
   C. Some things adults think are true about college are not.
   D. There are all sorts of financial aid possibilities for adult students.

4. How many college students are NOT adults ages 25 or older?
   A. 40%
   B. 50%
   C. 60%
   D. 80%

5. Which of the following is NOT mentioned as a way to juggle adult responsibilities and college?
   A. correspondence courses
   B. evening courses
   C. Internet courses
   D. on-campus daycare

6. There is less financial aid available for adult students. True or false?

7. Which of the following is NOT a consideration in financial aid?
   A. current financial status
   B. age
   C. number of people in a family
   D. need

8. Colleges offer courses only 5 days a week, Monday through Friday. True or false?

9. You must take the ACT or SAT to attend college. True or false?

10. How much higher can you expect your salary to be if you get an undergraduate degree?
    A. 10%
    B. 25%
    C. 50%
    D. 75%

EXERCISE 3.8   **Organizing Ideas.** The following statements come from the reading. Decide if they are myth or reality. First, write each myth in the chart on the next page, under "Myths." Then write the corresponding reality next to it, under "Realities."

A student must live in or within commuting distance of a campus in order to attend.

Adults don't qualify for financial aid.

Adults don't fit in at college.

Adults must take standardized tests to apply for enrollment, even if they haven't been in high school in years.

Almost half of college students in the U.S. are 25 years of age or older, and even more participate in other forms of adult education.

Anyone who shows financial need can qualify for it.

Colleges offer courses through correspondence, television, Internet, and other media.

Colleges often have programs that help students manage their many duties and provide services at different days and times to meet the needs of students.

Colleges provide credit and classes in a variety of ways to meet the needs of busy adults.

Going to college doesn't pay.

It's impossible to complete a degree if you can only go to school part-time.

Juggling family, work, and school responsibilities is impossible.

Many colleges do not require that adult students take a standardized test for admission.

People that get a bachelor's degree make more money than people with a high school diploma.

Myths	Realities
1.	1.
2.	2.
3.	3.
4.	4.
5.	5.
6.	6.
7.	7.

Reading 4
Reading from Sociology

WHY ROBERT BRYM DECIDED NOT TO STUDY SOCIOLOGY: AN INTRODUCTION
adapted from *Sociology: Your Compass For A New World*
by Robert J. Brym

1   "When I started college, I was 18," says Robert Brym. "I was *confused* by the different courses there. I have now taught sociology for more than 20 years. I have met thousands of undergraduates. I am quite sure most of them feel as I did then.

2   "One reason I was confused was that I didn't know why I was in college in the first place. I knew college could help me get a good job. But, I also thought *college* should provide more than training for an exciting and high-paying work.

3   "High school teachers had told me that college would 'broaden my horizons.' It would teach me to 'think critically.' I wasn't sure what they meant. But, they made me want to know more. Thus, I decided in my first year to take mainly 'practical' courses. I took economics, political science, and psychology. I thought these might prepare me for a law *degree.* I also took a couple of other courses for my 'intellectual' side. These were philosophy and *drama.* One thing I knew for sure. I didn't want to study sociology.

4   "Sociology seemed like **thin** soup with odd ingredients. I had asked a sophomore what sociology was. He told me it dealt with why people are unequal. It looked at why some are rich and others poor. It explored why some are strong and others weak. I came from a **poor** immigrant family in a poor region. I thought sociology could teach me something about my own life. But it also seemed a lot like economics and political science to me.

5   "What, then, was unique about sociology? My growing sense was that sociology was nothing special. This was confirmed when a senior said that sociologists try to *describe* the ideal world. They try to figure out how to make the world a better place. That appealed to my naïve sense of the world's injustice. Still it sounded a lot like philosophy. A junior said sociology looks at how and why people play different roles in their lives. That made sociology seem like drama. Someone said that in her sociology class she learned why people commit crimes. They talked about suicide, homicide, and other deviant acts. That seemed like psychology to me. I concluded that sociology had no distinct flavor all its own. So, I chose to take other courses."

From *Sociology: Your Compass for a New World (with InfoTrac)* 1st Edition by BRYM/LIE. © 2003. Reprinted with permission of Wadsworth, a division of Thomson Learning: www.thomsonrights.com. Fax 800 730-2215.

A Change of Mind

6 "Even so, I took four sociology courses a year. That was because I met a great mentor. My mentor was a special professor I met just before my sophomore year. He made me think about what I could and should do with my life. He shattered some of my deepest beliefs. He started me thinking sociologically.

7   "Specifically, he first put Yorick's dilemma to me. Yorick is a **character** in *Hamlet*. Toward the end of the play, Hamlet finds two gravediggers at work. They dig up the **remains** of the former court jester, Yorick. When Hamlet was a child, Yorick played with him. He carried Hamlet around on his **back**. Hamlet picks up old friend's skull. He talks about the end to which we must all come. Even Alexander the Great, he says, became dust.

8   "This story implies Yorick's dilemma. It is the same problem all thinking people face. Life is finite. To make the most of it, we need to learn how to live best. That is no easy task. It requires study and **reflection.** You need to select high values and goals. College is supposed to give you a chance to do this. Finally, I started to see that college could teach me more than job skills.

9   "My mentor showed me that sociology could show me a new and better way of seeing my world. He said it could point out my place in the world. It could show me how to move through life. It could even tell me how I might *contribute* to the world.

10   "Before I studied sociology, I took little notice of what happened in the world. I thought physical and emotional forces caused them. *Drought* triggers famine. Greed causes war. Hard work leads to richness. Love ends in marriage. Suicide results from depression.

11   "Now, my mentor threw facts in my face that contradicted my ideas again and again. If drought causes famine, why have famines occurred in normal weather? What about groups who hoard or *destroy* food so others would starve? If hard work causes wealth, why are so many **hard** workers poor? And so my questions grew.

12   "My mentor also challenged me to understand the way sociology explains social life. He said sociology was the study of how humans behave socially. He explained that social causes differ from physical and emotional causes. Understanding social *causes* can help explain otherwise confusing facts about world problems. My teachers in high school taught me that people are free to do what they want with their lives. But, my mentor showed me that the social world opens some *chances* and closes others. It opens and closes these chances to some and not to others. Thus, it limits our freedom. It makes us the people we are. We need to look at strong social forces, he said. Sociology helps us to know ourselves. It shows us our strengths and weaknesses. I was hooked. Sociology became my field."

WRITING CONNECTION

Respond to the following on a separate sheet of paper or in your notebook.

Would you consider sociology as a career? Why or why not?

EXERCISE 4.1   **Pronunciation.** The words below are italicized in the reading. Draw a line from each word on the left to its correct pronunciation on the right.

1. confused	a. kən-ˈfyüzd
2. describe	b. kən-ˈtri-byət
3. drama	c. ˈkä-lij
4. contribute	d. ˈdraût
5. college	e. di-ˈströi
6. drought	f. di-ˈgrē
7. degree	g. ˈkȯz-ez
8. chances	h. ˈdrä-mə
9. causes	i. ˈchan(t)s-ez
10. destroy	j. di-ˈskrīb

EXERCISE 4.2   **Blends and Digraphs.** Sort the following words by their consonant sounds. If the word contains a blend, write the word in the left column of the chart below. If it contains a digraph, write it in the right column. Blends and digraphs can be anywhere in the word. Some words have no blends or digraphs. Some words may have both blends and digraphs. If so, write the word in both columns.

school   thus   philosophy   drama   flavor

specifically   skull   drought   richness   explain

Consonant Blends	Digraphs

EXERCISE 4.3   **Vowel Sounds.** Sort the following words by their vowel sounds. If the word contains a long vowel sound, write the word in the first column in the chart below. If it contains a short vowel sound, write it in the second column. If it contains a vowel combination that makes a different sound, write it in the last column.

know	free	skull	place
drought	greed	like	taught
school	will	hooked	

Long Vowel Sound	Short Vowel Sound	Vowel Combination

EXERCISE 4.4   **Identifying Syllables.** A syllable is formed each time your mouth opens and makes a vowel sound in a word. For example, *mouth* has one syllable, *open* has two syllables, and *example* has three. Sort the words below by the number of syllables in each word.

science	degree	goals	suicide	finite
showed	supposed	famine	hooked	

One Syllable	Two Syllables	Three or More Syllables

EXERCISE 4.5   **Dictionary Usage.** The boldfaced words below are in the article you just read. Look them up in your dictionary. For "a.", write the meaning of the word that matches how it is used in the reading. Look at its context for this. For "b.", write another meaning that you find in your dictionary.

1. . . . like **thin** soup with odd ingredients.

   a. _____

   b. _____

2. . . . **poor** immigrant family in a poor region.

   a. _____

   b. _____

3. Yorick is a **character** in *Hamlet*.

   a. _____

   b. _____

4. They dig up the **remains** of the former court jester, Yorick.

   a. _____

   b. _____

5. . . . carried Hamlet around on his **back**.

   a. _____

   b. _____

6. It requires study and **reflection**.

   a. _____

   b. _____

7. . . . might prepare me for a law **degree**.

   a. _____

   b. _____

8. . . . why are so many **hard** workers poor?

   a. _____

   b. _____

EXERCISE 4.6   **Word Study.** Look up the following words in your dictionary. For "a.", write the etymology (history) of the word. For "b.", write the definition of the word. For "c.", explain how the etymology helps you understand and recall the word's definition.

1. suicide

   a. _____

   b. _____

   c. _____

2. lust

   a. _____

   b. _____

   c. _____

3. famine

   a. _____

   b. _____

   c. _____

4. starve

   a. _____

   b. _____

   c. _____

EXERCISE 4.7   **Reading for Meaning.** Circle the correct answer for each question below.

1. Why did Brym first decide not to take sociology courses?
   A. No one could tell him what the class was about.
   B. He didn't know any of the teachers who taught the course.
   C. The course seemed too much like others he was already taking.
   D. The course would not count in his intended major.

2. What is sociology?
   A. the study of how humans behave socially
   B. a combination of economics, psychology, and drama
   C. the scientific study of one person's behavior
   D. a study of the world's problems and how one person can solve them

3. An expert opinion is an opinion you get from someone who is knowledgeable in a field. From whom did Brym get an expert opinion about sociology?
   A. a senior
   B. a junior
   C. a mentor
   D. a sophomore

4. What did Brym first plan to have as a career?

    A. politics

    B. business

    C. law

    D. marketing

5. Which of the following *best* describes Yorick's dilemma?

    A. You need to be buried among friends.

    B. We all die at the end.

    C. Being a court jester pays little money.

    D. Actors die before their audiences.

6. In what year of schooling did Brym meet his mentor?

    A. freshman

    B. sophomore

    C. junior

    D. senior

7. To what animal is Brym comparing himself when he says sociology "hooked" him?

    A. bird

    B. dog

    C. fish

    D. cat

8. What did Brym's high school teachers say college would do for him?

    A. teach him skills for a good job

    B. teach him to think critically

    C. teach him what he needed to be a doctor

    D. teach him a second language

9. What is Brym's profession?

    A. lawyer

    B. economist

    C. professor

    D. psychologist

10. When Brym says he was "hooked," what does he mean?

    A. He would make sociology his life's work.

    B. He would take a senior-level sociology course.

    C. He would go to graduate school.

    D. He would study drought, marriage, and crime.

Reading 5
Reading from Literature: Poetry

WE AND THEY
by Rudyard Kipling

Father, Mother, and Me,
Sister and Auntie say
All the people like us are *We*,
And every one else is *They*.
And They live over the sea,
While We live over the **way,**
But—would you believe it?—They look upon We
As only a sort of They!

We eat pork and *beef*
With cow-horn-handled knives.
They who gobble Their rice off a *leaf,*
Are horrified out of Their lives;
And They who live up a tree,
And feast on **grubs** and *clay,*
(Isn't it scandalous?) look upon We
As a simply disgusting They!

We shoot birds with a gun.
They **stick** lions with *spears.*
Their full-dress is un-.
We **dress** up to Our *ears.*
They **like** Their friends for *tea.*
We **like** Our friends to stay;
And, after all that, They look upon We
As an utterly ignorant They!

We eat kitcheny food.
We have doors that *latch.*
They drink milk or blood,
Under an open *thatch.*
We have Doctors to fee.
They have Wizards to pay.
And (impudent heathen!) They look upon We
As a quite impossible They!

"We and They" by Rudyard Kipling; from *Debits and Credits*, originally published in 1926.

(*continued*)

All good people agree,
And all good people say,
All nice people, like Us, are We
And every one else is They:
But if you cross over the sea,
Instead of over the way,
You may end by (think of it!) looking on We
As only a sort of They!

WRITING CONNECTION

Respond to the following on a separate sheet of paper or in your notebook.

Identify two groups in today's times who view each other as "We" and "They." What stereotypes do they hold of each other?

EXERCISE 5.1   **Pronunciation.** The words below are italicized in the reading. Draw a line from each word on the left to its correct pronunciation on the right.

1. beef	a. 'spirz
2. leaf	b. 'lēf
3. clay	c. 'wē
4. they	d. 'klā
5. spears	e. 'bēf
6. ears	f. 'tē
7. tea	g. 'thā
8. we	h. 'lach
9. latch	i. 'thach
10. thatch	j. 'irz

EXERCISE 5.2   **Blends and Digraphs.** Sort the following words by their consonant sounds. If the word contains a blend, write the word in the left column of the chart at the top of the next page. If it contains a digraph, write it in the right column. Blends and digraphs can be anywhere in the word. Some words have no blends or digraphs. Some words may have both blends and digraphs. If so, write the word in both columns.

| sister | they | agree | horrified | friends | thatch |
| cross | spears | dress | heathen | scandalous | |

Consonant Blends	Digraphs

EXERCISE 5.3   **Vowel Sounds.** Sort the following words by their vowel sounds. If the word contains a long vowel sound, write the word in the first column in the chart below. If it contains a short vowel sound, write it in the second column. If it contains a vowel combination that makes a different sound, write it in the last column.

| good | sea | rice | leaf | grubs | gun |
| tea | milk | doors | fee | blood | thatch |

Long Vowel Sound	Short Vowel Sound	Vowel Combination

EXERCISE 5.4   **Identifying Syllables.** A syllable is formed each time your mouth opens and makes a vowel sound in a word. For example, *mouth* has one syllable, *open* has two syllables, and *example* has three. Sort the words below by the number of syllables in each word.

| auntie | open | impossible | knives | simply |
| horrified | wizards | nice | end | |

One Syllable	Two Syllables	Three or More Syllables

EXERCISE 5.5

Dictionary Usage. The boldfaced words below are in the poem you just read. Look them up in your dictionary. For "a.", write the meaning of the word that matches how it is used in the reading. Look at its context for this. For "b.", write another meaning that you find in your dictionary.

1. While we live over the **way**. . .

   a. _____

   b. _____

2. They **stick** lions with spears.

   a. _____

   b. _____

3. We **dress** up to Our ears.

   a. _____

   b. _____

4. And feast on **grubs** and clay. . .

   a. _____

   b. _____

5. We **like** our friends to stay. . .

   a. _____

   b. _____

6. They **like** Their friends for tea.

   a. _____

   b. _____

EXERCISE 5.6   **Word Study.** Look up the following words in your dictionary. For "a.", write the etymology (history) of the word. For "b.", write the definition of the word. For "c.", explain how the etymology helps you understand and recall the word's definition.

1. wizard

   a. _____

   b. _____

   c. _____

2. scandalous (Hint: see *scandal*)

   a. _____

   b. _____

   c. _____

3. horrify (Hint: see *horror*)

   a. _____

   b. _____

   c. _____

4. ignorant (Hint: see *ignore*)

   a. _____

   b. _____

   c. _____

5. impudent

   a. _____

   b. _____

   c. _____

EXERCISE 5.7   **Reading for Meaning.** Circle the correct answer for each question below.

1. Who are "We"?
   A. people like us
   B. people in our family
   C. people from neighboring countries
   D. people from developing countries

2. Who are "They"?
   A. people like us
   B. people not in our family
   C. people from neighboring countries
   D. people from developing countries

3. What is the purpose of this poem?
   A. to entertain
   B. to inform
   C. to persuade
   D. all of these

4. What do "They" eat?
   A. bugs
   B. leaves
   C. pork
   D. beef

5. When might your point of view change, according to the author?
   A. when you eat under an open thatch
   B. when you climb a tree
   C. when you have neighbors to tea
   D. when you cross the sea

6. Which words mean the same as "impudent heathen"?
   A. rude savage
   B. mean warrior
   C. weary traveler
   D. fine fellow

7. Which of the following is compared to doctors?
   A. medicine men
   B. nurses
   C. surgeons
   D. wizards

8. What is the main idea of the poem?
   A. "We" are better than "They."
   B. "We" are more civilized than "They."
   C. Who are "We" and who are "They" depends on your point of view.
   D. Who are "We" and who are "They" depends on who your family is.

9. What is the tone of this poem?
   A. serious
   B. mocking
   C. refined
   D. wishful
10. The author finds "They" to be shameful. True or false?

Glossary

academic standing   Based on a student's cumulative grade point average (CGPA). If you are in good academic standing, you can enroll the next term. If you are not, you may have to meet certain requirements before enrolling.

acronym   A word made up of the first letter of other words. Acronyms can be used to help you remember information. For example, to remember the names of the Great Lakes, use HOMES, for Lakes Huron, Ontario, Michigan, Erie, and Superior.

antonyms   A word that has the opposite meaning of another word. *Easy* and *difficult* are antonyms.

appendices   The plural of "appendix." The appendices include extra material at the end of a book. The appendices in this book include readings and the exercise answer key.

assumption   A conclusion you make based on the given facts and your background knowledge. You may have no other facts or proof.

auditory learner   A person who learns best by hearing; a type of learning style

bandwagoning   A type of propaganda in which a person, product, or concept is made attractive because it is popular with others; a "join the crowd" theme

bar graph   A type of graph in which bars represent different quantities. The units used to measure items must be the same, such as dollars, inches, pounds, etc.

base   The basic part of a word that gives it meaning. Also known as the root. For example, *bio* is the base of *biology* and means *life,* so *biology* is the study of life.

bias   Opinions, feelings, or beliefs, which shape attitude on a subject

blend   Two or more consonants together in which each consonant's sound is heard, such as the *bl* in the word *blend*

bridging context clues   Words in the text that help you figure out a word's connotation. There are three types of bridging context clues: contrast, comparison, and example.

caption   Tells the subject of a graphic

cause/effect   An organizational pattern that shows that an action or response happened because of an earlier event or reason (cause). It tells what happened (effect). It may also explain why it happened (cause). For example: Because you had to work late and could not study for your history test, you did not get a good grade.

college catalog   A book that includes general school information such as admissions, how to register, majors, and classes

comparison clues   A type of bridging context clue that shows how two or more things are alike. For example: Many students prefer distance learning through television or other media; *similarly,* more and more students like to take courses through the Internet.

comparison/contrast   An organizational pattern that shows connections between people, places, objects, or concepts. Comparisons show how they are alike. Contrasts show how they are different. For example: Both biology and zoology study life forms, but zoology focuses on just animals.

connotation   The meaning of a word based on your experience or feelings. It is the opposite of denotation. For example, the denotation of *home* is a building where people find shelter. The connotation for *home* might be a warm, safe place for a family to live.

consonants   One of the following letters: *b, c, d, f, g, h, j, k, l, m, n, p, q, r, s, t, v, w, x, z,* and sometimes *y.* Consonant sounds are heard when the lips, tongue, or teeth stop the flow of air coming out of your mouth.

context   The words around an unknown word that help you figure out its meaning

contrast clues   A type of bridging context clue that points to the opposite meaning of a word. For example: Math is my easiest subject, *but* reading, *on the other hand,* is my favorite class.

cross-reference   Tells you where to look for more information about a word or topic

culture   The traditions and customs of a group. On a college campus, this can include wearing school colors the day before a football game and the nicknames students give places and professors.

data   Factual information

definition clues   A type of context clue in which linking verbs join the word or words that tell its meaning. For example: The study of the stars *is* called astronomy.

denotation   The exact, dictionary definition of a word or group of words. For example, the denotation of *home* is a building where people find shelter.

details   Pieces of specific information that support or give facts about the main idea of a paragraph or passage

dictionary   A book containing words arranged in alphabetical order. It includes how to pronounce words, their meanings, their histories, and their parts of speech.

digraph   Two or three consonants that come together to form a new sound, such as the *sh* in *she*

distance learning   A type of education where students work on their own, usually at home. They communicate with faculty and other students using email, chat rooms, bulletin boards, video conferencing, and other forms of computer-based communication.

drawing conclusions   Using information to help you understand what is being said or implied

entries   The words in a dictionary or thesaurus. Each word and the information about that word form one entry.

etymology   The history of a word, usually found in a dictionary

euphemism   A type of persuasion that replaces "bad" or unpleasant phrases with "good" or pleasant phrases that can often hide the truth, such as *let go* for *fired*

example clues   A type of bridging context clue that tells you an example of a new word or words is to follow. You use background knowledge to find meaning. For example: Living in a *residence hall*—also known as the dorm—is a good way to meet lots of people.

experiential context clues   Ways to find the meaning of an unknown word by using your own experience and knowledge to help you. You use the word's context to connect your background knowledge to it. Common sense and your knowledge of parts of speech will also help.

expert opinion   The judgment of someone who has knowledge and skill about a particular subject

fact   True details about a topic

faculty   The teaching staff of a school

flowchart   A drawing that shows the steps in a complicated process

general vocabulary words   Common, everyday words

global thinker   A person who likes to see how information works together; a type of learning style

glossary   A mini-dictionary found at the end of some books that includes the meanings of key words

graph   A diagram or chart that organizes information such as bar graphs or line graphs

graphics   A way of organizing information visually with drawings, maps, pictures, or graphs

guide words   Two words found at the top of a page in a dictionary. They tell you the first and last words on the page.

headings   Words that tell what information is found in the rows and columns of a table

homonyms   Words that sound alike, such as *there* and *their*

hyperlinks   A feature in a web page that lets you jump to other information, either in the same website or in a new one

image advertising   A form of propaganda in which a person, product, or concept is associated with attractive but unrelated types of people, places, sounds, activities, or symbols

implied   Unstated; suggested

index   An alphabetical list of items (such as topics or names) in a printed work that tells the page number where the item is found

inferred   Using the facts and details in the text and your background knowledge to draw conclusions

Internet   A worldwide network (or group) of computers that are all linked together, also known as the Net

intra-chapter guides   Used to help guide a reader through a chapter; includes some or all of the following: headings, subheadings, terms in context, boxed information, different typefaces, graphics, and marginal notes

jargon   The specialized or technical language of a trade, profession, or similar group

keys   Also known as legends; tell what the symbols on a graphic mean

kinesthetic learner   A person who learns best by doing; a type of learning style

learning styles   The way in which you think, such as logical or global, or the way in which you learn best, such as visual, auditory, tactile, or kinesthetic

legends   Also known as keys; tell what the symbols on a graphic mean

line graphs   Graphics that compare data for several items over time

linking verbs   Verbs that don't show action but show what something is; used in definition clues and include *is, was, are, am, seems, feels, means, involves, is called,* and *resembles*

list/sequence   An organizational pattern of development that shows key points in one of two ways: either a list where items appear in a random (unorganized) order like a shopping list, or in a step-by-step progression of ideas, like a recipe

literal   The exact or factual meaning of a word

loaded word   A type of persuasion used to make people, issues, and things appear as negatively as possible, such as *druggie* for *substance abuser*

logical inference   A conclusion that cannot be avoided; for example, if $A = B$ and $B = C$, then $A = C$

logical thinker   A person who learns best using details and order; a type of learning style

long vowel sound   The sound that is heard when the vowel sound is the same as the vowel's name. For instance, the vowel sound of *a* in *name* is the same as the letter *A*.

main idea   What the author wants you to know about a topic; the central thought or meaning of a paragraph or passage; can be either implied or stated

map   A graphic that shows physical or political features of a place, such as a state or country

mapping   Making a drawing to graphically show how written information is organized

mnemonics   Helpful ways to remember and recall information, such as acronyms, acrostics, association, location, and word games

name calling A type of propaganda in which a person, product, or concept is made to seem more attractive by using unpopular terms to describe the competition

navigate To move from one web page to another web page

Net A worldwide network (or group) of computers that are all linked together; also known as the Internet

netiquette Internet etiquette or manners; guidelines for posting messages online or writing emails

opinion What a person believes about a subject; not a fact

organizational patterns Patterns that help you learn to connect details to the main idea. They also help you relate what you already know to what you are reading. There are four kinds: (1) subject development; (2) list/sequence; (3) comparison/contrast; and (4) cause/effect.

outlining A way of note taking that uses indentations, bullets or Roman numerals, and upper- and lowercase letters to show major and minor points

overview In reading and studying, a quick look at a paragraph, page, chapter, or book

part of speech One of eight grammar categories into which words have been grouped: nouns, pronouns, verbs, adjectives, adverbs, conjunctions, prepositions, and interjections

physical map A map that shows the natural features of a country or region

plain folks A type of propaganda in which a person, product, or concept is made to seem more down-to-earth, common, or natural by using everyday people or situations

political map A map that shows the location of political divisions such as towns, regions, or countries

post-chapter guides Used to help the reader summarize and learn chapter content; includes some or all of the following: summary, review questions, terms, references, and suggested readings

pre-chapter guides Used to tell the reader what the chapter will be about; includes some or all of the following: title, introduction, prereading questions, outline, map, objectives

prefixes One or more letters used at the beginnings of a word that changes the word's meaning; for example, putting the prefix *in* before the word *correct* makes the new word of *incorrect* (not correct)

previewing Quickly reading or surveying to get the main idea about a page, chapter, or book that you will read more closely later

primary source Original documents or first-person accounts of an event

pronunciation key A graphic that shows the way a word should be spoken, using phonetic symbols

propaganda A form of persuasion used to change opinion. It tells only one side of an issue to try to make you believe that side is the best one.

punctuation clues   Punctuation marks (commas, brackets, dashes, parentheses) that help indicate the meaning of an unknown word

reading and study plans   A series of steps that gives you a goal when reading and studying. They help make reading and studying more active and successful. Examples are SQ3R, SQ4R, and PQRST.

relevant   Important or significant

root   The basic part of a word that gives it meaning, also known as the base; for example, the root *bio* in *biology* means *life,* so *biology* is the study of life

satisfactory progress   Having at least a *C* grade point average

scale   A feature that helps you estimate size and distance on a map; for example, one inch on a map might equal 250 miles in real life

scanning   Reading quickly to become familiar with the text or to find the answer to a specific question

schwa   The most common vowel sound in the English language; pronounced as "uh" like in the word *allow;* often heard in words of more than one syllable; shown as an upside-down *e* (ə) in a pronunciation key; can be made by any vowel.

scroll   To move up and down on a web page

search engines   Programs that search for keywords on the Internet. They give you a list of the websites where the keywords were found. Some of the most common search engines are Lycos, AltaVista, and Google.

secondary source   The opposite of a primary source; a secondhand account of an event or information

short vowel sound   The sound usually made by a single vowel in a word or syllable, such as *bed* or *boy*

signal words   Words that show the organizational pattern of a paragraph or passage, such as *first, next, on the other hand*

silent letter   A letter or letters in a word that make no sound in that word, such as the letter *b* in the word *comb*

skimming   Reading quickly to find the main idea of a paragraph or passage

SOLVE   The acronym *SOLVE* stands for a step-by-step process of making a decision: *S* = Identify **S**ituations; *O* = Think of **O**ptions; *L* = Think of **L**ogical Outcomes; *V* = Mo**V**e Forward; *E* = **E**valuate Your Choice

specialized vocabulary words   Words that have different meanings in different subjects, such as *set* in math and *set* in tennis

special-purpose map   Also known as a thematic map; highlights just one part of a place, such as the rivers in Colorado

stated context clues   Written clues (words or punctuation) about the meanings of unknown words

stereotype   Generalizations about a group of people

student handbook   A book that includes guidelines for student life

subject development A type of organizational pattern in which an author names the topic, tells about the topic, then describes and defines the topic

subject directory A list of web pages by topic; Yahoo! is a popular subject directory

suffixes One or more letters added to the end of a word that changes its meaning and part of speech; for example, adding -*ful* to the noun *respect* changes it to the adjective *respectful*

summarize To review the main points and record only what's important to your topic

surf To follow the links on a web page or move from place to place on the Internet searching for topics of interest

syllable Forms each time your mouth opens and makes a vowel sound when saying a word

syllabus A course outline given out by an instructor at the beginning of a quarter or semester

synonyms Words that have similar meanings to that of another word, such as rock and stone

synthesize Combining your review summaries to create a document like a chart that helps you compare likenesses and differences

table A type of chart that shows the relationships among details. Information is put into rows and columns.

tactile learner A person who learns best when she or he can touch objects; a type of learning style

technical vocabulary words Words and phrases used in just one subject. They have no meaning except when you are talking or writing about that subject.

term planner A calendar for the academic quarter or semester

testimonial A type of propaganda in which a famous person suggests you buy a product

text context clues Written clues to help you figure out a word's meaning. There are two kinds: punctuation clues and definition clues. These types of context clues help you to find a word's denotation.

text labeling Notes that indicate or summarize main ideas found in the text

text marking A reading strategy that involves finding important information and highlighting or underlining it

thematic map Also known as a special-purpose map. This kind of map highlights just one part of a place, such as the rivers in Colorado.

thesaurus A book listing words and their synonyms

timeline A type of flowchart that shows the order of important dates or events

to-do list A list of events and tasks you need to complete

topic The subject of a paragraph or passage

topic sentence   Tells you the subject of the paragraph; often the first sentence

trends   The movements of data (factual information) in a graphic; for instance, amounts could increase, decrease, or stay the same

unabridged dictionary   A book that contains all known words in the English language in alphabetical order. It includes their meanings, how to pronounce them, their histories, and their parts of speech.

units   Items of measurement, such as pounds, inches, etc.

URL   The abbreviation for Uniform Resource Locator. It is the one-of-a-kind address for a website on the Internet.

visual learner   A person who learns best from seeing or looking at things; a type of learning style

vowels   The letters *a, e, i, o, u,* and sometimes *y.* Words in English must contain one or more vowels.

weasel words   A type of propaganda in which the words or phrases used lack exact meanings

web pages   Pages within a website

websites   Locations on the World Wide Web

weekly schedule   A planned list of activities for each day of the week

World Wide Web   The part of the Internet where information is stored; also known as the Web or WWW

Answer Key for Chapter Exercises

Chapter 1

Exercises 1.1, 1.2, Learning Tip Exercises

Answers will vary.

Chapter Review

1. *Reading* means to understand or figure out. It applies to print and online materials, college, people, situations, and even yourself.
2. *SOLVE* is an acronym. It is a way to help you think about your choices when you have to make a decision. The *S* comes from *Identify Situations*. The *O* comes from *Think of Options*. The *L* comes from *Think of Logical Outcomes*. The *V* comes from *MoVe Forward*. The *E* comes from *Evaluate Your Choice*.
3. *Answers will vary.*

Chapter 2

Exercises 2.1–2.4

Answers will vary.

Exercise 2.5

Answers will vary but should reflect the following basic content.

1–2:

- **What are general education requirements?** General education requirements include coursework in tools of learning, humanities and social sciences, sciences, and personal development.
- **What are tools of learning?** Tools of learning are courses in writing, math, oral communication, critical thinking, and computer skills that help students learn and use information.
- **What are humanities and social sciences?** Humanities and social sciences are courses in literature, culture, history and government, and other social sciences that help students think about themselves and the world around them.
- **What are sciences?** Science courses in biological and natural sciences helps students learn about the scientific process and develop skills for exploring ideas.
- **What is personal development?** Personal development courses provide students with tools for lifelong success and include Student Success Seminar, physical education, service learning, ROTC, personal health, and career planning.

Vocabulary

1. A   2. C   3. B

Vocabulary Builder

Answers will vary.

Comprehension

1. C   2. C   3. C

Exercise 2.6

Answers will vary but should reflect the following basic content.

- **What is AmeriCorps?** AmeriCorps programs use people's courage, skills, and dedication to meet the needs of local communities.
- **How would I decide where and how to serve?** More than 40,000 members serve with a variety of different programs in every state in the nation. I could either do the work myself or I could serve by planning projects and getting volunteers.
- **How can AmeriCorps help me get education, experience, and skills?** AmeriCorps helps participants learn teamwork, communication, responsibility, and other job skills.
- **How can AmeriCorps help me pay my bills?** AmeriCorps provides a small living allowance, health insurance, student loan deferment, and training in addition to a $4,725 education award to help pay for college, grad school, vocational training, or to pay off students loans.
- **In what kinds of national and local groups can I serve?** Examples of AmeriCorps options for service include national groups like the American Red Cross, Habitat for Humanity, and Boys and Girls Clubs; local community centers and places of worship; AmeriCorps*VISTA or AmeriCorps*NCCC.
- **Main Idea:** AmeriCorps provides participants with diverse opportunities to serve and learn.

Vocabulary

1. C   2. C   3. A

Vocabulary Builder

Answers will vary.

Comprehension

1. D   2. A   3. D

Chapter Review

1. A reading and study plan for learning should include an overview (survey or preview), goals for learning, reading and checking understanding, and active review strategies.

2. An overview is a quick look at a chapter or book to identify (1) what the chapter or book is about, (2) information that you already know, and (3) chapter organization.

3. *Answers will vary but should include one of each type of guide.* **Pre-Chapter Guides:** *chapter title* tells what the chapter is about; *chapter introduction* identifies important ideas in the chapter; *pre-reading questions* show what is important in a chapter; *key terms* show what words are important in the

chapter; *chapter outline or map* shows how the chapter is organized; *chapter objectives* tell what the read should know after reading the chapter. **Intra-Chapter Guides**: *headings and subheadings* point out important information; *key words in context* show how vocabulary words are used in the chapter; *text boxes* give more information about a chapter topic; *different typefaces* show important information; *graphics* are visual aids that show ideas in picture form; *marginal notes* give extra information about a topic in the chapter. **Post-Chapter Guides**: *chapter summary* reviews main ideas; *review questions* help test understanding of what was read; *terms* identify important words in the chapter; *suggested readings* tell where to go to read more on the chapter topic.

4. previewing, outlining, and mapping
5. You can check your understanding as part of a reading and study plan.
6. It makes learning more active and provides an objective to reach.
7. It should be active and have a goal. Each should be short with several sessions spread over time.

Chapter 3

Exercise 3.1

Answers will vary.

Exercise 3.2

Letter	Sound	Words
c	s (soft *c*)	rice, space, reduce, specific
	k (hard *c*)	congress, cage, exact, technical, educator, specific
g	j (soft *g*)	cage
	g (hard *g*)	rag
d	d	reduce
	j	educator
q(u)	kw	quilt, requirement
s	s	Texas, congress, space, express
x	z	xylem
	ks	Texas, express
	gz	exact, exam

Exercise 3.3

Blend: shift, craft, class, prince, grade, stamp, plastic, first, past, spell, inspire, praise
Digraph: shift, shadow, shall, cheese
Silent Consonant: comb; knew; attack; written; gnarl; shall

Exercise 3.4

Short Vowel Sound: brisk, shelf, shunt, pit, text
Long Vowel Sound: scream, plume, deed, dice, please, prime, shame
R-Controlled Vowel Sound: harm, port, star, sport

Exercise 3.5

Y as a Consonant: yolk, year, you

Y as a Vowel (Short *i* Sound): paralysis, mythological, synthesis, polygamy

Y as a Vowel (Long *i* Sound): pry, sky, ply

Y as a Vowel (Long *e* Sound): electricity, chemistry, history, industry, polygamy, biology

Exercise 3.6

Vowel Pair	*Words*
au as in *taught*	august, haughty
aw as in *draw*	prawn, awesome
oi as in *join*	foil, choice
oy as in *joy*	ahoy, alloy
oo as in *room*	shoot, stoop, groom
oo as in *book*	mistook, nook
ou as in *cough*	bought
ou as in *pound*	scoundrel, scour
ow as in *cow*	power
ow as in *crow*	flow
ew as in *blew*	stewed, screw

Exercise 3.7

Vocabulary

Answers could include any of the following:

1. Egg; ham; granted; ship; truck; fill; clock; odds, ends, or other short vowel word.
2. Face, pine, teeth, feet; write, race, or other long vowel word.
3. *One word from two of the following three groups:* (1) you, your; (2) why, by; (3) crazy, slowly, history, verbally, creativity
4. the, few; quite; egg; ham; day; lights; same; wind; watch; ship; truck; fill; clock; odds; ends or other one syllable word.
5. impressed; madness; alike; weather; special; filling; alarm; annals; single or other two-syllable word.
6. visible; invisible; opposites; overlook; oversee; invented; creativity; recital; performance or other three or more syllable word.
7. opposites; apples; egg; muffins; essay; truck; letter or any other word with a silent consonant.
8. *Any three of the following:* invented; French; fries; impressed; wind; send; truck; end; and; speakers; plural or other word with a consonant blend.
9. *Any three of the following:* English; French; watch; chance; booth; tooth; ship; should or other word with a diagraph.
10. *Any three of the following:* invisible; alarm; alike; creativity; paradoxes; contradictions or other word with the schwa sound.

Vocabulary Builder

Answers will vary.

Comprehension

1. B	3. B	5. B	7. D
2. C	4. A	6. B	8. B

Chapter Review

1. **Vowels:** a, e, i, o, u
   Either Vowel or Consonant: y
   Consonants: b, c, d, f, g, h, j, k, l, m, n, p, q, r, s, t, v, w, x, z

2. A dictionary pronunciation key shows how each letter in a word sounds. It helps you decode words by showing how the letters sound in a word.

3. A blend consists of two or more consonants in which each letter sound is heard. A digraph is formed when two consonants combine to form a new sound.

4. A consonant is formed when the lips, tongue, or teeth stop the air coming out of the mouth. In vowels, the teeth, lips, or tongue do not stop sounds. The sounds are formed by the shape of the mouth.

5. Chin movement shows the number of syllables because a syllable is formed each time the mouth opens to make a vowel sound.

6. (1) If a word or syllable ends in vowel-consonant-*e* (vc*e*), the vowel is long and the *e* is silent. (2) If two vowels come together in a word, the first vowel is long and the second vowel is silent. (3) If a single vowel ends a word or syllable, the vowel has a long sound.

7. It is pronounced as "uh." An example of a word with the schwa is *America*.

Chapter 4

Exercise 4.1

1. (injustice)	(insist)	(install)	~~invention~~
2. ~~patent~~	(patrol)	(pest)	~~piece~~
3. (century)	(chalk)	~~change~~	~~charge~~
4. ~~silver~~	(slide)	(slime)	(slip)
5. (verse)	(virtual)	(Virginia)	(violet)
6. ~~blaster~~	~~bless~~	(blue)	(boll)
7. (acrid)	(active)	(adapt)	~~afternoon~~
8. ~~egg~~	(eight)	~~elephant~~	~~eliminate~~
9. ~~thank~~	~~their~~	(threw)	(thrift)
10. ~~steal~~	~~stole~~	~~store~~	~~summit~~

Exercise 4.2

1. a. from Etienne de Silhouette, a French controller general of finances
   b. noun
   c. *Answers will vary.*
   d. 2
   e. *Answers will vary.*

2. a. acronym from self-contained *u*nderwater *b*reathing *a*pparatus
   b. noun
   c. *Answers will vary.*
   d. 1
   e. *Answers will vary.*

3. a. from Latin *reluctant-, reluctari* to struggle against, from *re-* + *luctari* to struggle
   b. adjective
   c. *Answers will vary.*
   d. 2
   e. *Answers will vary.*

4. a. from *Zipper,* a trademark
   b. noun
   c. *Answers will vary.*
   d. 1
   e. *Answers will vary.*

5. a. Latin, passport, diploma, from Greek *diploma* folded paper, passport, from *diploun* to double, from *diploos*
   b. noun
   c. *Answers will vary.*
   d. 3
   e. *Answers will vary.*

Exercise 4.3

Answers could include any of the following:

1. teacher, educator, faculty, mentor, professor, or any other synonym for *instructor*
2. university, school, institution, academy, or any other synonym for *college*
3. pupil, school girl/school boy, freshman, sophomore, junior, senior, or other synonym for *student*
4. education, schooling, study, research, scholarship, knowledge, or other synonym for *learning*
5. talk, speech, instruction, address, lesson, or other synonym for *lecture*

Exercise 4.4

Vocabulary

1. B	2. B	3. A	4. A	5. C

Vocabulary Builder

Answers will vary.

Comprehension

1. C	3. B	5. B	7. A
2. A	4. B	6. C	

Chapter Review

1. A dictionary contains words and the meanings in alphabetical order. A thesaurus is a book of words and their synonyms. A dictionary and thesaurus are alike in that they both can build vocabulary. They can help readers understand words better, improve speech and writing, and learn more quickly.
2. A collegiate dictionary is written specifically for use by college students.
3. Words in a thesaurus can be arranged alphabetically or by subject.
4. Guide words show which entries can be found on that page.
5. Etymology is a word's history.
6. Cross-references tell where to look in the thesaurus for more synonyms.
7. An unabridged dictionary is too large and expensive for most people to own.
8. Most word-processing programs include both a dictionary spell-check and thesaurus.

Chapter 5

Exercise 5.1

1. c; a; b   2. b; c; d; a   3. d; a; b; c; e

Exercise 5.2

1. Bachelor of Arts or Science
2. approved
3. courses taught through the Internet
4. collection
5. official notice of all money given to a student

Exercise 5.3

1. average of my grades from all the courses I've taken
2. several small loans combined into one loan
3. freshmen advisors
4. grades of *A, B,* or *C* show as a *P* on your transcript
5. tuition, fees, living costs, and other costs for going to college

Exercise 5.4

Answers will vary but should be similar to the following meanings:

1. coed—for both males and females
2. lifelong learning—learning that is not limited to a specific time but continues throughout life
3. default—do not pay
4. principal—amount borrowed
5. transfer credit—credit from another college

Exercise 5.5

Answers will vary but should be similar to the following meanings:

1. acronym—letters used as a word that stand for a phrase
2. fickle—changeable
3. canine—animal in the dog family
4. chartreuse—a bright green color

Exercise 5.6

Answers will vary but should be similar to the following meanings:

1. capstone courses—courses taken in the last year of college
2. extracurricular activities—not part of the curriculum; noncredit activities
3. academic accommodations—classroom adaptations
4. sanctions—penalties
5. close relatives—family members

Exercise 5.7

Answers will vary but should be similar to the following meanings:

1. commons—dining areas
2. quad—outside areas
3. asynchronous—not at a specific time
4. articulation agreements—contracts that state the kinds of coursework one college will accept from another
5. depository—storage place

Exercise 5.8

Answers will vary but should be similar to the following meanings:

1. **edition**—version (n)
2. **zoomed**—moved quickly (v)
3. **dot-commer**—someone who works for an online company (n)
4. **outfit**—company or business (n)
5. **comb-over**—an attempt to cover a bald spot (n)
6. **macular degeneration**—an eye problem that mainly affects the elderly (n)
7. **heart-healthy**—good for the heart (adj)
8. **currency**—money (n)
9. **goof off**—avoid work (v)
10. **snippet**—small amount (n)
11. **serendipity**—unexpected surprise (n)
12. **page**—look through a book (v)

Exercise 5.9

1. **acrophobia**—fear of heights (n)
2. **arachibutyrophobia**—fear of peanut butter sticking to the roof of the mouth (n)
3. **phobia**—an intense unrealistic fear of an object, an event, or a feeling (n)

4. **panic**—intense physical feelings triggered by fear (n)
5. **specific phobias**—irrational fears of certain objects, ideas, or situations (n)
6. **social phobias**—fear of being humiliated or embarrassed in front of others (n)
7. **agoraphobia**—fear of being in a situation or place where escape would be embarrassing or challenging (n)
8. **panic attacks**—a combination of physical symptoms that include sweating, rapid breathing and heart rate and intense fear and can progress to the level of not being able to leave the house for fear of an attack or a panic-triggering situation (n)
9. **glossophobia**—fear of speaking in public (n)
10. **familiar**—acquainted with (adj)
11. **constitutes**—forms (v)
12. **extreme**—very strong (adj)

Vocabulary

1. B　　　2. A　　　3. A

Vocabulary Builder

Answers will vary.

Vocabulary Builder

Answers will vary for students' definitions in their own words and sentences.

Word	Pronunciation	Definition from Dictionary
dependency	di-'pen-dən(t)-sē	relying on something that is psychologically or physically habit-forming
psychological	ˌsī-kə-'lä-ji-kəl	of, relating to, or arising from the mind or emotions
intense	in-'ten(t)s	extreme in degree, strength, or size
unrealistic	ˌən-ˌrē-ə-'lis-tik	not realistic
triggers	'tri-gərz	something that precipitates other events
freak	'frēk	to become or cause to become greatly excited or upset
irrational	i-'ra-sh(ə-)nəl	lacking usual or normal mental clarity or coherence
puberty	'pyü-bər-tē	the stage of adolescence in which an individual becomes physiologically capable of sexual reproduction

Comprehension

1. A　　2. B　　3. D　　4. A　　5. D　　6. B

Chapter Review

1. The wrong meaning of a word can cause confusion because it affects understanding. Examples will vary.
2. Using context would be harder for ESL speakers because they don't have as much background knowledge to help identify meanings.

3. *Answers will vary.*
4. Adjectives and adverbs both describe other words. Adjectives describe nouns. Adverbs describe verbs and adjectives.
5. *Answers will vary.*
6. Background knowledge forms the "bridge."
7. Denotation is a dictionary meaning of a word. Connotation is the personal meaning of a word.
8. Parts of speech help you narrow the options for the meaning you need.

Chapter 6

Exercise 6.1
Answers will vary.

Exercise 6.2

1. noun	3. noun	5. adjective	7. noun	9. adverb
2. noun	4. noun	6. noun	8. adjective	10. noun

Exercise 6.3

1. B	2. A	3. D	4. C	5. A

Exercise 6.4
Answers will vary but should reflect the basic meaning below.

1. middle
2. sound
3. self
4. earth or land
5. written/writing

Exercise 6.5

1. D	3. A	5. B	7. E	9. F
2. I	4. J	6. H	8. C	10. G

Learning Tip Exercise
Answers will vary.

Chapter Review
1. A base (root) provides the basic meaning of a word. Some bases can be used alone. A prefix is a word part that is added at the beginning of a word. A suffix is a word part that is added to the end of a word. A suffix helps determine a word's part of speech. Bases, prefixes, and suffixes are alike in that these word parts contribute to a word's total meaning.
2. Word parts can provide meaning. They can also determine part of speech.
3. Suffixes determine part of speech.

4. Because English words come from a variety of sources, what looks like a word part may not be a base, prefix, or suffix.
5. The first letter in *prefix, root,* and *suffix* (P, R, S) occur in the same order that they occur in the alphabet.
6. Knowing the meaning of word parts helps you determine meaning of entire words.
7. Context helps you know which meaning of a word is needed. When you know word parts, you have a network of information to which you add new meanings. This increased network of understanding enhances recall.

Chapter 7

Exercise 7.1

Vocabulary

Terms that refer to courses or degrees	Terms that refer to grades	Terms that refer to people	Terms that refer to money or payments	Terms that refer to academic documents	Terms that refer to time periods
A.A.	academic average	faculty	fee(s)	academic	academic
A.S.	academic dismissal	freshman	grant	dismissal	calendar
audit	academic probation	sophomore	purge	catalog	add/drop
cancelled class	academic	student	scholarship	curricula	credit hour
catalog	suspension	classification		schedule of	drop date
closed class	academic warning	student ID		classes	full-time
co-requisites	grade	transfer		student id	part-time
credit hour	grade point average	student		syllabus	registration
curricula	probation			TBA	semester
electives	quality points			transcript	
general education	scholastic				
humanities	suspension				
independent study	transcript				
interdisciplinary	withdraw				
major					
multidisciplinary					
non-credit					
prerequisite					
purge					
registration					
required course					
schedule of classes					
section number					
syllabus					
TBA					
transcript					
withdraw					

Vocabulary Builder
Answers will vary.

Comprehension
1. because Tom didn't pay his tuition or fees
2. $1200
3. program of study
4. An A.A. degree is a two-year degree designed to transfer to a four-year college; an A.S. degree is a two-year degree for students wanting technical or occupational training.
5. Academic dismissal is worse. It prevents a student from attending class for a calendar year. Scholastic suspension prevents a student from attending class for a semester.
6. Academic warning and academic probation have the same meaning. They describe the standing given to a student who has less than a 2.0 GPA. Academic suspension occurs when a student has less than a 2.0 and a quality point deficit of 20 or more points.
7. a transcript
8. that the class time, place, or instructor has not been specified yet
9. academic calendar
10. A co-requisite is a course that is taken with another course. A prerequisite must be taken before another course can be taken.
11–12. *Answers will vary.*
13. A closed class is a class with a filled enrollment. No other students may enroll in the class due to space limitations. A cancelled class is no longer available for enrollment by anyone.

Exercises 7.2–7.3
Answers will vary.

Exercises 7.4–7.5
Answers will vary.

Learning Tip Exercise
1. GPA = 2.28 (32 points / 14 credit hours)
2. GPA = 2.15 (28 points / 13 credit hours)
3. GPA = 1.93 (31 points / 16 credit hours)
4. *Answers will vary.*

Chapter Review
Answers will vary but should reflect the following basic content.
1. Any 3 of the following: campus buildings, campus services, course names, campus orientation, campus newspaper, bulletin boards, campus events and activities, campus catalog, campus website, campus phonebook

2. General vocabulary are words that can be used in any subject. Specialized vocabulary are words that have particular meanings in the context of specific courses. Technical vocabulary are words whose meanings apply only to a specific subject. Examples of each will vary.

3. *Answers will vary.*

4. Word cards are used for individual words. Word maps help you see relationships among word meanings.

5. *Answers will vary.*

Chapter 8

Exercise 8.1

1. Topic: TV shows
   Main Idea: news shows
   Detail: *20/20; 60 Minutes; Good Morning, America*

2. Topic: plants
   Main Idea: flowers
   Detail: tulips; daisies; roses

3. Topic: athletics
   Main Idea: team sports
   Detail: tennis; softball; hockey

4. Topic: physical fitness
   Main Idea: aspects of jogging
   Detail: running shoes; stronger muscles; better health

5. Topic: nature
   Main Idea: forests
   Detail: trees; wild animals; birds

6. Topic: post-secondary education
   Main Idea: 2- and 4-year schools
   Detail: University of Maine; Coastal Community College; Northwest Junior College

7. Topic: educational expenses
   Main Idea: campus expenses
   Detail: application fees; tuition; lab fees

8. Topic: tests
   Main Idea: final exams
   Detail: staying up all night; coffee; study groups

9. Topic: nutrition
   Main Idea: junk food
   Detail: potato chips; soft drinks; candy

10. Topic: museum
    Main Idea: fine arts
    Detail: paintings; pottery; sculpture

Exercise 8.2

Main Idea: Community colleges are a big player in undergraduate teaching and learning.

The following words should be crossed out:

With, of, a, of, and, The, and, of, the, of, with, for, the, and, a, of, to, and, and, the, of, in, On, the, of, the, and, in

Exercise 8.3

1a. C	1c. H	2. B	4. I	6. K	8. D
1b. E	1d. J	3. G	5. F	7. A	

Vocabulary

1. A   2. B   3. C

Vocabulary Builder

Answers will vary.

Comprehension

1. A   2. C   3. B

Exercise 8.4

Answers will vary but should resemble the following:

Paragraph 1 main idea: Many stories claim to explain the origin of the WWII phrase "Kilroy was here."

Paragraph 2 main idea: One story about Kilroy was about an admiral who wanted to save metal.

Paragraph 3 main idea: Kilroy may have referred to a soldier that drew a fairy on a restaurant table to let his sweetheart know that he had waited for her.

Paragraph 4 main idea: Kilroy may have been a ship inspector who wrote "Kilroy was here" to show he had inspected the rivets on the ship.

Paragraph 5 main idea: Although many people that served in the army were named Kilroy, the real Kilroy seems to be the ship inspector.

Paragraph 6 main idea: A British cartoon figure, Mr. Chad, may have been the inspiration for cartoons of Kilroy.

Paragraph 7 main idea: Sometime during the war, Chad and Kilroy merged (came together).

Paragraph 8 main idea: In World War II, Kilroy was the ultimate soldier.

Passage (Paragraphs 1–8) idea: Many accounts claim to explain the origin of Kilroy.

Paragraph 9 main idea: American soldiers were helped by Kilroy's presence.

Paragraph 10 main idea: Changing the environment also helps reduce stress.

Passage (Paragraphs 9–10) idea: Kilroy helped soldiers cope with the stresses of war.

Paragraph 11 main idea: American soldiers left Kilroy in odd places.

Paragraph 12 main idea: He (Kilroy) has a special place in American culture.

Paragraph 13 main idea: Kilroy has appeared in war movies.

Paragraph 14 main idea: Kilroy has appeared in other forms of media.

Passage (Paragraphs 11–14) idea: Passage idea: He (Kilroy) has a special place in American culture.

Reading (Paragraphs 1–14) main idea: Although many stories claim to explain Kilroy's existence, Kilroy was and remains an important cultural figure.

Vocabulary

Answers will vary for students' definitions in their own words and sentences.

Word	Pronunciation	Definition from Dictionary
1. folklore	ˈfōk-ˌlȯr	the traditional beliefs, myths, tales, and practices of a people, transmitted orally
2. documented	ˈdä-kyə-mənt-əd	established as genuine
3. scarce	ˈskers	short in supply
4. yards	ˈyärdz	a tract of ground, often enclosed, used for a specific business or activity
5. erase	i-ˈrās	to remove (something written, for example) by rubbing, wiping, or scraping
6. officials	ə-ˈfi-shəlz	those authorized by a proper authority; authoritative
7. origin	ˈȯr-ə-jən	how or where someone or something began or came from
8. obscure	äb-ˈskyu̇r	not clearly understood or expressed
9. ultimate	ˈəl-tə-mət	of the greatest possible size or significance; maximum
10. comrade	ˈkäm-ˌrad	a mate, companion, or associate
11. cope	ˈkōp	to contend with difficulties and act to overcome them
12. environment	in-ˈvī-rə(n)-mənt	the area in which something exists or lives
13. signature	ˈsig-nə-ˌchu̇r	your name written in your own handwriting
14. distract	di-ˈstrakt	to cause to turn away from the original focus of attention or interest; divert
15. culture	ˈkəl-chər	all the knowledge and values shared by a society

Vocabulary Builder
Answers will vary.

Comprehension
1. B   2. C   3. D   4. C

Chapter Review
1. The purpose of skimming is to quickly find main ideas.
2. *Answers will vary.*
3. Text marking identifies key points, but text labeling provides clues for remembering the importance of what was marked. The text labels also help reinforce memory.
4. Text labels are similar to topic sentences in that they focus on main ideas. Text labels are different from topic sentences because (1) they do not have to be in sentence form, (2) they are briefer and (3) they are written by the reader.

Chapter 9

Exercise 9.1
1. administrators; Dean Jones; students; counselors; faculty; Mr. Thomas
2. work; pizza place; Tom's room; Writing Center; football game
3. during the summer; in the morning; before math class; two-thirty; from one to four
4. electives; Speech 105; foreign languages; Geography 101
5. working overtime; as a result of working during the summer; through student loans; by working in the residence hall; through scholarships
6. over $4000; each paycheck; $45 per week; $3350

Exercise 9.2

Comprehension
1. Elon University
2. North Carolina
3. Leo Lambert
4. Gerald Whittington
5. vice president for business
6. Fall 2005
7. Students are upset because they weren't informed of the process and feel they weren't treated with respect.

Vocabulary

Answers will vary for students' definitions in their own words and sentences.

Word	*Pronunciation*	*Definition from Dictionary*
1. empowerment	im-ˈpau̇(-ə)r-mənt	invested with power
2. forums	ˈfȯr-əmz	a public meeting or presentation involving a discussion usually among experts and often including audience participation
3. drastic	ˈdras-tik	extreme

Vocabulary Builder

Answers will vary.

Exercise 9.3

1. 6
2. Hawaii
3. solid, nonresonant body
4. United States
5. 1940s
6. Leo Fender
7. a radio shop
8. California
9. to improve the amplified hollow-body instruments
10. the Broadcaster
11. 1948
12. Harold Kinney
13. fishing lures
14. 1
15. George Beauchamp, Adolph Rickenbacker

Vocabulary

Answers will vary for students' definitions in their own words and sentences.

Word	Pronunciation	Definition from Dictionary
1. amplifies	ˌam-plə-ˌfīz	to make larger or more powerful; increase
2. existed	ig-ˈzist-əd	to have actual being; be real
3. shares	ˈsherz	any of the equal parts into which the capital stock of a corporation or company is divided
4. lures	ˈlûrz	decoys used in catching animals, especially artificial bait used in catching fish
5. procession	prə-ˈse-shən	that which is moving onward in an orderly, stately, or solemn manner; a train of persons advancing in order; a ceremonious train; a retinue, as a procession of mourners

Exercise 9.4

1. choosing a topic for a research paper
2. Many factors determine the selection of a topic for research.
3. *Answers will vary.*
4. your interest, the relevance of the topic to your class, and how much information you can find about it

Exercise 9.5

Part 1

1. Special tips benefit international students who attend U.S. colleges.
2. List. The tips do not need to be followed in a specific order.
3. 6
4. First, Second, Third, Fourth, Fifth, Sixth
5. *Answers should include any two of the details for each point.*
   a. First, they should preview texts before class.

   Details (1) This helps them predict what the lecture will be about.
   (2) It helps keep them from misunderstanding.

   b. Second, watching successful American classmates can provide models for them.

   Details This helps with notetaking. It also aids talking with instructors and other students.

c. Third, they should study with an American student.

Details (1) practice English (2) study content. Being in a study group with an American helps them learn American (3) dialect, (4) speed, and (5) slang used at their institutions. (6) Their language skills improve as they hear more English.

d. Fourth, they should get active on campus.

Details (1) go to as many campus meetings as possible. This helps them (2) improve learning skills and (3) meet new friends.

e. Fifth, if possible, they should meet with an American family.

Details (1) The campus's international office or a (2) local church may keep lists of families who want international students to visit.

f. Sixth, international students should learn more about American culture through the media.

Details This means they need to (1) watch TV and (2) listen to the radio. They should (3) see movies. They need to (4) read newspapers, (5) magazines, and (6) books. They should (7) visit museums, (8) shops, (9) parks, and so on. The more they understand American culture, the more they will fit into the campus community.

Part 2

1. how to start a campus organization.
2. Sequence. The steps need to be followed in the order they are given.
3. 5
4. first, next, third, next, last

Exercise 9.6

Part 1

1. Intentional or unintentional plagiarism is one of the most common forms of cheating in college.
2. Both comparion and contrast. The paragraph compares the definition and consequences and contrasts the motives and methods.
3. 2
4. on the other hand, even though, differ, same

Part 2

1. Daily to-do lists vary.
2. Contrast. It contrasts different ways to create to-do lists.
3. 2
4. some, other, however, either, or

Part 3

1. Different kinds of writing assignments vary in length and purpose.
2. Contrast. Aside from the fact that all involve writing, likenesses among the different types of papers are not discussed.
3. 3
4. other, vary, however

Exercise 9.7

1. There are many different penalties for academic dishonesty.
2. academic dishonesty (cheating, or plagiarism)
3. An *F* on the paper or test; referral of the case to a formal committee; disciplinary actions such as probation, suspension, or expulsion
4. what happens; if; if

Exercise 9.8

The following words and phrases should be circled:

1. also, When this happens, no longer, As a result, Another benefit, in turn, as well, while
   Organizational pattern: cause/effect
2. There are no signal words.
   Organizational pattern: subject development
3. second, third, Fourth
   Organizational pattern: list/sequence

Chapter Review

1. Scanning is reading quickly to find specific information. Skimming is reading quickly to find main ideas.
2. (1) Look at how the reading is organized. (2) Identify the question you need to answer. (3) Search for clues that point to the answer. (4) Read slowly and check your answer.
3. where, when, who, why
4. Organizational patterns help you find and understand main ideas more easily. They help you relate details to the main idea; relate what you already know to what you are reading; recall large blocks of information rather than individual details.
5. written cues that point to the organization of ideas
6. The subject-development pattern names the topic and gives numerous facts about it. The list/sequence pattern identifies main points, orders a list of main points, or presents a problem and steps for its solution. The comparison/ contrast pattern describes ways in which concepts are alike or different. The cause/effect pattern describes results and the factors that cause them.

Chapter 10

Exercise 10.1

Cartoon 1

1. There has been an explosion in the chemistry building on a college campus.
2. Smoke is coming out of the building. The caption refers to a chemistry building.
3. professors
4. Because one character refers to himself as "I" and talks about giving finals. Professors give exams.

Cartoon 2

1. A student is walking a long way from the parking lot to a classroom building on campus.
2. You can see the parking lot, the buildings, and the sign that says "Campus 14 mi."
3. A college student
4. The student has a backpack, and he is walking toward campus.

Exercise 10.2

1. inform
2. persuade
3. persuade
4. inform

Exercise 10.3

1. O	3. F	5. F	7. O	9. F
2. F	4. F	6. O	8. F	10. O

Exercise 10.4

1. F	3. F	5. O	7. O	9. X
2. O	4. O	6. F	8. O	10. F

Exercise 10.5

Answers will vary.

Exercise 10.6
Vocabulary
Answers will vary for students' definitions in their own words and sentences.

Word	Pronunciation	Definition from Dictionary
1. gender	ˈjen-dər	females or males considered as a group
2. hinder	ˈhin-dər	to obstruct or delay the progress of
3. segment	ˈseg-mənt	any of the parts into which something can be divided
4. pervades	pər-ˈvādz	to be present throughout
5. coed	ˈkō-( )ed	of or relating to an education system in which both men and women attend the same institution or classes; coeducational

Vocabulary Builder
Answers will vary.

Comprehension

1. C	3. B	5. C	7. A	9. B
2. C	4. C	6. A	8. D	10. D

Chapter Review
1. Student examples may vary from the following:

Type	Definition	Example
logical inference	A conclusion that must be made	1. Test preparation and test success are not the same. 2. Test preparation takes time. 3. Studying the wrong information does not help.

Type	Definition	Example
assumption	Conclusions based on background knowledge	1. If you are preparing for a test in a specific subject, you should study that subject. 2. Test preparation is boring/interesting/hard, etc 3. Proper test preparation reduces stress. 4. Proper test preparation improves performance.

2. *Answers will vary.*

3. Euphemisms and loaded words are both forms of propaganda. Euphemisms are ways to make unpleasant situations sound better. Loaded words are used to make circumstances sound as bad as possible. An author's choice to use them implies that the author intends to give a distorted view of the information. An author is probably using them in a persuasive way.

4. Euphemisms and loaded words are both forms of bias. Their use slants opinion toward or away from the topic.

5. *Answers will vary.*

Chapter 11

Exercise 11.1

Vocabulary

1. A   2. C   3. D

Vocabulary Builder

Answers will vary.

Comprehension

1. C

2. D

3. a. bar graph

   b. Comparison of Average Undergraduate Federal Loans and Grants

   c. 1995–1996 and 1999–2000

   d. The amount of undergraduate loans and grants is increasing over time.

   e. 1999–2000

   f. a little more than $1000

4. a. line graph

   b. federal grants and loans to undergraduate students

   c. 1995–1996 and 1999–2000

   d. Grants and loans to students in private colleges are increasing at about the same rate as grants and loans to students at public universities. Grants and loans are also higher for students in private colleges.

5. a. table

   b. Comparison of Actual Costs of Education, Tuition, and Differences between Tuition and Costs

   c. The tuition, costs, and difference is lowest at community colleges and highest at private four-year colleges.

Exercise 11.2

1. Highway 121
2. Campus Bookstore #5, Humanities Building #7, Science Building #9, and Performing Arts Building #10
3. Building 3 is the fieldhouse and gymnasium, used for athletics.
4. In Lot B
5. At the Federalsburg College Art Gallery #4
6. Danielson Child Care Center #6
7. Marshyhope Creek, Rose Katz Pond
8. Campus Bookstore #5, Katz Road
9. a) Turn onto Danielson Memorial Drive, go left onto College Drive, turn left onto Katz Road and follow it past Rose Katz Pond to Lot B; b) Turn onto Charles Long Avenue and make the first right that leads to Lot B or follow Charles Long Avenue around the traffic circle into Lot B.
10. The two entrances and the two parking lots.

Chapter Review

1. Graphics organize information visually. Graphics are used to show complex or difficult information. Graphics help you read and remember visual details.
2. Graphics and text information complement each other. Graphics can show information that might be difficult to explain in text.
3. Bar graphs use a single factor for comparison. Line graphs can compare several factors over time.
4. Special-purpose maps highlight an aspect of a specific place.
5. The scale shows how to convert distances on the map to actual distances.
6. Keys or legends show symbols used on the map and what they stand for.

Chapter 12

Exercise 12.1

1. s	5. n	9. m	13. t	17. e
2. g	6. b	10. c	14. j	18. d
3. a	7. r	11. o	15. h	19. l
4. q	8. i	12. k	16. f	20. p

Exercise 12.2

Answers will vary.

Exercise 12.3

Vocabulary

1. B	3. C	5. D
2. A	4. A	6. C

Vocabulary Builder

Answers will vary.

Comprehension

1. A   2. D   3. B   4. D   5. A

Exercises 12.4–12.5

Answers will vary.

Chapter Review

1. The Internet (or the Net) is a worldwide network of computers that are linked or connected together. The part of the Internet where information is stored is called the World Wide Web, the Web, or WWW.

2. The first step in searching the Internet is defining what you want to know. Second, you list key terms connected to that topic. Third, you choose the right search tools. Last, you have to evaluate what you find.

3. A search engine is a database of information collected by an electronic program. You enter a term in order to search the information in the database. A subject directory is a more specific collection of information collected by individuals who are experts in their fields. To use the subject directory, you continue to select items from menus until you reach the information you need. A subject directory is useful for more general searches.

4. First, when possible, you start by using more general sources. These include online encyclopedias or print reference books. They help you find key concepts. As you look at other sites, you can compare them with these basic books. The strength of hits is a second way to judge worth.

5. The following factors can be used in assessing the validity of a website: website author name and contact information; support or proof (e.g., a list of references, author's educational or professional background) of content; credentials (qualifications) of the site's sponsor; purpose (e.g., to provide information; to sell; to entertain); author's writing style; currency of information; accuracy of information; and avoidance of bias.

6. Anybody can put information out on the Internet.

7. Summarizing is putting selected information from a single source into your own words. Synthesis is combining several sources into a single body of information.

8. Materials are protected by copyright as soon as they are written.

9. Plagiarism is intentional or unintentional use of other people's information as if it were your own. You can avoid plagiarism by carefully documenting sources and by summarizing information rather than cutting and pasting from a website.

10. *Answers will vary.*

Credits

• Page 70 Excerpted with permission of Atria Books, an imprint of Simon & Schuster Adult Publishing Group, from *Crazy English* by Richard Lederer. Copyright © 1989 by Richard Lederer.

• Page 88 Reprinted with permission of the Associated Press.

• Page 111 Reprinted with the permission of Texas State University, San Marcos, TX 78666. Originally published by *The Daily University* on March 19, 2003. Written by Bonnie Allen.

• Page 201 Reprinted with permission from *The Pendulum*.

• Page 231, 232 Used by permission of Richard M. Longman. All rights reserved.

• Page 243 From the *Cornell Chronicle,* Vol. 27, No. 31, April 25, 1996. Reprinted with permission from Cornell University.

Page 262 © MMI CBS Worldwide Inc. and the Associated Press. All rights reserved.

Page 292 Reprinted with permission of the Associated Press.

Page 303 Reprinted with permission of Anthony "Art" Arton. All rights reserved.

Page 309 "What's in a Name? How to Address a Professor in Class" by Natalie Rodriguez; used by permission of *The Central Florida Future;* University of Central Florida, Orlando, FL.

Page 322 From *Sociology: Your Compass for a New World* (*with InfoTrac*), First Edition by BRYM/LIE. © 2003. Reprinted with permission of Wadsworth, a division of Thomson Learning: www.thomsonrights.com.

Page 329 "We and They" by Rudyard Kipling; from *Debits and Credits,* originally published in 1926.

Index

Bold numbers indicate tables or figures